Deviant Opera

The publisher and the University of California Press Foundation gratefully acknowledge the generous support of the Constance and William Withey Endowment Fund in History and Music.

Deviant Opera

SEX, POWER, & perversion ON STAGE

AXEL ENGLUND

UNIVERSITY OF CALIFORNIA PRESS

University of California Press
Oakland, California

© 2020 by Axel Englund

Cataloging-in-Publication Data is on file at the Library of Congress.
ISBN 978-0-520-34325-2 (cloth : alk. paper)
ISBN 978-0-520-97470-8 (ebook)

Manufactured in the United States of America

29 28 27 26 25 24 23 22 21 20
10 9 8 7 6 5 4 3 2 1

Contents

Illustrations

Acknowledgments

Writing about opera is a task intimidating in its interdisciplinarity. This book forced me to venture far outside my own academic comfort zone—not just backward from the twentieth century and outward from literature but in all sorts of unnerving directions—and it could not have been written without the generous help of readers and reviewers who specialize in areas other than mine. I wish to thank Kristi Brown-Montesano, Anna Cavallin, Bonnie Gordon, Wendy Heller, Rikard Hoogland, Arman Schwartz, Anna Watz, and Richard Will, each of whom took the time to give me feedback on chapters involving their respective fields of expertise; Lawrence Kramer, whose comments were astute, inspiring, and far too eloquent not to seep into my own formulations; David J. Levin and Mary Ann Smart, both of whom encouraged the project from early on, pinpointing its strengths as well as its weaknesses from their singularly broad outlook on opera studies; and an anonymous reader whose unmistakable voice raised a number of questions that vastly improved the result as it stands. Thanks to Martha Feldman, Mel Gordon, and Johanna Yunker for being kind enough to help me out with references and access to unprinted texts and to Franco Pauletto for checking my translations from the Italian. I am also deeply grateful for the efficiency and enthusiasm of those who have been working on this project for UC Press—Raina Polivka, Madison Wetzell, Emilia Thiuri, Peter Perez, and Joe Abbott.

The participants at the various symposia and colloquia where I tried out early versions of my argument were also instrumental to its final form. Many thanks to those who have engaged in discussion with me at the Theater and Performance Studies workshop and the Center for Gender and Sexuality Studies at the University of Chicago; at the International Association for Word and Music Studies and its Forum section; at the 2017 conference on Opera and Performance at Stockholm University; at the Brown Bag Lecture Series of the College of New Jersey; at the music colloquium of King's College London; at the European Cultural Studies program of Princeton University; at the first gathering of the Yale Opera Studies Today in 2019; and at the seminars of the Aesthetics section of Södertörn University and the Department for Culture and Aesthetics, Stockholm University—to my colleagues at the latter institution I am also profoundly thankful for their having made my everyday life exciting and inspiring for more than a decade now.

The inordinately generous grant entrusted to me by the Knut and Alice Wallenberg Foundation in 2013 has proven a permanent game changer in my professional life, for which I am very grateful. While I was working on this book, it allowed me not only to spend all the time I needed on the manuscript but also to attend a significant number of opera performances around the world, without which I could not have had access to the ideas and experiences that ended up on these pages.

Without the performers in the productions I write about, nothing of what follows would have mattered, and many of their voices will remain with me for the foreseeable future. I owe special thanks, however, to those who were willing to share their thoughts with me in conversations or correspondence: Mardi Byers, Sammie Gorham, Jens Larsen, Anna Larsson, Marisa Martins, Joa Helgesson, and Anna Zakrisson.

To the people closest to me I owe more gratitude than my words can carry: to Eyvind, Edith, Monica, Sven, and Dan for constituting the fabric of my being; to Klara Askegård for sterling coparenting, lasting friendship, and for thinking this book a thoroughly bad idea when I first mentioned it; to Adeline Heck for sharing with me many great opera experiences, for helping me think and talk about voice, and, above all, for her love and companionship; to Anna Jörngården, not just for her insightful reflections on this project and her patience with my going on about it but for miraculously uniting the roles of best colleague and best friend; and to Laura Wahlfors for her wisdom in all things musical and queer but above and beyond that for conversations and quietudes that make me feel at home wherever we meet. Many other friends have also provided particularly important support while I have grappled with the questions in this book: Lisa Agerbæk, Magnus Bremmer, Katarina Båth, Linda Carlsson, Isabel de Jounge, Markus Huss, Kanerva Juutilainen, Sanna Lindeberg, Stina Michelson, Ella Petersson, Sandra Quist, Manne Sjöstrand, and Rachel Åkerstedt—thank you all for helping to make my life livable during these years.

This book is dedicated to Matilda, who departed far too soon, and to Idah, who (at least in the grand scheme of things) arrived just in time.

Preface

Arriving at the dungeon for his two o'clock appointment, the dismayed Client (bass-baritone) learns that Mistress Tosca is out with a cold and that his Domme today will be Mistress Salome (mezzo-soprano). Nevertheless, he launches into the scene according to their prearranged script, donning a pink dress and pigtails. The substitute mistress, whose role is that of an opera diva, catches him spying on her as she is getting changed after a performance. While twisting his arm, she sings in a deep, menacing forte: "What are you doing in my dressing room, Polly Puddlepanties?" (She forgets to call him a "naughty little bitch," though, and has to be reminded.) This scene is from *Safe Word*, a 2017 one-act opera by composer Robert Paterson and librettist David Cote, which premiered at Nashville Opera in January 2017.[1] During the half-hour performance, directed by John Hoomes, the Client and his Domme engage in spanking, flogging, and verbal abuse, while numerous layers of role-play develop and intermingle in self-consciously surprising ways.

A year later, in January of 2018, Seattle saw the premiere of a brand-new adaptation of Ermanno Wolf-Ferrari's 1909 intermezzo *Il segreto di Susanna*, with the revamped title *Susanna's Secret: A BDSM Opera*. Here, Susanna (soprano) hides from her husband (baritone) a penchant for erotic power exchanges, which she explores instead with a submissive friend (mute). The driving force behind this project was soprano and stage director Sammie Gorham, founder of the Seattle Modern Opera Company, who is also an outspoken practitioner of SM—or BDSM, the now widespread acronym subsuming bondage/discipline, domination/submission, and sadomasochism.[2] In addition to directing and singing the lead role, Gorham herself adapted the libretto to a present-day setting, adding the BDSM theme in the process.

I ask Gorham what the two practices, each of which plays an important part in her life, have to do with each other. Is there any common ground? "They both evoke a lot of emotion and for me, specifically, both things make me cry, both things make me laugh hysterically, both things make me sob and weep, you know?"[3] Gorham goes on to explain: "I'm a switch"— that is, a BDSM practitioner who alternates between being top or bottom—"but typically I'm a submissive. And I definitely have the big emotional reactions a lot. But I've always been a crier. Music, or anything, moves me and I just weep." In marked contrast to psychoanalytic theories of sadomasochism, which tend to conceptualize it as emotional disconnection, a present-day practitioner like Gorham sees BDSM as a source of the powerful emotional experience that is also the hallmark of opera. But there is also an affinity to be found in the tension between fantasy and reality, between artifice and authenticity: "There are a lot of ridiculous scenarios that people really like. Depending on the kind of scenario that you want," Gorham says about BDSM, "it can be very far-fetched, or it can be very real." Of course, no operagoer is unaware of the genre's predilection for far-fetched stories. Like BDSM, it involves actual human bodies in fantasy scenarios, which can be as mesmerizingly intense for those who are into them as they can be embarrassing or ludicrous if the spell misfires. "I think both of them are 'ok, let's go play in this fantasy world for a little while,' you know." The make-believe that is a basic condition of theater is heightened or exaggerated by music and stories alike: "Opera is like the highest form of fantasy theater," Gorham remarks; "it's this crazy music that doesn't happen in real life—ever—and these crazy situations. And then with a lot of BDSM and kink stuff, it's definitely the same thing. It's this highly fantasized realm," she concludes, "so I just think they're pretty similar."

Deviant Opera is a book about such similarities. *Safe Word* and *Susanna's Secret* are by no means alone in displaying them on stage. As the Domme in the former piece puts it in one of her arias, "Ritual humiliation / is sweeping the nation."[4] And not just the nation: in opera houses all over the world the imagery of BDSM and fetishism—whips, chains, leather, handcuffs, and riding crops, but also the physical enactment of eroticized power and violence—has become a recurrent element in contemporary mise-en-scène. As a result, canonical operas are regularly being reenvisioned on stage as erotic games of dominance and submission. *Deviant Opera* seeks to understand this cultural phenomenon by interpreting it in relation both to specific operatic works and to operatic performance in general. It treats the contemporary imagery of BDSM as an optics through which opera's past configurations of sex, gender, power, and violence, as well as the physical interaction between singing bodies and listening audiences in the present, can be perceived.

On one level, then, *Deviant Opera* is about a current tendency in opera staging. It builds on scholarship from the last two decades that has treated opera as a mutable onstage phenomenon, affording primacy to the way it is seen and heard in concrete productions—whether live or mediated—over its codification in scores. By studying operatic staging via a particular element of its contemporary visual code and analyzing a cross-section of its concrete onstage manifestations, the book furnishes opera studies with a fresh perspective that could also be applied to other habits of contemporary stage direction. On another level, however, this particular imagery evokes concerns that resonate deeply with both historical and contemporary discourse on opera: the affinity with supposedly deviant sexuality that has insistently adhered to opera; the obsession of operatic plots with the intersection of power, violence, and desire; opera's normative reproduction or performative subversion of misogynist assumptions; the hyperbolic theatricality of opera's musical and textual representation of sexual desire; and the discourse of sensual enjoyment associated with the experience of operatic song.

Therefore, *Deviant Opera* is also a book about what opera *is* to the twenty-first century. It describes a historical trajectory from the operas of Handel and Mozart via Wagner and Puccini to Berg and beyond, but the works and their contexts are always approached from the perspective of their theatrical instantiations today. These productions are arenas where past and present notions of sexuality and power clash. Taken together, however, they can also be understood as a performative interpretation of the art of opera itself and its role in contemporary culture. This book argues for the necessity of connecting sensual enjoyment with critical engagement. The intense pleasure of the music—and the operatic voice in particular—remains key to the art form, cherished for its own sake by singers and audiences alike, whichever production frames it. The insistent intertwinement of that sensuality with disconcerting notes of power and violence is what necessitates reflective criticism. In the end the productions discussed here point to the uncomfortable fact that opera habitually eroticizes pain and humiliation, that the audience is expected to come to the opera house to take sensual pleasure in hearing and seeing the intense suffering of others. Hence, their offering of operatic *jouissance* is of a piece with their appeal for critical engagement with sex, power, and gender; without the former there would be no incentive for the latter. Together, these two aspects of opera form a vital basis for the genre's continuing relevance to the new millennium.

Since stagings like the ones I write about are bound to puzzle, infuriate, or intrigue almost any regular operagoer today, I have strived to write accessibly enough to reach readers outside the narrow straits of opera scholarship. I also set out to do justice to the strange combination of the sensual, the silly, and the sinister inherent to my topic (an ambition that remained my objective long after I had realized its fundamental impossibility). The book is neither an attack on or a celebration of either contemporary opera staging, SM, or their combination. It argues that the onstage foregrounding of sex, power, and desire should compel us—as audience members, as opera fans, as cultural critics—to think about these issues through and with the enjoyment of operatic performance. My objective has thus not been to reach a conclusive ethical assessment but to encourage and stimulate such thinking. Neither practice can be stowed away securely in compartments labeled "misogyny," "subversion," "liberation," or "oppression." They are not reliable molds that produce the same result over and over but continuous performative games with high stakes. They must be addressed by the individual listener and spectator in a process of interpretative thought that can never be disentangled from the *jouissance* that is the promise of opera, whether it is fulfilled or not.

Deviant Opera represents my own attempt to engage with these productions, informed by the historical and theoretical contexts that I have found the most rewarding and revealing in each individual case. At any given moment I invite my readers to creative disagreement: if there is one point I am inclined to repeat over and over, it is that opera's undercurrents of power, violence, and eroticism require an open and continuous critical dialogue. While active querying of the ethics and politics of a staging does not obstruct the particular pleasure that we seek when attending the opera, that pleasure can never be entirely isolated from the political. The opera stage is an arena where the problem of sex, power, and violence is made manifest and played out in physical form. Once it is granted its own agency, operatic mise-en-scène intervenes in the absorption, much to the dismay of those who would prefer to be swept away by the waves of musical beauty and turn a deaf ear to opera's more discordant notes. A staging can illuminate, interrogate, and question—or endorse and capitalize on—the brutality of the plot and the sensuous force of the music, without eradicating either. The productions addressed in *Deviant Opera* highlight, in various ways, the interplay of eroticism and violence, desire and power. Other flaws and merits aside, they do not allow us to forget the fact that canonic opera is a form of culture that thrives on our capacity to derive pleasure from the suffering and humiliation of others—seeing it, hearing it, relishing it.

Introduction

LADY GRAVEAIRS. Madness! madness! upon my honour. I protest there should be a writ of lunacy taken out against the whole group. Surely you can entertain no hopes that this opera will be ever represented by any one else in the world but yourselves.

LADY BELINDA FLAYBUM. I have not a doubt but it will be acted in a thousand private theatres; and that the songs will be as popular as those of The Duenna; or, Love in a Village. [*Bell rings.*] But, hark! the performers are all ready to begin.

Ladies, play away the overture.

Anonymous, *Lady Bumtickler's Revels*

With this exchange the curtain rises on *Lady Bumtickler's Revels: A Comic Opera, in Two Acts* (London, 1872).[1] This whimsical piece of pornography-cum-libretto, printed in the Victorian era but possibly of late eighteenth-century origin, takes as its exclusive topic the so-called English vice—that is, flagellation for the purpose of sexual gratification. Throughout the opera's two acts, the characters—including not only Lady Belinda Flaybum and Lady Bumtickler herself but also the Duchess of Picklerod, Lord Strangeletch, Miss Tomboy, Lady Harriet Tickletail, and many others—alternate between whipping each other's posteriors with birch rods on any conceivable pretext and singing the praises of this pastime to well-known tunes in the tradition of the English ballad opera.

Lady Bumtickler's Revels makes a point of marrying operatic performance with what would later come to be termed sadomasochism. Indeed, it seems to imply that they are the same thing. The audience has come to

1

watch the spectacle, of course, but also to listen: flogging becomes a specifi-cally musical and, above all, *vocal* performance. For instance, when Lady Flaybum recounts how a young girl called Cecilia—notably a namesake of music's patron saint—once begged her to play the role of a punishing step-mother, the Lady remarks that one "could read bravissimo in her eyes dur-ing the whole whipping."[2] Lord Strangeletch, for his part, asks of one Miss Stoutback that she impersonate Lady Bumtickler and give him "the severest chastisement from the rod" for having wet his bed, and when he demands foreplay—something "preparatory to the correction," as he says—she decides to give him "the prologue to the lecture in a song."[3] As it turns out, singing is just what gets the lord going, and he responds with an air of his own:

> Then when you bare my backside to the pickled rod—
> I feel myself greater than Macedon's demi-god!
> At each magic stroke while I dance on your knee—
> I feel more delight than in Langolee!
>
> Your eyes are bewitching, tho' flaming with anger;
> Your breasts I could worship from morning till night;
> Your voice in a rage is like Bellona's clangor,
> And fires my soul in the amorous fight![4]

In its sensual appeal the raging voice of opera is akin to an ancient god-dess of war: its wielder is also expected to wield the punishing rod. Song is not only afforded the status of an erotic stimulus on a par with more frequently fetishized attributes but is also interwoven with the theatrical representation of power and humiliation. The pleasure of being overpow-ered by operatic voice is construed as masochistic. Moreover, if the very act of singing and listening to opera can be imagined as an "amorous fight"—what might today be called an erotic power exchange—this seems to imply that not only the characters and performers but also the audience belong in the same sexual fantasy. Strangeletch and Stoutback both sing and listen to each other, and Lady Flaybum, who in the above-quoted dia-logue is a spectator eager for the show to begin, will soon show up on stage herself. A crowd of strange letches, the opera audience seeks gratification through both sight and sound, and they participate as much as they per-ceive. In short, *Lady Bumtickler's Revels* enlists operatic performance as a fellow debauchee in its feast of flagellation.

Why is this odd little product of antiquated obscenity of any interest today? After all, Lady Flaybum's predictions about the popularity of the piece turned out to be mistaken, and its disappearance from cultural memory is perhaps no great loss. Nevertheless, the lady was on to something. A century and a half later, opera appears to have acquired a taste for sadomasochism: in recent decades stages in Europe, North America, and beyond have seen a host of productions place heavy emphasis on the intertwinement of sex, power, and violence, often by involving the paraphernalia of BDSM. Spectators have thus seen Bassa Selim's harem in the guise of a brothel, where chains, whips, and cages are put to use in constant copulation; Despina in latex pants, patent-leather boots, and opera gloves, riding across the stage on Don Alfonso's back; Lucia using blindfolds and bondage to seduce Arturo (before proceeding to choke and stab him); Lady Macbeth debasing her court dwarf, who is made to wear a long rat-tail and crawl over the stage on all fours; Rigoletto, wearing a full-body suit in black leather, putting on a show of sexual humiliation at the Duke's orgy; Hunding keeping Sieglinde like a dog in his house, crouching and with a rope around her neck; Samson being led around in a collar with a chain, blindfolded, spat on, and photographed by Dalila and the Philistines; Manon commanding a harem of gagged slaves in leather corsets; Geronte running a seedy nightclub home to bondage and rituals of domination; Scarpia having the torture of Cavaradossi performed by a bare-chested man in full-face mask and leather pants; Salome being blindfolded by her own veil, bound by belts, held down, and symbolically violated by the men at Herod's court during her dance; Zerbinetta, sporting skin-tight leather and a riding crop, enjoying herself with a policeman and his handcuffs; the servant Sante spread-eagled on a Saint Andrew's Cross and flogged by his mistress Susanna; Mescalina spanking Astradamors's bottom while he is crawling across the stage in tall black boots and a pink negligee; the Maid, wearing black leather gloves and knee-high boots, sodomizing and peeing on the diaper-clad Hotel Manager; the adulterous Marie having her hands tied down on the bed with a belt, while begging to be dressed, stripped, shamed, and chained by the Boy; Madame Irma, who is running an SM-style bordello, bringing a black latex balaclava for the conductor to wear while leading an ensemble in similar outfits; soprano Valerie Solanas dominating and humiliating an all-male ensemble of four electric guitarists—and this list of examples does not even mention the productions I will actually discuss in the following chapters.[5]

These stagings all evoke a cluster of images that, in current cultural consciousness, are taken to signal something kinky or transgressive. In spite of their diversity they can be spoken of together, as a specific visual code employed with some consistency in contemporary operatic mise-en-scènes. Even though it always responds and relates to scores and librettos, this code is largely added to opera by the directors and their creative teams. For want of a better term, I will refer to it as the *iconography of perversion*. The symbols and signs in this iconography include not only immediately identifiable props and costumes but also the interaction of living bodies, the gestures and movements of which evoke various fusions of eroticism, power, and violence—bodies being beaten, bound, and controlled in situations with sexual overtones, bodies signaling arousal or revulsion, compliance or resistance, authority or acquiescence. Thus, the iconography of perversion evokes the corporeal practices of dominance and submission, as well as the style of fetishism; and more often than not, they coexist and intermingle.

To be sure, there is a lot of internal variation in the above catalogue. For instance, the staged scenes include both men submitting to dominant women and the converse, as well as productions queering those categories by role-switching, cross-dressing, and same-sex relations (counting both the iteration above and the productions discussed in detail below, each of those categories amount to about a third of my examples). The signals of kink or perversion range from subtle detail in single scenes to undiluted ostentation throughout a production, the results from the playfully provocative to the seriously disturbing—the latter partly because many of these productions include representations not only of consensual kink but also of behaviors that are, within the fictional world, patently nonconsensual. The importance of this last distinction cannot be overstated—most obviously because it is what separates BDSM from sexual violence but also because the productions I deal with, as we will see, very often place this border itself in the spotlight.

Whatever opinion one may have of these productions, they constitute a distinctive phenomenon in contemporary culture that merits critical

attention. My aim in this book is to understand that phenomenon by paying close attention to a number of representative stagings, in search of
possible answers to a set of interrelated questions. How can the iconography of perversion be interpreted in relation to operatic performance? How
does this visual code connect with the auditory experience that is so often
thought of as the core of the genre, the sensuous pleasure of the operatic
voice? What do all the chains, whips, and shiny black outfits mean in relation to operatic works, to their texts and their contexts, past and present?
Taken together, as a turn-of-the-millennium phenomenon, what can these
stagings tell us about opera and its representations of gender, power, and
desire today?

DEVIANCE AND THE CANON

In speaking of opera in terms of "deviance" and "perversion," I am not
subscribing to the value judgments that typically adhere to these words—
neither the condemnatory and pathological ones nor the affirmative ones
that have more recently been evoked to critique normativity—and
although I will drop the scare quotes from now on, they remain implied.[6]
Beyond pointing to the visual codes of SM, these terms serve to emphasize
a dependence on the convention that is their opposite. To deviate or per-
vert is always to relate to a perceived norm.[7] This fact links such notions
to the contemporary stage practices often subsumed under the labels
Regietheater or *Regieoper*—that is, "director's theater" or "director's opera,"
respectively. These terms are a shorthand for a tendency that has now
been widespread in opera for decades (and the fact that they are often
used in German signals the geographical origin of the phenomenon,
although it is now common in the rest of Europe and even in the United
States).[8] The most basic characteristic is the stage director's claim to creative authorship on a par with the composer or librettist. By onstage rereadings of operatic works, director's opera presents the drama to a present-
day audience, often in a provocative or deconstructive manner. The clash
between aural and visual registers is key to its effect: music and text that
typically adhere to the creators' prescriptions chafe against a mise-en-
scène that flagrantly ignores their stage directions.

Much like perversion and deviance, these terms require a bracketing of pejorative connotations: together with invectives like "Produceritis" and (in the US) "Eurotrash," they have often expressed a reflex dismissal from those who take the first duty of staging to be the faithful and literal reproduction of the composer's intentions.[9] Director's opera, too, typically depends on the relation to a perceived norm. To quote Clemens Risi, one of the leading researchers of this style of staging, the expectations they produce lie "between recognition and surprise through deviation."[10] This deviation is set off against the backdrop of a relatively small repertoire of operatic works and, above all, an imagined standard way of putting them on the stage. To appreciate (or detest) the particular deflections of a new production, the audience must have an idea both of the work and how it might "traditionally" look. The increasing importance that this practice assigns to directors and dramaturges in the postwar era is the flip side of opera's reliance on its canon: the fewer new operas commissioned, the greater the need for innovative stagings to ensure that the old ones still seem relevant and interesting.[11] A canonical work, moreover, always raises claims to reverence, and director's opera thrives on the irreverence thus made possible. From the perspective of fidelity to time-honored masterpieces, perversion therefore flaws not only the productions that use the visual codes of BDSM but all director's opera: any mise-en-scène that deviates too markedly from the way the work was originally conceived is unsound or unsavory. In that sense the examples discussed in this book can be thought of as a paraphilic paradigm of sorts. Whenever critics use the word *perversion* and its derivatives to condemn productions or concepts—and they do so with great frequency and conviction—a purportedly unacceptable sexuality is evoked in the service of castigation, thereby implying that those responsible are misguided not just on an aesthetic level.[12]

It is worth noting that while the iconography of perversion is largely a present-day phenomenon, opera has been scandalizing audiences for centuries through its lack of proper sexual morals. The stereotypical place of canonized operas in contemporary culture—old masterpieces to be venerated—tends to obscure the fact that these works were often highly controversial in their original contexts. In fact, each and every one of the composers and librettists featured in this book saw their operas criticized, in some cases even censored, precisely for their provocative eroticism.

Occasionally allowing these operas to offend "good taste" need not, in and of itself, be a bad idea. Nor does it, of course, necessarily engender success-ful stagings, and those addressed in this book are certainly not beyond critical reproach. While I would consider some of them stunning operatic achievements—dramaturgically as well as musically, visually as well as vocally—others are unsatisfying or deeply problematic. Some of them are sensitive both to the overall drama and minute details of the music, while others appear to take no interest in these aspects. Sometimes they are uncomfortable because of the difficult questions they raise, sometimes because their sexism overwhelms whatever other qualities they may have. Be they of an ethical or aesthetic order, however, such problems do not invalidate critical engagement. On the contrary, they necessitate it.

One factor to be taken into account is that of authorial gender: the operatic canon consists overwhelmingly of works by male composers and librettists. Not only that: a majority are still today also directed by men—including the stagings I study in this book. How are we to understand this? For one thing, we know that it does not mean that SM in itself is in any concrete way an inherently male fantasy. The example of E. L. James's *Fifty Shades of Grey* trilogy—BDSM-themed romance written by a woman for an overwhelmingly female readership—demonstrates this clearly enough, as does any number of recent sociological studies featuring inter-views with female SM practitioners.[13] When it comes to the gender of the stage directors, approximately a third of the productions mentioned in this book (including those referenced above) have been directed by women. This asymmetry merits mention, not least since of the examples that are discussed (rather than just mentioned), only Barbara Hannigan's semistaged concert performances of *The Mysteries of the Macabre*, Vera Nemirova's *Lulu*, and Sammie Gorham's adaptation of *Susanna's Secret* are directed by women. It does not necessarily mean, however, that female directors are *more* underrepresented in deviant opera than in the opera world in general. As a point of comparison: of the twenty-four operas at the Metropolitan Opera in the 2019/2020 season, only one is staged by a woman (Julie Taymor's production of *The Magic Flute*), while the Royal Opera House at Covent Garden, perhaps because its creative producer recently claimed to be "seeking more female creatives to build and develop productions," managed to reach four out of twenty-three.[14]

This imbalance is a glaring problem in the opera world, but when it comes to the critical engagement with a particular staging, the gender of its director forms no kind of guarantee of its politics, especially since that role is only one of many (albeit typically an authoritative one) in the creative team needed to put an opera on stage. Nor can their intentions govern the result in any conclusive way. The same goes for the experiences or opinions of singers. Even so, I have not wanted to leave out the perspectives of those who regularly put their bodily selves at stake in performance. Being on stage, exposed to listeners and spectators, is in many ways a singularly vulnerable position, certainly no less so when a production involves representations of sex, power, and violence. Whenever possible, I have tried to be attentive to what singers have to say in interviews (some conducted by myself, some published elsewhere). In light of the predominance of male directors among my examples, this has seemed particularly important with respect to female singers.

Another famous sore spot in the gender politics of the opera canon is the fate of the women that these singers portray: they die. In her 1979 feminist classic *Opera, or the Undoing of Women,* Catherine Clément argued that the operatic canon is insistently haunted by misogyny. Her point was precisely the disturbing insistence with which opera kills off its female protagonists: Lucia, Gilda, Senta, Isolde, Brünnhilde, Carmen, Mimi, Cio-Cio San, Lulu, and countless others are trapped in plots designed with their death as an inescapable aim, to the accompaniment of a music that aestheticizes their suffering.[15] Without discrediting Clément's insights, many later critics have pointed out that her argument is valid for the tragic operas of the long nineteenth century but hardly for other parts of opera history (for instance, Renaissance and baroque works or the comic opera tradition from the eighteenth century onward). Moreover, her reading of opera is too literally just that—a reading. As Mary Ann Smart puts it, "Clément might be seen as elevating the scrutiny of plot to the status of doctrine, making disregard for the music into the cornerstone of her approach."[16] From Clément's perspective, music *must* be ignored because its function is precisely to seduce us into forgetting the violence directed against its female leads. During the 1990s, critics associated with New Musicology—most notably Susan McClary and Lawrence Kramer—started to redress this oversimplification of music by attending to its central role in representing gender and sexuality.[17] Meanwhile, Paul Robinson, Carolyn Abbate, and others pointed to how Clément's narrative of victimization was deaf to the immense and unique power wielded in opera by the female voice.[18] Such criticism notwithstanding, few would argue with her basic insight that the violence done to women is in itself a norm of the canon. The question of how to deal with this observation has become neither less difficult nor less urgent since it was first articulated.

Large parts of current opera studies, however, are otherwise occupied. One vibrant strand of recent scholarship, for instance, has turned away from canonical opera and its traditional institutions. Searching for fresh perspectives from the genre's margins—or to be less stingy: its frontiers— scholars like Nina Eidsheim and Jelena Novak have focused their efforts on contemporary, experimental, or underground opera.[19] There is much enthusiasm for performances that renegotiate the boundaries between audience and performers through immersive and participatory aesthetics, as well as more critical calls not to take their benefits for granted.[20] Reviewing a range of discussions on relational aesthetics, Heather Wiebe traces a logic, present in both scholarship and arts funding, that leaves little space not just for confrontational director's opera but also "more fundamentally for any opera performance that involves traditional forms of spectatorship, but is not primarily about pleasure" or about "star singers and appealing spectacle."[21] Another widespread tendency, partly a reaction against the fixation on live performance that came with the so-called performative turn around the turn of the millennium, is a focus on opera's intense relationship with media technology, from radio and LPs to digital broadcasts in the movie theaters.[22] The same interest in technology is visible in more historically inclined studies promoting ostensible fringe phenomena like the opera curtain or the telephone to center stage.[23] This aspect will not be a particularly strong focus of my argument, even though I do write chiefly about productions captured and available on DVD. The drawbacks of doing so are obvious: as both performance- and technology-oriented scholarship has taught us, a recording is an entirely different beast from a live performance. The focus of the spectator is governed by the camera, and countless aspects of the audience's experience are altered or lost. For the questions I pursue, however, the practical gains seemed greater—not only to be able to delve into the productions I find most important rather than those I have had the possibility to attend live but also to allow my readers to see and hear the stagings I write about and thus to assess my argument for themselves.

Moreover, without fetishizing either notated works or live performance, it is fair to say that at a given point the fascination with technologies may begin to eclipse the thing they were mobilized to produce. In a sparkling dissection of what they call "quirk historicism," Nicholas Mathew and Mary Ann Smart want to see scholars "write openly about what moves us musically, rather than displacing our musical attractions onto nearby objects."[24] Similarly, Arman Schwartz has expressed the hope that "our new appreciation for trains and fog machines and DVDs might also prompt us to reengage with opera's aesthetic and affective worlds."[25] Such a reengagement must include, I would argue, a new look at the way sex, gender, and power are seen and heard in opera today because those things affect and move us like few others. To this end opera studies need to revisit Clément's insights into opera's aestheticization of cruelty from the present moment—a present that has seen, among other things, the global spread of radical director's opera, the *Fifty Shades* phenomenon, and the earthquake of the Me Too movement. Crucially, it needs to do so by attending to another facet palpably missing from Clément's plot-based account: opera's visual appearance. Shifting the emphasis from work to onstage action, the performative turn also drew critical attention to dramaturgy and mise-en-scène, not least within director's opera: Tom Sutcliffe's *Believing in Opera* (1997) and David J. Levin's *Unsettling Opera* (2007) are milestones in this regard, and they have influenced the present book on more accounts than I can enumerate.[26] In the last decade their work on contemporary staging has been developed in anthologies, articles, and chapters by Clemens Risi, Gundula Kreuzer, Mary Ann Smart, Joy Calico, and many others.[27] It is at the intersection of this work on staging and work on sexuality and gender in opera— which was actually more prolific during the 1990s than it has been in the new millennium—that this book seeks to position itself.

If deviance is always relative to a norm, it is also potentially subject to normalization. When an aberration achieves critical mass, a new norm is established, paralleling or even replacing the previous one. In light of this the assumption that interventionist stagings rely on novelty as their chief merit needs to be reconsidered. In *Believing in Opera* Sutcliffe wrote: "The more closely one looks at what is condemned as *produceritis*, the more doubtful one becomes about any systematic or sweeping condemnation of non-naturalistic or non-narrative approaches. Performers need to express their responsibility with an unfettered imagination, though innovation naturally does not always equal excellence."[28] From this perspective the escape from a preestablished code of staging may not be a sufficient condition of great operatic theater, but it is a necessary one. Yet the ropes, chains, and handcuffs seen on today's stages may suggest that opera's imagination is less unfettered than Sutcliffe wished to believe. When he was writing his book, in the mid-1990s, the conventional code of staging appeared to have vanished and made room for the auteur director: "when there was no longer a style of the age, a convenient bundle of conventions, which all could follow almost unconsciously, there had to be an outsider, an observer, as adviser and editor. Hence directors' theatre—and opera."[29] Some twenty years later, however, it is clear that a "style of the age" has returned with a vengeance, evolving precisely from the directors' opera that once seemed inseparable from its destruction. Most operagoers, regardless of their preferences, will have noticed by now that a certain set of conventions, have imposed themselves on contemporary staging, and critics frequently point to it. Thus, Levin, for instance, follows Hans-Thies Lehmann in pointing to an "avant-garde conformism" while Risi and Kreuzer have noted a "potential calcification of not only the ever-same repertory but also the *Regietheater* approaches themselves."[30] Despite such remarks, however, the conventions of deviance remain insufficiently charted by research. Whether or not they signal a waning of originality and stagnation, opera studies might see in them an incentive to new approaches.

    In this vein Mary Ann Smart has suggested the possibility of an alphabet of contemporary staging (beginning with "Asylums," "Biker-gear," and "Children"). Smart's point is that "even the *enfants terribles* of *Regieoper* are working within a system, a complex communicative infrastructure that is rooted in training and education, in *topoi*, and in the lingua franca of the surrounding cultural environment."[31] The study of this system, she emphasizes, is a research desideratum: "Elevating these conventional patterns to a more conscious level of perception may also open lines of communication between presence-effects and meaning-effects in these stagings. By enumerating the constituent elements of a particular conventional scenario or effect, we can understand more about the possible or likely ways that device affects spectators, tracing its immediate, non-linear impact back to the cultural associations that it may evoke or play upon."[32] I subscribe wholeheartedly to Smart's wish for more attention to the conventional sign system of director's opera, and this book is an attempt in that direction. But rather than taking the route of enumeration, or seeking to produce a comprehensive map of the system as a whole, I will focus my attention on one of its subsets, examining through a cross-section the way it is put to use in specific productions. As I have already emphasized, I take such an investigation to necessitate acts of interpretation but ones in which the "meaning-effects" that form the object of traditional hermeneutics will be codefined continuously by the "presence-effects" of opera's powerful visceral impact. By way of these interpretations I will argue that the iconography of perversion has a status that distinguishes it from other elements in the visual language of director's opera. In other words, BDSM is not just any four letters in the operatic alphabet: the cluster of associations that belong to this label resonate deeply with the way in which opera has represented the intersection of sex and power in the course of its four centuries.

For this resonance to become audible, a historical component is indispensable. As should be clear by now, I am not talking about a method that attempts to recreate the original historical mode of performance. Rather, I have aimed for a perspective that allows for the contemporary visual language to be understood simultaneously in relation to its current and historical contexts, as a conflicted and creative interaction between them. In particular, of course, it is necessary to factor in the historically conditioned configuration of sex, gender, and power, both in contemporary culture and at the moment from which the operatic works originated. On one level the book will proceed in a roughly chronological manner through the operatic core repertoire; it begins with Handel and the Baroque, then moves via Mozart and classicism through the fin de siècle of Wagner and Puccini, and onward into modernism with Berg and Ligeti. At the same time, however, the historical moments mediated by this succession of operas are perceived through the contemporary lens that is the iconography of perversion. In every given case, then, a dialogue between distinct historical moments is being staged, resulting in a continuously changing, kaleidoscopic image of desire and power. If the story to be told includes an element of historical linearity, it is nevertheless projected from the present moment. While the two are always entangled, the book is more about the present than about the past. Various aspects of the conceptions of power, gender, and sexuality that are woven into the operatic scores and libretti will come into view in each chapter. However, the contemporary iconography of perversion and its relation to general tendencies in operatic mise-en-scène requires some attention at this point. Specifically, I will outline a shared condition of director's opera and the BDSM subculture: that of a deviant practice that finds itself drifting into the mainstream.

INTO THE MAINSTREAM: BDSM, DIRECTOR'S OPERA, AND CONTEMPORARY CULTURE

"Sticks and stones may break my bones, but chains and whips excite me," sang Rihanna and Britney Spears at the Billboard Music Awards 2011, wearing high-heel leather boots and their microphones chained to their wrists.[33] The same year saw the publication of *Fifty Shades of Grey*, which was to become the fastest-selling paperback of all time and the centerpiece of a multimillion-dollar industry including everything from beginner's bondage kits to limited-edition teddy bears.[34] These are only two examples of the ever-increasing visibility of kink in popular culture, which is unlikely to have escaped anyone's attention.[35] Today, SM appears to saturate pop music, fashion, commercials, movies, and TV. While this phenomenon is clearly more widespread than ever before, it is actually far from new. Susan Sontag noted as early as 1975 a growing fascination with sadomasochism, as well as the fact that it depended on a fixed code that was not available to the perverts of the past: "Sade had to make up his theater of punishment and delight from scratch, improvising the decor and costumes and blasphemous rites. Now there is a master scenario available to everyone. The color is black, the material is leather, the seduction is beauty, the justification is honesty, the aim is ecstasy, the fantasy is death."[36] As the punch line of Rihanna's refrain confirms, SM is still designated by a specific collection of theatrical props (many of which hark back to Sacher-Masoch and Sade). Sticks and stones may not be among them, but chains and whips are, and the boots and black leather that

Sontag noted also remain central. When, in the first installment of the *Fifty Shades* trilogy, Christian Grey introduces Anastasia Steele to his playroom, the description of her shocked amazement takes the form of an itemization: "all manner of ropes, chains, and glinting shackles" and "a startling assortment of paddles, whips, riding crops, and funny-looking feathery implements."[37] The catalogue is described as open-ended to suggest impressive mass, yet every item mentioned is readily identifiable as a marker of kink in contemporary popular culture. In the passage of Sontag's essay cited above, she put her finger on a connection between the existence of a fixed set of symbols and the increasing availability of SM imagery. It is in this neatly prepackaged form—fetishistic in the Marxist as well as the Freudian sense, that is, as objects charged with both monetary and erotic value—that SM has assumed the character of a mainstream commodity in recent years. But if the fascination Sontag observed in 1975 has increased exponentially since then, this process has also partially changed what the imagery means. It no longer appears exclusively in the psychopathology of crime-drama rapists and killers but also as the stuff of relationship dramas, sitcoms, romcoms, and lifestyle magazine coverage.[38] While it still betokens the edgy, dark, and dangerously exciting sides of sex, it now does so from a popular position. With the move from underground culture to best sellers and blockbusters, in other words, SM has also made a move from the unambiguously aberrant to the increasingly normalized.

This tendency is related to the way in which the SM scene itself has been transformed over the last few decades. One possible point of departure for this development is the sexual revolution of the 1960s, in particular the 1969 Stonewall riots. Certainly, both SM and fetish fashion have historical roots far beyond that moment; in Europe as well as the United States the entire postwar period had seen a growing gay leather subculture, as well as heterosexual fetish-bondage-spanking communities, and the dissemination of SM imagery can be observed in publications like *Bizarre* (1946–59) or in the bondage-themed comic strip *Sweet Gwendoline*.[39] Even further back, Weimar Berlin was a veritable hothouse for everything that was considered sexually deviant at the time, including fetish-style clothing and sadomasochistic behavior.[40] What has been notable in the post-1969 SM community, however, is an increasing tendency of practitioners to come out of their dungeons and seek acceptance by the surrounding society—although typically coupled with a conflicting will to safeguard a transgressive identity.

The early 1970s saw the establishment of the first modern associations for SM: the Eulenspiegel Society in New York City in 1971 and the Society of Janus in San Francisco in 1974.[41] Unlike older clubs, these were not primarily clandestine venues but open organizations providing support, education, and information to their members and working actively against the prejudice and discrimination that SM enthusiasts were (and still are) facing.[42] Practitioners of SM started marching in the Pride parade, although they were often met with significant skepticism and booing from other cohorts.[43] In 1983 the catchphrase "safe, sane, and consensual" made its first appearance in a self-defining statement of a New York–based gay-male activist group, in order to clearly distinguish SM activities from sexual violence.[44] Over the following decades those three words—often abbreviated SSC—spread from their original context, becoming something of a slogan for the community as a whole, which served, on the one hand, as a guiding principle for practitioners and, on the other hand, as an effective way of letting those outside the scene understand SM as a responsible and ethical activity.

Unsurprisingly, in a community whose self-understanding is based on nonconformism, this development toward public acceptance has been met with some ambivalence. Where deviance is a consciously cultivated identity, normalization becomes an inconvenience. The hordes of curious beginners approaching BDSM after reading *Fifty Shades* are thus often derided by those who consider themselves serious devotees of an alternative lifestyle.[45] Interviews with self-identified SM practitioners often show them trying to avoid being confused with "'weekend' dabblers" and "'bedroom,' 'unsafe,' or 'newbie' players."[46] Whether it wants to or not, however, the SM community has come a long way from hidden subculture to visible mainstream, to the point that it partakes of a distinctly neoliberal ethos; despite BDSM's claim to transgressive identities, those same identities cannot be isolated today from a lucrative market of commodified sexuality—of expensive attire and equipment, of best-seller books and billboard hits—which allows for individual self-fashioning through consumption.[47] This also means that the demographics of SM have changed. While still retaining strong links to LGBTQ interests, contemporary BDSM communities are much less exclusively homosexual than at the time of the old-guard leather scene in the 1970s; practitioners today are typically white, middle-age professionals, often highly educated and affluent—in short, not too unlike the stereotypical operagoer.[48]

The point of retracing this popularization here is that it runs parallel to the steady expansion of director's opera on stages worldwide. As European opera houses were gradually rebuilt and reopened after the Second World War, the theatrical component was revolutionized not only by new technological possibilities but also by an increasing emphasis on the importance of acting and the artistic visions of stage directors.[49] With the pioneering work of Walter Felsenstein at the Komische Oper in East Berlin and Wieland Wagner at the Bayreuth Festspielhaus, directors began to attract attention (often divided between acclaim and outrage) almost on a par with composers, conductors, and star singers. Their influence paved the way for Joachim Herz, Götz Friedrich, Ruth Berghaus, Nikolaus Lehnhoff, and Jean-Pierre Ponnelle—all of whom attempted to revitalize opera with iconoclastic stagings in the 1970s. Patrice Chéreau's 1976 staging of Wagner's *Ring des Nibelungen* in Bayreuth is usually regarded as a landmark event, not least because the video recording and broadcasting of the complete cycle made it available to a wide audience.[50] Chéreau's *Ring* cleared the stage for a generation of directors that included Hans Neuenfels, Harry Kupfer, and Peter Konwitschny and whose influence gradually spread from the German-speaking world to the rest of Europe and, eventually, to the United States.[51]

One of the most obvious (and bitterly criticized) tendencies of director's opera has been a predilection for visual elements associated with other geographical places and historical moments than those of the stories themselves. While Wieland Wagner's visual revolutions had favored abstraction from time and space, creating a mythical, scaled-down landscape with innovative lighting techniques, later directors have often worked with very concrete settings in order to tease out the historical, cultural, political, and economic subtexts of opera. Chéreau's *Ring,* for instance, let Wagner's mythical universe be inhabited by costumes and images culled from the industrial revolution and the nineteenth-century bourgeoisie but also by black ties and business suits; and between 1986 and 1989 Peter Sellars produced his much-publicized stagings of Mozart and Da Ponte's *Le nozze di Figaro, Don Giovanni,* and *Così fan tutte,* locating the stories in 1980s New York (in Trump Tower, Spanish Harlem, and a diner in the Hamptons, respectively).[52] While the musical and vocal elements of opera remained untouchably sacred and firmly rooted in the past, all sorts of images of the contemporary now began to seep into the heavily guarded bastion of tradition that is the opera house.[53] As a result, the operatic stage became the arena for heterochronic clashes between the current and the historical: contemporary popular culture was able to interact with an art form that had spent the century of media revolutions developing an elitist image, warding off the popular and the present to defend its place in a changing media ecology. In keeping with the broader cultural tendency from the 1970s and onward to deconstruct the divide between high art and popular culture, as well as that between the aesthetic and the erotic, the opera house became a site where these categories flowed into each other.

In the same decades that SM became an ever-more palpable presence in the contemporary imaginary, opera thus showed an increasing willingness to admit elements of popular culture into its highbrow sanctuary. These are the two concurrent developments that make possible the phenomenon addressed in this book. At the moment of their intersection the iconography of perversion, together with an abundance of other late twentieth-century images, made its appearance on the opera stage. Both practices describe a similar trajectory from the margin toward the middle while still struggling to retain a sense of being transgressive. Just as BDSM subculture became more and more widespread until it came to occupy a place of its own in the contemporary mainstream, operatic staging practices that seemed highly provocative when they first appeared gradually became part of the standard theatrical language of opera. In a global perspective they may not be the norm, especially if one looks beyond the big urban opera houses. The most common style is still the one that typically gets to represent the "traditional," that is, a style that uses modern vocal and instrumental techniques, lighting, stage sets, gestures, and blocking practices but visually evokes a setting that corresponds to the popular contemporary image of the one portrayed in the work.[54] But the stagings that define themselves as deviant in relation to this norm have now become common enough for the codes and patterns that pervade them to be discernible and interpreted. That is the work to which this book aims to contribute.

Chapter 1, "Opera and Sadomasochism," attempts to flesh out the analogy between these two practices. Prominent components are the cultural tropes of eroticism, power, and agency that have been—and still are—ascribed to the faculties of sight and hearing and to the roles of audiences and spectators. Most typically, the body seen is thought of as controlled or objectified, while the body heard is thought of as expressive and empowered. Moreover, the sensory pleasure of listening to the operatic voice has repeatedly been construed by its devotees as an erotic experience. Because operatic performance involves a combination of voice and gaze, these figures mark it as a dynamic of sensual pleasure and power, akin to SM also in its penchant for hyperbole. The stagings I write about use the iconography of perversion to dramatize this dynamic. They suggest that we see, hear, and experience opera as an erotic power exchange aimed at the pleasure of both audiences and performers. If we accept this perspective, what implications does it have for the art form today and for its abilities to cope with its own undercurrents of misogyny and sexual violence? This question cannot be answered a priori, as a blanket judgment about how to stage power and eroticism—or how to assess the ethics or aesthetics of such a staging—but only by engaging in sustained critical interpretation, which attends to the meaning of words, music, and staging, as well as their visceral power.

Chapter 2, "Sex in Excess: *Rinaldo, Alcina,* and the Contemporary Baroque," explores the iconography of perversion in the baroque opera revival via two stagings of Handel. In productions from Glyndebourne and Stuttgart various facets of "the baroque" in opera are reinterpreted through allusions to fetishism and eroticized power: the playing-out of different layers of acting and disguises against reality, the proclivity for hyperbole, and the preheteronormative staging of gender. I also argue that the fetishistic projection of an erotic charge onto props and clothing, which can always potentially shift owners, allows these productions to stage power as unstable and renegotiable, while also serving as a postmodern substitute of premodern myth and magic. The chapter also connects the concept of the contemporary baroque, or neobaroque, with operatic performance, via the notion of "preposterous history," borrowed from Mieke Bal. Bal's concept hinges on the notion that the baroque is always already marked by an excess of coexisting historical moments. In this sense the baroque origin of opera becomes a paradigm for the hetero-chronicity that characterizes director's opera in general. Rather than being just the first of a series of case studies, this chapter thus suggests the notion of the baroque as a way of conceptualizing the jumble of historical moments that results when contemporary visual codes of SM are super-imposed on past representations of sex, gender, and power.

In contrast to the volatility that characterizes the representations of gender on the baroque stage, the Enlightenment gradually furnishes clas-sical opera with a more rigidly heterosexual gender regime, while the social distribution of power goes through unprecedented upheaval in the years around the French Revolution. Nowhere are the dynamics of sexual and social power more central than in Mozart's and Da Ponte's operas, the sec-ond one of which is the topic of chapter 3, "Schools of Libertinage: *Don Giovanni* with Sade." Here, I turn my attention to stagings directed by Calixto Bieito and Claus Guth. Bieito's staging not only represents a new level of brutality but also a different species of fetishism from that of the Handel stagings. The human individual itself is objectified and divided, in a contemporary visualization of Sadean libertinage: while riding crops and blindfolds can be passed on to others, the dislodging of a fetishized body part implies physical harm. In the end it is the Sadean obsession with repetitive violence that reigns on Bieito's stage. While Guth's take on the opera seems more playful, marked by light erotic role-play rather than abuse, the games turn out not to be so harmless after all. In the end both of these stagings collapse the boundary that supposedly separates consensual erotic domination—whether it is enacted verbally or physically—from real violence.

Chapter 4, "In-House Allegories: Enactment and Actuality in *Parsifal* and *Tosca*," traces a similar collapse. In this seemingly disparate duo of fin de siècle works, the productions I discuss place singer, conductor, and pro-ducer characters on stage, involving them in SM-like scenes. Thus Romeo Castellucci's Brussels staging of *Parsifal* draws on nineteenth-century dis-course on perverted Wagnerian eroticism to envision the interplay between Klingsor and Kundry as that between a conductor and a female lead singer. Puccini's most famous heroine, by contrast, was always a singer: in *Tosca* Scarpia's desire is predicated on the fact that its object is a soprano. Niklaus Lehnhoff's staging invokes the fetishism of Sacher-Masoch to emphasize that Scarpia is as much a fin de siècle masochist as he is a sadist. His greatest fetish, however, is not fur or shoes but the vocal object. In Carsen's version he is an opera producer; he directs a private scene in order to enjoy her song, and the knife with which she stabs him is little more than a phallic objectification of her voice. Again, these stagings point to opera's obsession with the transmutation of the acted into the actual: like SM, opera enacts violations that supposedly remain within the limits of the safe, sane, and consensual. At the same time, both practices repeatedly imagine the breakdown of the firm border toward the real cruelty that lies outside those limits.

The focus in Chapter 5, "More or Less Human: *Wozzeck, Lulu,* and the Soprano Conductor," is on the roles of the superhuman and the subhuman. When BDSM fantasies of dehumanization are put on the stage, I argue, they collide with the idea of operatic song as an expression of a specifically human agency. In a staging of Alban Berg's *Wozzeck* directed by Dmitri Tcherniakov, the dehumanized protagonist is a male prostitute who submits to humiliation by his superiors, later to replay the experience in an SM scene with Marie, as he kills her. Berg's second opera, *Lulu,* seems almost never to be produced without the iconography of perversion, and a host of stagings evoke bondage and human-animal role-play. Barbara Hannigan, whose Lulu in Krzysztof Warlikowski's staging is the object of a pornifying gaze, nevertheless sees in the character an agent in full control of her destiny. This perspective is crystallized in Hannigan's own performances of the *Lulu Suite,* where Lulu sings her self-assertive lied while conducting an orchestra. Conducting Ligeti's terrifyingly difficult *Mysteries of the Macabre* in dominatrix attire, Hannigan exercises as total a control over the orchestra as over her own coloratura. Her half-concert, half-opera performances—which have often earned her the label "superhuman"—thus turn murdered Lulu and paranoid Gepopo into conductor characters, regaining on their behalf the agency and humanity that operatic plots so often deny their female characters.

The book ends with a short epilogue, "The Actuality Effect and Opera's Quest for Authenticity," which situates the collapse between the acted and the actual in relation to contemporary performance art that attempts to make room for reality on stage. Two underground performances serve as end-point examples of this tendency: Sammie Gorham's aforementioned adaptation of *Il segreto di Susanna* (1909) into a BDSM opera in present-day Seattle, which is staged as a coming-out process both for the character and the singer, and baritone Joa Helgesson's 2017 adaptation of Monteverdi's *Orfeo*, which was performed in an old Berlin factory building by actors and singers suspended with metal hooks through their skin. Although in quite different ways, these performances engage the personal—the actual bodies and psyches of the singers—in an effort to get at the potential authenticity of opera.

Ultimately, this book suggests that what at first glance may look like a mere fad among stage directors reveals itself as an index not only of a broader trend in contemporary Western culture but also, on a deeper level, of an insistent tendency in opera as a genre. Deviant opera, understood as a widespread mode of staging and performing canonical works, makes an assertion about the deviance of Opera with a capital *O*. It exposes the genre's relentless preoccupation with the nexus of sensuality and power, with violence and eroticism. In present-day opera culture, moreover, that preoccupation takes a very particular form on stage. Tricked out in the iconography of perversion, it zeroes in on the boundaries of the theatrical space, to the point that the partition between fantasized cruelty and real cruelty becomes the principal focus. Situating the genre in that borderland, deviant opera demands that we channel the ecstatic surge of the operatic voice into new ways of understanding our own relation to the spectacle of suffering.

1   Opera and Sadomasochism

While I was working on this book, reactions I garnered from regular operagoers ranged from "Do you really mean no one has written about that
yet?" to "Right, I bet there's no lack of material there!" or "I know! What
the hell is *wrong* with contemporary opera directors?" (as well as the occasional "Do they actually pay you for that?" of course). By contrast, the people who gave me a "What? Is that a thing?" were generally those who took
little interest in the genre to begin with. As anecdotal as this account is,
such reactions fueled my curiosity about how and why opera allows for the
association with supposedly deviant sexualities: what, if anything, does
opera really have to do with sadomasochism?

This question will be given a variety of answers in the following chapters
via the concrete mise-en-scène of the relationship in various guises. Central
to the argument of this book, however, is the notion that these stagings also
have a collective significance: because the iconography of perversion recurs
today with such insistence, it demands to be interpreted in relation not
only to the individual production but also to the genre or art form as a
whole. In addition, it is repeatedly conflated with self-reflexive strategies.
Many of the stagings I address present themselves explicitly as opera about
opera—a typical characteristic of director's opera—while others open

themselves up to such readings in subtler ways. My claim is that, construed together, they amount to an oblique statement about their genre: they imply that opera and SM are alike. The point is not primarily that they constitute scenic *representations of* BDSM, that is, that they show the fictional characters as engaged in consensual power exchanges. While this is true of many scenes, others show characters who, in the operatic fiction, are clearly victims of nonconsensual abuse, assault, torture, and rape. Instead, I want to argue that deviant opera suggests the possibility of reading operatic performances of sex, power, and violence as *analogous to* BDSM scenes. We may consider this suggestion persuasive, puzzling, or preposterous, but the task of the following chapters is to show that it is being made on the operatic stage and to elucidate it through interpretation.

To begin teasing out its implications on a general level, one must first note that the idea of an affinity between opera and sexual identities or behaviors on (or beyond) the border of the socially acceptable is far from new. Opera houses have often served as covert bordellos: in eighteenth-century France the term "filles de l'opéra" (opera girls) belonged to the taxonomy of prostitutes, and a journalist at the time described the Opéra as a "repository for indecency, adultery, prostitution, the most disgraceful villainy; in a word, a refuge for all depravities, all vices."[1] Even in our age, this heritage lives on in a symbolic register. As literature scholar Margaret Reynolds puts it: "It is no accident that the opera house is furnished with velvet plush, gilded mirrors, naked cherubs, and powdered footmen, for these are the trappings of the brothel, and we go to the opera house for sex."[2] Apart from this association, opera has frequently been suspected of effecting a type of chaos that is dangerous because it upsets heterosexual normativity. For instance, the success of Italian opera in London during the early eighteenth century gave rise to widespread gender anxieties, clustering in particular around the castrati singers and the potential danger of their voices (and the rise of the castrati, in turn, was related to the anxiety about women on stage).[3] Similar worries beset the Danish philosopher Søren Kierkegaard (or, rather, the persona "A" in his *Either/Or*), who saw himself "infatuated, like a young girl" when Mozart's operatic seductions overwhelmed him in *Don Giovanni*.[4] The later gay-male opera cult confirms the image of the opera house as home to a marginalized sexuality, celebrating pleasure at a distance from heterosexuality. Such rapports among opera, nonnormative sexual practices, and gender subversion have been enthusiastically explored at least since Wayne Koestenbaum flung the operatic closet open with *The Queen's Throat* in 1993.[5]

The fact that the specific association between opera and sadomasochism has been much less frequently discussed, however, does not mean that it originates in the dirty minds of contemporary directors. The above-mentioned *Lady Bumtickler's Revels* is one offbeat example of the ways this cultural trope was circulated. Others abound. Take the case of Richard Wagner, whose music was often perceived as outrageously erotic in the late nineteenth century.[6] German critics spoke of his music using innovative descriptions such as "the erotic flagellation-music of the Liszt-Wagner school" or "slap-in-the-face orchestral accompaniment."[7] In Paris Charles Baudelaire described his listening experience as the pleasure of allowing himself to be "penetrated, invaded," and "subjugated" by Wagner's music.[8] The association of a vague kinkiness has stuck to Wagner ever since, reinforced no doubt by the boots-and-leather imagery borrowed from Nazism, to which Wagner's violent grandeur is often the given musical accompaniment (and the pop-psychologizing literature on Adolf Hitler has not hesitated to suggest connections between his purportedly deviant desires—incestuous, masochistic—and his Wagnerism).[9] In Liliana Cavani's 1974 film *The Night Porter,* which recounts the sadomasochistic relationship between an ex-SS officer and his former female prisoner when they meet again in the 1950s, a performance of *Die Zauberflöte* sets off flashbacks of her being chained to a bed in a wartime camp. But when the two rekindle their strange love affair and he chains her to a bed in his apartment, it is an LP box of *Die Walküre* that is placed on the nightstand.

Playing on similar ideas, Angela Carter's novella *The Bloody Chamber* (1979), a variation on *Bluebeard's Castle,* weds Wagner with Sade: a young, musically talented girl marries a marquis, whose castle contains a forbidden room that turns out to be a medieval torture chamber. The night before their wedding, he takes her to see *Tristan.* She is wearing his wedding gift, a ruby choker "like an extraordinarily precious slit throat" that augurs her own *Liebestod* by the sword.[10] But the fairy tale ends with a feminist twist: the beheading of the bride is interrupted by her mother, who shoots the murderous husband dead. Carter hilariously presents the event as a cheerful Italian intervention into the Teutonic framework: "The Marquis stood transfixed, utterly dazed, at a loss. It must have been as if he had been watching his beloved *Tristan* for the twelfth, the thirteenth time and Tristan stirred, then leapt from his bier in the last act, announced in a jaunty aria interposed from Verdi that bygones were bygones, crying over spilt milk did nobody any good and, as for himself, he proposed to live happily ever after."[11] Indeed, Wagner can still function as an icon of perversion today, to which recent usages of his music in the cinema testify: in the psychoanalytic biopic *A Dangerous Method* (David Cronenberg, 2011), Carl Gustav Jung (Michael Fassbender) is seen spanking a masochist patient (Keira Knightley) to an orgasm with the Wälsungen motif from *Die Walküre* playing in the background; in Roman Polanski's *Venus in Fur* (2013) the theater director (Mathieu Amalric) staging Sacher-Masoch's story has the *Walkürenritt* as his mobile-phone ringtone; and in the second part of Lars von Trier's *Nymphomaniac* (2013), Joe's (Charlotte Gainsbourg) move toward serious masochism is marked by the hammering of the Nibelungen anvils from *Das Rheingold,* soon echoed by the cracking whips of subsequent scenes.

The affinity between opera and sadomasochism hinted at by such examples can obviously not be understood in essentialist terms, as if it were an inherent necessity in the art form itself. It is a cultural trope transmitted by historical and contemporary discourse on opera. Understood as a semiunified cultural phenomenon, the stagings addressed in this book repeat, refract, and reinterpret this trope. Like any effective metaphor, it thrives on the tension between similarity and difference, conflict and convergence. Are opera and BDSM the same thing? Obviously not. That is precisely why the move of identifying them with each other calls for a sustained thinking-through of both differences and similarities. Where might we look for overlaps between these two distinct practices? What are their points of intersection? What implications are evoked and activated by a metaphorical statement like "opera is sadomasochistic" or "sadomasochism is operatic"?

FIGURING VOICE AND GAZE: EROTICISM, AGENCY, AND FETISHISM

The appearance of bondage, fetishism, and eroticized power exchanges on the operatic stage is linked inextricably to a problem that has been at the

forefront of opera studies since roughly the turn of the millennium: that
of physical presence and performativity, on the one hand, and operatic
plot and meaning, on the other. Opera criticism has kept asking itself—
and often in far too polarized terms—if and how the visceral experience of
operatic music can be reconciled with critical readings of its meaning:
how does the drastic side of music relate to the gnostic?[12] How does the
scandal of the singing body relate to the referentiality that it interrupts?[13]
In the deviant stagings that dress up such questions in leather and latex,
they are mirrored by the relation between a scripted SM scenario and its
physical enactment. As a set of signs and codes, the iconography of perversion may seem closely related to the referential end of the spectrum: it
participates actively in a particular, idiosyncratic interpretation of operatic plots and performances. At the same time, its referentiality points
squarely to the drastic and the scandalous: it insists on opera's capacity to
deliver sensual pleasure beyond decorum and morals but also on its liabil-
ity to cause embarrassment, repulsion, and distress. The analogization of
opera with SM thus spotlights the fact that both depend on the plotting of
pleasure—be it aesthetic or erotic—by verbal and visual means. Rather
than seeking sensual enjoyment intuitively or immediately, they deliberately construct it via emotionally charged narratives and role-playing bodies. The imagery of sadomasochism becomes a placeholder for a precarious coexistence of presence and meaning, which are often too entangled
in each other for a distinction between them to be even remotely tenable:
like opera, SM involves real bodies in fantasy scenarios of pain and humiliation, with the claim to sensual ecstasy as its justification and the risk of
violation as its constant shadow.

Any opera performance, moreover, is a multisensory spectacle, potentially harboring layer upon layer of sensuousness: the trained bodies on
stage are perceived both visually and aurally by the bodies in the auditorium (or, for that matter, in front of a mediating screen). Director's opera
tends to draw a lot of its energy from playing with constellations of what is
seen and what is heard, deliberately creating gaps and discords between
those registers.[14] Because the visual aspect dares to contend with the auditory one, this is among its most provocative characteristics. Traditionally,
the music—and above all the operatic voice—has been understood as
the unique core of the genre. The revolutions of music recording in the

twentieth century worked to support this view, allowing the sounding side of opera to be perceived in isolation. But whether caught on a recording or not, voice is difficult to pin down: it pours effusively and elusively between the embodied and the disembodied, between meaning and sound, between its concrete material vibrations and its role as metaphor for individual subjectivity, desire, or agency. One of opera's most fascinating traits is the way it dramatizes these ambiguities, highlighting and renegotiating the relationships between the literal presence and the figurative functions of voice. The productions I discuss take this dramatization of voice one step further: they envision it specifically as an erotic power exchange.

A lot of current scholarship aims to pick apart the figures through which voice and song have traditionally been understood—such as, for instance, subjective expression or agency—in order to bring its materiality into focus.[15] This impulse is related to a broader tendency of increased attention to materiality, whether of the body in live performance or of opera's technological substrates and mediations. While this critical project has been immensely valuable in light of the long history of philosophy excluding the physical from consideration, I share none of the suspicions against interpretation that sometimes accompany it.[16] Critical attention to meaning is not incompatible with a valorization of the drastic, visceral, and sensual experience of opera. In opera the climactic moments of the stories typically coincide with those of the music's physical impact (say, when singers soar toward their top notes, leaving behind a trace of gooseflesh on the skin of their listeners). Just as in SM, in other words, scripted scenarios and symbolic representations do not distract from but feed into and mingle with the visceral or sensual experience. When that experience strikes the operagoer, it is already codefined by the way we are used to thinking and talking about it, as well as by the way opera's stories frame and filter it. It is not dulled or disarmed by this fact but intensified; indeed, that intensification is opera's stock in trade. If we want to understand deviant opera, we must try to grasp how the cultural meanings of voice are evoked and actualized on stage, not at the expense of but in conjunction with its materiality, and not least by visual means. Rather than trying to extract the operatic voice from the tropes that resound in and around it, the productions discussed in this book use staging, design, and dramaturgy to work *through* them. In so doing, they simultaneously activate similar figures that adhere to the gaze—such as control, ownership, or objectification. Without treating them as natural givens, deviant opera productions summon the various meanings culturally ascribed to sight and sound in order to play with them—particularly those having to do with eroticism, power, and fetishism, which will therefore need to be outlined at this point.

Throughout the history of opera the sensual qualities of singing have been spoken of in erotic terms, often echoing the ancient roots of this figure in Odysseus's encounter with the sirens. In scholarship focused on gender and sexuality, the eroticism of music in general and song in particular came into focus during the 1990s. What is voice, so the typical argument goes, if not a pulsating extension of the singer's throat, tongue, and lips that penetrates the ears of the listener? And what is opera, if not a prolonged intercourse between these bodily orifices, with the sole aim of pleasure for all involved? Such a view of voice received seminal impulses from the writings of Roland Barthes: "Singing," he suggested in 1970, "has something coenesthetic about it, it is connected less to an 'impression' than to internal, muscular, humoral sensuality. The voice is a diffusion, an insinuation, it passes over the entire surface of the body, the skin. . . . Music, therefore, has an effect utterly different from sight; it can effect orgasm."[17] Equally influential was Michel Poizat's Lacan-fueled classic *The Angel's Cry*, which understands opera as a quest for moments of *jouissance*, when the singer's voice transforms into a pure vocal object. Psychoanalytically speaking, this experience depends on voice functioning as the object of a drive (like the oral, anal, and genital objects theorized by Freud). Opera, from this perspective, is built on the fact that voice already exists within an eroticizing system.[18]

After Poizat's book was published in English in 1992, a wave of highly subjective accounts of operatic sexuality followed, not least from the perspective of homosexuality. In addition to Koestenbaum's aforementioned book, this vantage point is represented by Samuel Abel's *Opera in the Flesh* (1994), even though his account of the operatic experience often emphasizes a gender-transcending pansexuality. Abel maintains that opera performance is a sexual act: "I do not mean that opera is metaphorical or vicarious sex, an intellectual reenactment or contemplation of pleasurable sensations. There is nothing vicarious about opera's sensuality. It is real, physical erotic stimulation of the audience by the performance."[19] Abel's insistence on the literalness of this trope may seem bewildering today, but the idea of opera's sensuousness as erotic persists. Adopting a phenomenological view, Clemens Risi emphasizes the structure of expectation and fulfillment (or disappointment) as key to both operatic and erotic interactions, while also highlighting the importance of the listener's subjective experience: "A trace of the performative, or more precisely, erotic interrelation between the singer and the listener or spectator can only—if at all—be discerned through the description of one's own experience." (Risi responds to his own call by elaborating on the erotic suggestiveness he perceives in Cecilia Bartoli's performances, which "evokes the reality of numerous resonant cavities in various regions of the body.")[20] This emphasis on personal investment is typically a core component in accounts of the operatic voice as erotic: while Abel and Koestenbaum write from an explicitly gay-male perspective and Risi from an implicitly heterosexual one, Suzanne G. Cusick, Elizabeth Wood, Terry Castle, and Laura Wahlfors have all argued the eroticism of music from queer and lesbian subject positions.[21]

The notion of voice as expressive of sexuality and subjective identity has often made it a marker of agency and power. In an oft-quoted response to Clément's analysis, Carolyn Abbate seized on the power or female singing to construe opera as the envoicing rather than the undoing of woman. With reference to Strauss's *Salome,* she writes: "Visually, the character singing is the passive object of our gaze. But, aurally, she is resonant; her musical speech drowns out everything in range, and we sit as passive objects, battered by that voice. As a voice she slips into the 'male/active/ subject' position in other ways as well, since a singer, more than any other musical performer, . . . stands before us having wrested the composing voice away from the librettist and composer who wrote the score."[22] Abbate's terminology bespeaks struggle, even violence: as listeners, we are battered by the operatic voice (cue Lord Strangeletch, sung to and spanked by Miss Stoutback: "Your voice in a rage is like Bellona's clangor, / And fires my soul in the amorous fight!"). But because the opera audience comprises spectators, too, the onstage singer is also subjected to their looks. Abbate points to this fact by way of a set of inherited notions: vision is an active sense, while hearing is passive; sight is a controlling force moving away from the spectator's body, while voice is an expressive force moving onto or into the listener's body. The tenacious gendering of these binaries is also brought into play: to make the figure of opera's empowerment of woman appear, Abbate places it in relief against an elision of "male/active/ subject." The argument, although adapted to opera, harks back to the notion of the male gaze, famously theorized in film studies by Laura Mulvey, who argued that the role of women onscreen has been shaped by a threefold objectifying look: that of the male cameraman, that of the male coactor, and that of a male audience.[23]

On this view any operatic performance has an inherent power dynamic where the subjective expression of the (female) singer's voice is pitted against the objectifying gaze of the (male) spectator. To be sure, this model is an oversimplification on several levels, and not only because it risks essentializing certain gendered assumptions (that the high female voice is the paradigm of operatic singing or that spectatorship is necessarily defined by a male, heterosexual perspective).[24] With respect to *Salome*, for instance, Linda and Michael Hutcheon have argued that the person looked at may gain agency and mastery precisely by owning the gaze of spectators.[25] Many have queried the notion of singing as a unidirectional delivery from active subject to passive object: building on Erika Fischer-Lichte's theory of performativity, Risi thinks of the "active relationship between performers and spectators/listeners" as a "feedback loop," while Martha Feldman emphasizes the "transactional" quality of vocal performance, and Nina Eidsheim construes the acts of both singing and listening as "intermaterial vibrational practices" in which all participants are emphatically active.[26] If the passivity of the listener is not a given, neither is the subjective expressivity of voice. For instance, Abbate has later tried out the idea of performers being controlled by music—as if their bodies were played by the score rather than the other way around—and James Q. Davies argues that "voice has been too easily configured in the image of sonic emancipation, too readily fixed . . . as the spectral imprint of freedom."[27]

In sum, neither gaze nor voice moves unidirectionally, and neither can be conclusively or essentially aligned with a particular identity, gender, sexuality, agency, or power position. It would be too simple to describe the dynamics of an opera performance as a push-and-pull between the seen body as passive object and the heard body as subjective agency or between male gazes and female objects. At the same time, the meanings culturally ascribed to looking and listening cannot simply be circumvented; they are too pervasive as cultural assumptions, too strongly supported by the phenomenology of operatic performance, and too closely aligned with gendered asymmetries of social power in the real world. They resonate in any situation where bodies are looking at and listening to other bodies. Precisely because they have become commonplaces, they impact opera's meaning in a very real way: we cannot avoid experiencing a performance through and with them. The power of interpretation, both as creative staging and as discursive criticism, lies in its ability to take a step further from this observation; it shakes those tropes out of the dormant state of the stereotype, both to make us conscious about them and to open them up to new meanings. They may be amplified or distorted, undercut or repurposed, shifting prismatically as the optics of a given production refract them. This is crucial to the understanding of what deviant opera does: it dresses up the gendered power dynamics evoked by these tropes in the iconography of perversion, thereby spotlighting the complex circuits of power and pleasure afforded by operatic performance.

Relatedly, at the opera both sight and sound may cater to fetishism—a term that has been employed and explained in a variety of ways. In the most basic sense it signifies the attribution of magical powers to a specific thing. It is an irrational projection but nevertheless effective enough for those powers to appear as intrinsic to the fetish itself (and in this sense it operates like any other symbolic meaning: the observation that it is contingent rather than absolute does not vacate its significance). The label was introduced in the eighteenth century, as the European Enlightenment applied it to purportedly primitive and superstitious beliefs in tribal societies. During the course of the nineteenth century, however, its usage widened to include any number of corrupt object relations that appeared to have a strong hold on the heart of modern European culture itself, most notably the Marxist concept of commodity fetishism and the ideas of erotic fetishism developed by early psychiatry.[28] The latter, which was first theorized by Alfred Binet in the 1880s and subsequently developed by Richard Krafft-Ebing and Sigmund Freud, is doubtless the most prominent association of the term today.[29] Psychoanalysis from Freud to Lacan and beyond has construed fetishism as the psyche's way of dealing with a castration complex: when desire and fantasy are displaced onto specific objects or body parts, the fear of loss and lack—typically associated with a male perspective on women—reverts into lust. I will occasionally refer to this post-Freudian theorization of fetishism, but for the purposes of this book I am less interested in committing to any one understanding of fetishism than in reflecting on what it is made to mean in the context of a given production. In more general usage the term has come to signify anything that becomes the object of an obsessive fascination. In the contemporary BDSM community it is often used in this sense—that is, as synonymous with a kink or strong turn-on—but just as often to refer specifically to the appreciation of skintight attire made of a variety of black materials (such as leather, latex, rubber, and vinyl). Like other SM gear, this sartorial subculture forms a central part of the iconography of perversion as it appears in director's opera.

Beyond the use of such objects and attires on stage, the issue of visual fetishism in opera is indissociable from the intervention of screens. While opera's bodies have always been subject to the spectators' gaze, the current preponderance of technological mediation has effected a sea change in the way they are viewed. Screens pervade opera both as mediators of performance (through television, video, DVD, and live broadcasts) and as onstage elements (video art, projections, handheld cameras, and so forth).[30] Opera both live and recorded indulges in the specific kind of mediated scopophilia pinpointed by Mulvey: through cuts and close-ups the camera guides the spectator's attention and constructs a particular perspective—not least on the female body, which is repeatedly divided into isolated parts.[31] In addition, the mediated voyeurism is complicated by its relation to the sensual obsession that was already there: voice fetishism. How does an art that is used to defining itself strictly in terms of aural pleasure deal with the presence of a visible fetishism? The relation between the two could be construed as competition or even mutual exclusion. In its most radical form a fetish tolerates no rivalry: "The fetishist 'idolises' one element of the object, so to speak, makes the particular absolute and loses contact with the whole by making the part the *absolutum*."[32] For modern devotees of opera, that absolutum has always been the singing voice—hence the not uncommon preference for audio recordings over actual visits to the opera, where voice has to vie with a host of other sensory stimuli.[33] But the relation between visual and aural fetishism can also be understood in terms of symbolization: the fetishistic elements in a staging—whether they are close-up camera shots or BDSM props—can be seen as mirroring opera's voice fetishism, interpreting it as erotic in nature and as permeated by asymmetric power relations.

Whether it is visible or audible, the fetishized thing is always singled out: because it demands exclusive focus, the attention it receives disconnects it from its surroundings. Compared to the fetishization of objects, therefore, the fetishization of the human body or its parts entails a different degree of objectification. The latter is liable to revert into dehumanization, as the part no longer has any need for the whole. This implies distinction between two ways of envisioning fetishism on stage, each of which will become instrumental in the following chapters. The first is a fetishism that projects erotic power onto inanimate objects and clothes, which can always potentially be detached from the body and passed on to others. The second, by contrast, is a fetishism where the surface of projection is the human body and its isolated parts, which can only be dislodged at the price of bodily harm. This variety of fetishism always contains a latent threat of violence. As we will see, the terms of this opposition—fetishized props and fetishized bodies—feed into the tendency of contemporary mise-en-scène to deliberately poise erotic power exchanges between the representation of enacted fantasy scenarios and the representation of actual abuse.

HYPERBOLIC GAMBITS: BDSM, OPERA, AND THE THEATER OF SEXUAL CRUELTY

A central point of contact between opera and SM lies in their dependence on a particular kind of theatricality. Whether conceptualizing it as playful or pathological, accounts of sadomasochism rarely fail to point to its thespian aspects.[34] In the words of Niklaus Largier, historiographer of flagellation: "When the whip is raised, when leather, scourge, and cane strike against covered or naked flesh, we stand before a stage—a stage on which a ritual unfolds."[35] Contemporary BDSM is a heavily scripted erotic performance: participants tend to speak of their practices as "scenes," which typically involve extensive preparatory negotiations and planning in order to determine the limits of what may be played out and sometimes even described in subsequently published "scene reports."[36] (Yet, as with opera, the predetermined script cannot be mistaken for the thing itself: the actual performance is the ultimate end and only justification of the preparations that go into it.) Such scenes are often semipublic performances: BDSM is not exclusively limited to the private space of the bedroom but just as often takes place at open events, workshops, designated clubs, bars, or play-parties, where the spectator is a vital component.[37] It should also be noted that the most pedestrian distinction between the two practices—that BDSM is sex, while opera is not—is complicated not only by the discourse eroticizing operatic song but also by BDSM scenes that appear to evade this categorization. Although BDSM often involves what is commonsensically thought of as "actual sex"—say, genital stimulation or penetration of some sort—it does not necessarily or unconditionally do so: scenes may explore power exchanges for the purpose of arousal but stop short of any such interplay, which makes the distinction between BDSM and other types of eroticized theatrical performance considerably less clear-cut.[38]

The theatricality of opera and SM does not typically try to conceal itself. Rather, it tends to go beyond acting aimed at realism and to acquire a self-consciously ritualized quality. There are certainly BDSM scenes that aim for realism, yet the iconography of perversion more often foregrounds the eccentricity of its attire and accessories. These become props in an erotic performance that flaunts its own artifice. This is another important point of resonance with opera. Operatic singing not only pushes its theatricality into the realm of sensual pleasure; it also drowns out any aspirations to mimetic verisimilitude. Opera is a kind of theater that departs from naturalistic representation with deliberate conspicuousness. Spoken theater can do that, too, of course; the point is that opera cannot *not* do it. The principal strangeness of opera is its necessary condition: the bizarre fact that the people on stage consistently express themselves through exaggerated singing. Even visually realistic stagings, to such accompaniment, boast their theatricality, displaying their reality against a sounding foil of unreality.

One way to conceptualize this type of theatricality is as hyperbole—that is, as deliberately exaggerated expression. Barthes once drew a parallel between professional wrestling and Greek drama, and Levin has observed that opera belongs in their company: "Like wrestling, opera packs a peculiarly hyperbolized and highly stylized punch: it is the artifice that hits you."[39] When hyperbole is referred to as a "loud liar"—and what better way to characterize the voice of opera?—we are alerted to the fact that it makes the lie itself audible; it departs from realistic representation with deliberate conspicuousness, without attempting to hide its own excess. In this sense hyperbole has accompanied opera throughout its history, from the excessive late Renaissance spectacles meant to showcase the wealth and power of patrons, via the rhetoric of baroque libretti and the unbridled vocal virtuosity of the castrati, to the gargantuan proportions of Wagnerian music drama and beyond. The discourse of excess that has insistently adhered to opera tells us that on the operatic stage no one loves, hates, or desires in moderation: all impulses are pushed to or beyond their limits.

Sadomasochism, too, is often thought of in terms of hyperbole: it is an attempt to derive pleasure from the amplified enactment of gendered power structures. Indeed, the limitless exaggeration itself appears to hold significant allure. This notion has been evoked from widely differing perspectives. For example, the thoughts and writings of Sade—which, despite their distance from contemporary BDSM practice, still function as a reserve of fantasy scenarios—repeatedly emphasize the move toward extremes, the breaking of the uttermost barrier, as an end to be pursued for its own sake. In the account of an early sexologist like Krafft-Ebing, pathological sadism is described as "true hyperbole" insofar as it amounts to "a desire to exert the utmost possible effect upon the individual giving rise to the stimulus."[40] Object-relation psychoanalysis later conceptualized sadomasochism in terms of excess, as "a social subject's response 'out of proportion' to an object, the repressed drama of social dependency."[41] The notion of hyperbole has also been brought to bear on BDSM in terms of Judith Butler's perspective on performativity. In Butler's words, "there might be produced the refusal of the law in the form of the parodic inhabiting of conformity . . ., a repetition of the law into hyperbole, a rearticulation of the law against the authority of the one who delivers it."[42] In short, practices that reiterate behaviors originating in repressive power structures may, under certain circumstances, serve to undermine those structures through irony, parody, or hyperbole. Enthusiastically applying this

mode of thought to SM, queer-influenced criticism has typically arrived at
the conclusion that it is an inherently, or at least potentially, subversive
citation of patriarchal violence.[43]

In fact, this argument is often made even when the gendered power
dynamics are cast in a firmly heteronormative mold: "A man whipping a
woman during an SM scene," argues sociologist and ethnographer Staci
Newmahr, "does not conform to a cultural *expectation* of masculinity, but
instead symbolizes a (discursively) *unacceptable* masculinity. In this sense,
it is a hyperbolic masculinity that is represented—but not constituted—
through topping."[44] From this perspective SM is nothing if not a theatrical
representation of sexual violence. It is the framework of the safe, sane, and
consensual that marks SM as symbolically representing rather than actually constituting abusive behavior. But beyond this, the purportedly non-
conformist force of BDSM hinges on hyperbole. In Newmahr's example it
is a normative masculinity that is blown out of proportion. The exaggeration, as it were, is expected to produce quotation marks around the actions,
enabling them to work against the authority of norm and law.

This rationale is far from uncontroversial, and the ethical status of SM
tends to polarize gender, queer, and feminist criticism. It has been the
focus of an ongoing debate about feminist ethics, which flared up in the
late 1970s and was revived recently as a result of SM's increasing presence
in popular culture. Numerous critics, then and now, consider SM practice
and serious feminism to be irreconcilable phenomena, arguing that the
former celebrates sexual violence, despite an avowed commitment to progressive values.[45] Others hold that a categorical disapproval of SM by
feminist criticism merely recreates in a more fashionable guise the sanitiz-
ing repression that stigmatizes sexual pleasure, in particular for women
and sexual minorities. Some argue, like Newmahr, that BDSM may serve
as a subversive practice that creates a safe play space where configurations
of gender and power can be renegotiated.[46] Any resolution of this dispute
far exceeds the ambitions of this book (although it must be said that the
mainstreaming of BDSM into a commodified lifestyle industry poses a
significant challenge for those who want to hold on to the faith in its subversive potential).[47] What I want to do here is demonstrate that in debates
over opera's staging of sex, power, and violence, it can be usefully thought
of precisely as a question of hyperbole. If BDSM can be understood as a

consensual, hyperbolic enactment of sexual violence, how does this relate to opera's mise-en-scène of its own cruelties, habitually aimed against its women but often against its other characters, too—and, in a certain sense, even against its audiences?

In a rare comment on the aspect of staging, Clément imagines a production of one of the most beloved works of the repertoire, which for many has served as the gateway into the art form:

> You do not like my story? You prefer *The Magic Flute* of your childhood and the birdcatcher's lighthearted laughter while he looks for his bird? . . . Yes. But men's education suppresses its own violences, and I have never yet seen my heart's version of the *Flute*. In it the good priests with majestic voices would do what they really do; they would shove Pamina forcibly into the cubbyhole where Zarastro locks her up, they would beat up the Queen of the Night, they would kick Papageno, the truth at last.[48]

If Clément's main point is that male violence is a norm in opera, she argues here for a hyperbolic onstage representation of that norm. The impulse is to expose the latent misogyny rather than glossing it over, to resist the norm by making it hyperbolically visible. This line of reasoning is not uncommon in relation to opera staging. In a recent colloquy on sexual violence in opera, for instance, Ellie M. Hisama argues that a staging of Benjamin Britten's 1946 opera *The Rape of Lucretia* is feminist precisely because it does not allow for the suggestion—which she pinpoints in several accounts by male critics—that Lucretia secretly desires Tarquinius. For this reason director Mary Birnbaum set out to make the rape scene "as gross and violent as possible."[49] The abuse must be unmistakable in order to expel the possibility of pleasure—for Lucretia but also for the audience. If sexual violence slides into an ambiguous seduction, potentially titillating for the spectators, the result is a betrayal of the victim of abuse. On this view the decision of pushing the representation of sexual assault to an extreme is justified by the need to preclude such enjoyment or, at the very least, burden it with a bad conscience.

The same argument—and the same problem of staging sexual violence—underlies many controversial stagings of recent dates, and to supplement Clément and Birnbaum's rationale, I will briefly point to two of the most notorious ones: the 2004 *Entführung aus dem Serail* at the

Komische Oper Berlin and the 2015 *Guillaume Tell* at the Royal Opera House (ROH), Covent Garden. There are plenty of differences between these four performances—the level of violence prescribed in the original work, the times and contexts in which they are produced, the gender of the directors, the fact that Clément just muses over an imagined production whereas the others are actually staged, to mention a few—but they are united by a display of brutality against women explicitly intended to critique it. In the cases of the *Entführung* and *Guillaume Tell,* the production as a whole has been overshadowed by a single scene, which in turn has come to function as an emblem of director's opera. If opera and SM are united by a hyperbolic mode, these scenes become something like hyperbolized hyperboles: more extreme than any of the productions I will focus on in my own analyses, they constitute limit cases of deviant opera.

When Damiano Michieletto directed Rossini's *Guillaume Tell* at the ROH, the third-act ballet—in which the Swiss soldiers coerce the female villagers to dance—was staged as a protracted sexual assault, during which a group of officers stripped a woman (played by actress Jessica Chamberlain), poured champagne down her throat, and molested her with a gun. The scene provoked a chorus of boos while still going on, and the critical reception was overwhelmingly negative.[50] For instance, *Opera Today*'s Claire Seymour found "the director's decision to foreground the sexual brutality of war" to be "sensationalist, distasteful and gratuitous," and in the *Sunday Express* Clare Colvin called it "gratuitous and prurient," claiming that Michieletto "insult[ed] the intelligence of the audience by his in-your-face shock tactics."[51] The claimed gratuitousness lies in the exaggerated relation to the score's stage directions, which say: "Des soldats contraignent des femmes suisses à danser avec eux. Les habitans témoignent par leurs gestes leur indignation de cette violence" (Soldiers force the Swiss women to dance with them. The gestures of the inhabitants show their indignation at this violence). In Michieletto's staging the brutality is overstated in relation to this description but not necessarily in relation to the type of situation with which it deals. As a response to the ensuing criticism the ROH's director of opera, Kasper Holten, maintained that the scene sought to put "the spotlight on the brutal reality of women being abused during war time, and sexual violence being a tragic fact of war."[52] Michieletto, for his part, argued, "If you don't feel the brutality, the suffering these people have had to face, if you want to hide it, it becomes soft, it becomes for children."[53] Although less eloquently put, the rationale is the same as in Clément's imaginary *Flute:* let them do what they really do, because the truth must not be suppressed.

Calixto Bieito's *Die Entführung aus dem Serail* at the Komische Oper Berlin, which premiered in 2004 and had its final performance as late as April of 2018, is among the most written-and-talked-about productions of the last decades.[54] In Bieito's vision of Mozart's *Singspiel* the harem over which Bassa Selim presides had been turned into a present-day big-city brothel home to bestial behavior. The latter reached its disturbing peak during "Martern aller Arten" (All kinds of torture), the big coloratura aria in which the captive Konstanze vows to stay true to her betrothed no matter the pain to which he will subject her. In Berlin she (and the audience) was forced to watch as a prostitute was held down and brutalized by the Bassa's overseer Osmin, who slashed her nipples off with a knife, raped, and finally murdered her—all in a very realistic manner (fig. 1.1). Although Osmin's character is comical, his words often evoke an extreme violence, which form the substrate of Bieito's interpretation: "Erst geköpft, dann gehangen, dann gespießt auf heißen Stangen / dann verbrannt, dann gebunden und getaucht, zuletzt geschunden" (First beheaded, then hanged, then spitted on hot skewers, then burned, then bound, and drowned, and finally skinned). Here, the libretto itself is hyperbolic, and the staging turns its comedy into horror by taking those figures literally. The Komische Oper announced that "Bieito—like Mozart—sides with the women, who are destroyed by the men": the director wanted to expose how brutal behavior is born from men's fears—"in Spain, twenty women died between January and June 2004, for this reason alone," he notes—through an operatic work that in itself "shows a world that is against women."[55] This critical intention is actually quite clear in the production, not least from the stage being dominated by ads for beauty products and lingerie, highlighting the objectification of the female body in late-capitalist society.

If opera aestheticizes cruelty and suffering, not exclusively but overwhelmingly victimizing its female characters, stagings like these seek to push this point to an extreme, making it impossible to suppress. Arguably, they give Clément's perspective physical shape on the stage, and in so doing, they accord with her own imaginary staging of *Die Zauberflöte.* The

Figure 1.1. "All kinds of torture may await me." Bassa Selim (Guntbert Warns) making Konstanze (Maria Bengtsson) watch while Osmin (Jens Larsen) murders a prostitute (uncredited extra). *Die Entführung aus dem Serail* (dir. Calixto Bieito, Komische Oper Berlin, 2004). © Monika Rittershaus, 2004. Reproduced by kind permission.

explicit intention is a critical undermining: to make the aesthetic use of abuse and oppression—present to various degrees in all of the scores and librettos—too confrontational to be comfortably enjoyed in any detached, leisurely way, or perhaps in any way at all. I am not attempting to refute the ethical potential of this move, and I thoroughly sympathize with the refusal to sugarcoat the sordid undercurrents of opera; however, I want to insist on the basic insight that authorial intention can never prescribe the meanings that result from a particular performance of a particular production and its reception by a particular audience. In my view Micaela Baranello—who argues that "Bieito's *Entführung*, far more graphic than Michieletto's ballet, is a serious interpretation and, when seen in proper context, not gratuitous"—is right to stress that the "line between exploitation and productive meaning is by no means clear."[56] To emphasize its volatility, the above strategy—pushing something disturbing on stage to an extreme in order to make it impossible to gloss over—can be thought of as a hyperbolic gambit. The point is that this mode of critique is a risk activity with high stakes: it may be potentially productive, but it is also liable to misfire in various ways.

First of all, an attempt to preclude pleasure on the spectator's part can never be failsafe. In a world that harbors online video clips of executions and torture, snuff movies, and violent pornography—and where, historically, gladiator games, hangings, and beheadings have been viewed as acceptable forms of entertainment—it stands to reason that no quantity or quality of violence can thoroughly expel the possibility of secret titillation from that which is intended to be gruesome. This is especially true since the audience knows that the violence is not actual but enacted. Self-evidently yet importantly, what is shown on stage in Michieletto's *Guillaume Tell* or Bieito's *Entführung* is not sexual assault but representations thereof. Since neither the sex nor the violence is real, the problem cannot be quite the same as in pornography or spectacles like public executions or torture. What takes place within the operatic fiction is clearly nonconsensual torture, yet what the actors and singers provide is a theatrical enactment of it. Even scenes as extreme as these, therefore, can be thought of in analogy with extreme examples of BDSM: they would correspond to what the kink community calls "rape play"—that is, consensual scenarios focused on simulating the nonconsensual.[57] At the opera such scenes are certain to come across as disturbing to large parts of the audience, and for some they may indeed provoke the sought-for ethical stance. But they may also cater to a spectatorial pleasure that aligns more closely with the phenomena they are aiming to critique. Like deviance, hyperbole always depends on its distance from a norm, yet it can never protect itself from normalization. The more common the disturbing sight is, the less certain it can be of disturbing.

Second, there is also an ethical risk at the opposite end of the spectrum, where the affective impact becomes too strong to be justifiable. At its extreme this effect may reawaken and renew trauma or otherwise forestall not just the exploitative spectatorial pleasure but also the pleasure of operatic singing—which would arguably be problematic because it deprives the genre of what most fans take to be its ultimate justification. Ultimately, it may also preempt critical interpretation, because it gets in the way of any engagement at all. Consider, for instance, Risi's account of the dress rehearsal of Bieito's *Entführung*, where the following happened during "Martern aller Arten": "In the middle of one of the vocally most demanding passages of the aria, uproar broke out. Boos and loud cries of 'Stop!' 'No more!' and the like crescendoed to such an extent that the decibel levels of the audience at times drowned out the stage and the orchestra pit."[58] The audience's reaction cannot simply be dismissed as conservative fist shaking: the Komische Oper is well known for provocative productions, its audience accustomed to both nudity and violence. Neither is it likely that they believed that a woman was actually being tortured before their eyes. Rather, as Risi puts it, the "protests were presumably the physically necessary reactions of self-defense against what was being perceived as an attack upon one's own body."[59] This experience is the flip side of the idea that attending an opera is a physical activity with strong erotic elements. If we take seriously the idea of spectatorship as participation, a performance can make its audience part of something to which they do not consent. From this perspective the violation may be real in some sense, even though the onstage violence is just a representation. If we remain with the BDSM analogy, shouting "Stop!" marks the moment when the scene is pushed to or beyond its limits and a safe word is needed. Precisely by refusing to play along with the terms of the performance, the audience members confirm the idea of performance as a game based on mutual consent: as participants, they claim their right to interrupt it when it has gone too far. But operatic convention does not—perhaps cannot, even should not—furnish the audience with that prerogative: they can whistle, boo, and leave, but they have no agreed-upon means to stop the show.

When Sam Abel insisted that operatic performance is sex, he also worried about the fact that opera "makes sexualized violence 'feel right.'" The reason for this, he suggested, is that music "raises the intensity of theatrical sex wars and, at the same time, makes sexual violence more palatable, because the beautiful music mitigates the violence."[60] The reason this view seems ill-suited to stagings like Bieito's or Michieletto's is that it denies music any agency beyond aural cosmetics. Crucially, Rossini's "Pas des soldats" and Mozart's "Martern aller Arten" are exhilaratingly upbeat pieces in major keys and certainly both intense and beautiful when performed well. But I wager that relatively few of the audience members at the ROH and the Komische Oper perceived the sexual violence enacted on stage as mitigated by that beauty and, as we have seen, the stated intention of the creative teams was exactly the opposite. Nor, however, need the musical joy be eradicated by horrifying visuals: music has the capacity to retain every bit of its exuberance, which is undergirded by the ubiquitous ascription of lighthearted genius to the composers—especially to Mozart, of course, but also to Rossini. It is precisely the unsettling clash between these registers that pushes questions of ethics and aesthetics into the foreground.

When the hyperbolic gambit works, I would argue, it does so because it elicits a critical response from the spectating audience precisely by mingling enjoyment with discomfort. For the spectator who is not disturbed enough, the performance simply thrives on opera's predilection for cruelty and humiliation, leaving it intact and uncriticized, thus allowing for a visual pleasure that smoothly intermingles with the sensuality of operatic singing. For the spectator who is *too* disturbed, not only the pleasure of looking is forestalled but also that of listening and therefore also any reason to remain and engage with opera. The sensual gratification of the operatic voice is traded off, but no impetus for critical thought is delivered in return. Put differently, the need to probe opera (and one's own subjective experience of it) arises only from the simultaneous experience of the pleasant and the problematic. Neither can be prescribed. From a performance-focused perspective there is nothing—no directorial decision and no amount of reflection and control—that can guarantee the result beforehand. However hard a production tries, it cannot eradicate this ambiguity but will always run the risk of thrilling some spectators while traumatizing others. When the hyperbolic gambit misfires, opera may become part of the cynical exploitation of suffering that it aimed to critique, or it may become so devoid of *jouissance* that the audience has no reason to engage with it, critically or otherwise.

In this sense deviant opera—especially when pushed to its hyperbolic extremes—can be thought of as a risk activity in which its spectators and listeners engage along with the performers. When a director deliberately works with the affective response of the audience as his or her material, they become participants in a sense that feeds into the analogy with BDSM. Although the paradigm of SSC is central to the BDSM community, many practitioners feel uncomfortable with it precisely because it seeks to dissimulate a risk-taking that they perceive as crucial to their interest in the first place: to a certain degree, being emotionally and physically engaged in an erotic power exchange necessarily entails putting oneself at stake. Accordingly, some prefer to use the acronym "RACK"—that is, "risk-aware consensual kink."[61] It was coined in 1999 by practitioner Gary Switch, who convincingly argued: "If we want to limit BDSM to what's safe, we can't do anything more extreme than flogging somebody with a wet noodle. Mountain climbers don't call their sport safe, for the simple reason that it isn't; risk is an essential part of the thrill."[62]

It is therefore incumbent on BDSM to acknowledge its own risks and to develop strategies for dealing with them. Practitioners do so through extended negotiations that may go into the preparation of a scene, through responsive and responsible use of safe words and communicative gestures, as well as the aftercare (that is, when "the top [the one inflicting the pain] tends to the bottom's emotional/mental and physical needs").[63] Favoring an attentive and continuous dialogue in both words and readable body language, BDSM is an emphatically "communicative sexuality" (an aspect that has also been brought into an even more recent coinage: the "4Cs," representing Caring, Communication, Consent, and Caution).[64] Deviant opera suggests the need for an equivalent to these communicative habits to deal with the specific stakes of operatic performance and its hyperbolic representations of sex, power, and violence—backstage among producers, directors, and singers but also among critics, audiences, and spectators. That the conditions are vastly different hardly needs pointing out: unlike SM, aesthetic performances arguably neither can nor should commit to an eradication of ambiguous meanings and difficult experiences. But precisely where preestablished consent from audiences or safe words that stop the show are not an option, the acknowledgment of the specific kinds of risk germane to performance, as well as the discursive exploration of ethics and meaning, becomes all the more central and rewarding for its producers, directors, performers, audiences, and critics. Taking the analogy between opera and SM seriously implies committing to communication, even about that which seems most insistently to elude discursive meaning, such as the visceral experiences of pleasure and pain, of power and powerlessness, of shock and ecstasy.

THE ACTUALITY EFFECT: MAKING IT REAL

If we are trying to respond to the question "What are these stagings trying to tell us about opera?" on an overarching level, a provisional answer might read something like this: opera, like SM, is a hyperbolic, self-consciously theatrical performance, which continuously draws on the interplay of power asymmetries and eroticism. Both are irreducibly corporeal practices permeated by symbolic meanings and cultural tropes, which are typically mobilized with the ultimate aim of pleasure for all participants yet to some extent are always accompanied by the risk of unpleasure. Because of this risk, and because of its fraught representations of sexuality, gender, and violence, opera no less than SM also demands continuous communication—on the one hand, a responsive and responsible reading of bodily behaviors, visual signs, and sounding voices within the performance and, on the other, serious efforts of verbal communication around it. If one regards the opera productions that insist on the iconography of perversion as a semiunified phenomenon in contemporary culture, they can be understood as a visual filter that foregrounds these points of contact. To conclude this chapter, I will briefly introduce a more particular phenomenon, which builds on yet moves beyond these general analogies and will crystallize through the string of productions that I discuss. I have chosen to call this phenomenon the *actuality effect*. This term designates a characteristic figure employed repeatedly by directors in conjunction with SM, although it can be brought to bear fruitfully on staged opera far beyond that context. Its most basic condition is that it shows the transformation of a figure, a fiction, or a fantasy into something that is, in one sense or another, actual. I will make use of this concept to demonstrate opera's fixation with the border between the enacted and the actual, between imagination and reality, and on the repeated movement across it. Each of the stagings I discuss makes use of this effect. The insistence with which it appears, I will argue, testifies to its significance as a connecting tissue between opera and SM: what it actualizes in the stagings addressed here is the eroticized power electrifying the operatic air.

The Brechtian flavor of the term is intentional, and I will take a moment to explain its relation to the *Verfremdungseffekt*—that is, the alienation or estrangement effect. Parts of my undertaking find resonance in Brecht's theory and practice. While Brecht himself nurtured a profoundly ambiguous attitude vis-à-vis the bourgeois art of opera, it nevertheless exerted an important influence on his work, and director's opera is often understood as a direct descendant of epic theater, aiming to shake the audience out of its comfortable reception habits by showing canonical works in a defamiliarizing light.[65] Moreover, I take the relationship between critical interpretation and immersive pleasure to be an important focal point in the stagings I discuss, as is their foregrounding of historical disjunctions—both of which were core aspects of Brecht's theory and practice.[66] Most important, various ways of deconstructing the fourth wall will figure prominently in the following chapters. From this perspective some instances of what I call the actuality effect are a variation on the estrangement effect that depends specifically on the physical manifestation of figures and fantasies.

The present state of opera and the culture surrounding it, however, differ profoundly from what Brecht saw and heard. He developed his concept during the interwar period, against the specific backdrop of a predominantly naturalistic theater, and he was well aware that in a situation where avant-garde theater had become widespread, its estrangement effects could be co-opted by the anesthetic pleasures they were meant to disrupt.[67] Today, the omnipresence in popular culture of the techniques associated with the estrangement effect has inevitably dulled its edge. Some even argue that it has become "so ubiquitous in modern advertising, feature films and television sit-coms as to lose all artistic and political effect."[68] Joy Calico, who considers estrangement essential to contemporary opera staging, has rightly stressed the importance of differentiating between Brechtian *style* (as in a specific set of staging and acting techniques) and Brechtian *method* (as in the approach that seeks to empower the critical minds of the audience).[69] From this perspective the latter can be achieved without the former, by adapting to new frames of reference and developing its styles to keep arriving at an estranged experience. Arguably, however, it is not only the particular styles that become habitual at a given point but also the estrangement itself. Once it has formed its own convention, estrangement becomes less immediately effective and loses some of its supposed capacity to generate new understanding. After the code of director's opera has had almost half a century to assert itself, estrangement is likely to form a significant part of the expectations of any operagoer. Yet convention, whether that of director's opera or the ones it has partially supplanted, cannot simply be equated with general stagnation and repetitiveness. Nor does it need to be faulted for failing to come up with something radically original with each attempt (an intention that is habitually ascribed to director's opera by its detractors but perhaps less often forms part of the director's actual agenda). Instead, the establishment of a convention furnishes both operatic mise-en-scène and the criticism that attends to it with other options, which are not necessarily based on innovation or novelty. The power of estrangement may not have disappeared altogether, but it has faded into the background. It is against that background that an interpretative approach can discern other effects— the actuality effect among them.

The actuality effect operates on three different levels, which can be distinguished by their relation to the operatic diegesis (that is, the fictional reality in which the characters exist). The first level takes place within the primary diegesis. It may consist of, for instance, a metaphor or hyperbole uttered by a character, which is stripped by the staging of its metaphorical character. Take the lines from Konstanze's first aria in *Entführung*, where she reminisces about her rosy freedom with Belmonte:

Ach ich liebte,	Alas, I loved,
War so glücklich;	was so delighted;
Kannte nicht der Liebe Schmerz.	Knew nothing of the pain of love.

If these lines are sung in a bordello where sex is regularly accompanied by sadistic torture, the "Schmerz" can no longer be understood as, say, the heartache when the beloved is absent but refers instead to an actual, physical, pain. But because it is still clearly recognizable as a figure of speech, it has the effect of crossing the border from the figurative to the literal.

On a second level the actuality effect takes place between distinct layers of the diegesis—for instance, if the opera's characters create a new level of fiction by engaging in role-playing, which then turns out to become real for them. The prostitute who is tortured and butchered in Bieito's *Entführung* initially appears to believe that what is about to happen is merely a role-play of humiliation, an enacted demonstration of the Bassa's power, to which she submits because Osmin persuades her with a fistful of bills. It is only later, when the violence against her gradually gets worse, that she understands what is going on and struggles in vain to break free. This instance of the actuality effect depends on the prior establishment of a fiction-within-the-fiction, an enactment not just by the singers but by the characters, which is then revealed as actual to the latter (but not to the former).

On a third level, finally, the actuality effect may break through the diegesis altogether and impact the real human beings in the opera house. Again, an example can be borrowed from Bieito's *Entführung*, via Risi's description of how he experienced the torture scene at the dress rehearsal in 2004. "Maria Bengtsson," he writes, "sang for her life, for her survival, not only as Konstanze, confronted with the tortures that were burdening her soul and that were being acted out with cruel clarity before her, but also as a singer faced with an out-of-control audience whose shouts and protestations were drowning her out."[70] The fluctuation between the fictional role and the real bodily presence, Risi adds, is "one of the very characteristic perception modes of opera performance brought to an extreme." Specifically, this fluctuation is conditioned and framed by the represented story: the operatic diegesis itself, as it were, breaks down under the pressure of the hyperbolized brutality on stage and the audience's loud reaction to it. In this instance of the actuality effect, the enacted vulnerability of the character appears to cross over into the real vulnerability of her interpreter.

This observation does not necessarily mean that performing such a scene is always a bad or problematic experience, and it does not warrant the automatic assumption that the singers are unwilling participants subjected to something they have not agreed to. Yet this risk needs to be acknowledged, and if the backstage communication does not function properly or is couched in unspoken hierarchies and asymmetric power relations, it becomes significant. To act on stage is always to put oneself at stake to some extent, and professional performers are used to it. Singers, in particular, cannot let their vocal production be touched by actual emotion, which would immediately rupture tone and timbre. But hyperbolic representations of sexuality, power, and violence create a situation more difficult than any other to fend off from one's own person. Looking back at the first rehearsals, bass Jens Larsen (who held the knife) says: "We worked for a very long time on the staging of the 'Martern' aria. It went on for weeks, with Calixto and in very close dialogue with Maria. Does it work this way? Should it, may it, can it be done in this way? And back then, we decided—all of us, really—that it should be presented in this way once."[71] Bengtsson, who had her breakthrough with the Komische Oper *Entführung* and was relatively inexperienced at the time, describes it as an "unbelievable experience": "We provoked so much emotion," she says, and argues that the reason the production worked was that "such things happen in every European city. And everyone knows it." Bengtsson insists that all participants were fully behind the production, and she has no problem with provocative stage directors; on the contrary: "They have seen sides of me that I did not even know that I had."[72] Larsen also emphasizes the inevitable personal impact of the performance, even while maintaining control over one's voice: "It stirs you up inside in an unbelievable way, and you can feel that it is really on the absolute limit. And it strains you too. It is not easily done, playing this scene."[73]

Whether it amounts to a negative experience or a positive one, singers who participate in productions with strong elements of sex and violence test their control of their emotional and bodily selves to an extraordinary degree: the difficulty of retaining a neutral or detached stance in relation to the performance and its affective impact is significant. As audience reactions like those at the Komische Oper show, something similar can be said of those who are there to watch and listen. Ultimately, this may be the most crucial point of the analogy between SM and opera as it is presented in deviant stagings: because their fantasy scenarios of domination and submission necessarily involve the real bodies of real people, who put themselves at stake in the performance, their theatrics may turn out to be more real—or real in a different sense—than one would initially believe. The actuality effect, as it will come into view during the chapters that follow, repeatedly imagines this unsettling possibility on stage.

2 Sex in Excess

RINALDO, ALCINA, AND THE
CONTEMPORARY BAROQUE

Opera is a balancing act on the edge of excess. Its spectacular overabundance is as enthralling to its admirers as it is repelling to those who are immune to it. It is when present-day versions of this intemperance merge with operatic plots of desire and violence that the visual codes of sadomasochism make their appearance on stage. While the iconography of perversion is foreign to the historical origins of the operatic repertoire, the intertwinement of eroticism and power into excessive spectacle is not. At opera's birth, at the beginning of the seventeenth century, the taste for lavishness—epitomized by the sensuous extravagance of its voice—was inscribed in its genetic code. That taste has descended through all succeeding generations of the genre, despite the occasional attempt to bridle it by reform. It marks opera as a baroque art form in a sense that transcends the historical epoch with which that term was originally associated. Ever since the late eighteenth century started applying it to art and architecture, the term *baroque* has been laden with connotations of excess, bizarrerie, even bad taste.[1] What is more, its pejorative drift has been aimed at ethics and aesthetics alike: the flair for emotional indulgence and richness of ornament that attracted the epithet "baroque" was typically taken to imply a moral weakness.[2] What we today know as baroque

51

opera was a favorite target of this kind of castigation in its own time, its extravagance often perceived as a threat to the foundations of society, especially in terms of gender and sexuality.[3] That anxiety did not abate with modern times: in the mid-twentieth-century Joseph Kerman could still get away with labeling the century between Monteverdi and Gluck "the dark ages of opera," condemning the art form as "a shameless virtuoso display, emasculating classic history into a faint and tedious concert in costume," which had "thrown dignity into the canals" and "completely debased recitative."[4]

The radical stagings that have often accompanied the baroque revival of recent decades have not so much tried to reject these moralist categories as they have tried to reclaim them for their own reinterpretation of opera. Shamelessness, debasement, and loss of dignity are key elements in the productions I discuss in this chapter, as is the treatment of classic history in ways that Kerman would no doubt consider "emasculating"—that is, the performance of historical configurations of gender, sexuality, and power in contemporary costume, which interprets them from a present-day perspective as highly volatile and malleable categories. In this chapter I will home in on two specific tropes of baroque excess and the way they are recast in the iconography of perversion: *hyperbole* and *metalepsis*. Hyperbole in the rhetorical sense—the use of exaggeration for rhetorical effect—is inextricably connected to the baroque.[5] Meanwhile, interventionist stagings of baroque opera, which have often been characterized by a campy, more-is-more aesthetics and eclectic mash-ups, can be understood as the result of a specific combination of carnivalesque baroque and contemporary hyperbole. Something similar can be said about metalepsis, a term that I use here in the sense that Gérard Genette and other narratologists have developed: as a transgressive contamination between distinct levels of fiction.[6] The playful leakage between the diegetic layers of a story or image was a hallmark of baroque aesthetics—think of Cervantes, whose hero Don Quixote comes across a book about his own adventures, or Vélazquez, who is famously seen painting in a mirror in his own *Las Meninas*. Such leakage has also played a central part in postmodernist aesthetics, and the stage-within-the-stage belongs to the most beloved (and arguably overused) tricks in the toolbox of director's opera.

If hyperbole and metalepsis can thus be understood as contemporary variations on the baroque ethos, what happens when they meet the iconography of perversion? How do the elements of contemporary SM and fetishism react with the aesthetics of baroque opera? In what follows, I direct these questions at two stagings of George Frideric Handel, whose works have played the lead role in the revival of baroque opera.[7] One is the *Alcina* of the Staatsoper Stuttgart. It opened in 1998 under the joint direction and dramaturgy of Jossi Wieler and Sergio Morabito, who have collaborated on a large number of productions since, sticking to Stuttgart as their home base. In their *Alcina* the chivalric romance originally drawn from Ludovico Ariosto's *Orlando furioso* is sprinkled with intimations of bondage, cross-dressing, and shoe fetishism, and Alcina's sorcery is reinterpreted as irresistible sexual attraction. The other is a 2011 production of *Rinaldo* at the Glyndebourne Festival by the Canadian director Robert Carsen, who had several Handel productions under his belt before taking this one on. Here, the knights of the First Crusade are pupils at a British boarding school, and as the opera starts, the protagonist receives a caning by his history teacher, whom his pubescent fantasy will soon transform into a voluptuous dominatrix in a figure-hugging rubber dress. Like most productions discussed in this book, these two met a wide spectrum of critical responses, ranging from ecstatic praise to brutal thrashing. Irrespective of reviewers' opinion, however, they have retained the interest of their audiences and institutions: since their premieres, both have been released on DVD, taken on tour, and revived in their original venues (the Stuttgart *Alcina* was done in 2016 and Carsen's *Rinaldo* as recently as December of 2019). Before I attend in more detail to the SM elements of these stagings, however, I will dwell on the question of historicity and the relation between the baroque and the contemporary.

A PREPOSTEROUS HISTORY LESSON

The recent return of the seventeenth and early eighteenth centuries to the operatic stage has often highlighted the tensions between the contemporary and the baroque. This baroque revival amounts to a conflation of two disparate moments in time, the clash of which is so striking because they are not united by any continuously developing tradition. After the break-through of classicism, baroque opera more or less disappeared for more than two hundred years and had to wait until our time for regular per-formances. The most obvious example is the reappraisal of Handel's operas, which were completely forgotten until the 1920s and became a steady part of the repertoire only toward the end of the millennium. When baroque opera thus reappeared, it did so with a curiously ambivalent rela-tion to its historical origins. On the one hand, its reemergence was closely linked to the growing interest in early music performance practice, the rhythmic vigor and quick tempi of which made it possible to actually stage the endless succession of arias that amounts to a full-length baroque opera. On the other hand, it coincided with an explosion of irreverently innovative stage practice, which subjected the premodern works to post-modern rereadings (in Handel's case Peter Sellars's stagings of *Orlando, Giulio Cesare,* and *Theodora* from the 1980s and 1990s are exemplary).

This has led to the observation that the slow dramatic pace of opera seria makes directorial interventions possible, arguably even necessary: unlike the present, the early eighteenth century never expected an opera performance to keep an audience silent and absorbed for an entire evening.[8] Yet here as elsewhere, director's opera is routinely accused of dragging serious opera into the dirt of entertainment, often with recourse to the same masculinist-moralist terms with which Kerman condemned baroque opera as a whole. Critics thus fulminated against Glyndebourne's *Giulio Cesare*—the 2005 forerunner to *Rinaldo,* directed by David McVicar—which lacked any "'depth, nobility, or heroism,' its music 'cas-trated' of any meaning by 'whorish applause-seeking.'"[9] While similar anxieties are induced by most director's opera, some have opined that Handel's works are threatened in a more profound way than the repertoire staples: "If a director were to set . . . *Fidelio* in a brothel," writes Winton Dean, "no lasting damage would be done, except perhaps to the director's reputation. . . . That is not yet the case with Handel's operas."[10] Precisely because there is no established convention of traditional stagings, con-temporary mise-en-scène is much more likely to affect the public image of Handel as an opera composer. *Giulio Cesare* and *Theodora,* as it were, are part of a high-risk group: they have not developed the canonical immunity of recognized masterworks, so they are susceptible to an incurable

contamination by avant-garde productions. More productive than thinking of this predisposition in pathological terms, however, is to take it as a
particularly illuminating example of a core condition of opera: precisely
because it does not have a massive modern performance tradition, baroque
opera is a perfect site for embracing the mutability of performance. While
a staged production always amounts to a contemporary refashioning of
the past—even when it attempts to faithfully emulate that past—baroque
opera presents us with a greater temporal distance between present and
past than any later variety of the genre. But beyond this straightforward
fact, a temporal gap or heterochronicity is a central component in the concept of the baroque itself. To clarify this, I will turn briefly to some recent
attempts to rethink the baroque by unhinging it from its original historical period.

   In the wake of Gilles Deleuze's idiosyncratic reading of Leibniz and the
baroque in *The Fold*, recent decades have seen the rise of the concept of
the neobaroque, which attempts to establish a relation between the contemporary moment and the historical baroque.[11] The traits that are usually cited to define the neobaroque include excess, instability, virtuosity,
and loss of totality, which not only reveals the concept as part of a general
postmodern ethos but also, and more interestingly, stresses its affinity
with some core aspects of opera.[12] Once the overabundance and instability
of the baroque is affirmed rather than rejected, moreover, it can be pro-
ductively brought to bear on the aesthetic realization of history itself. Such
is the project of cultural theorist Mieke Bal's work on the relationship
between contemporary art and artists like Bernini or Caravaggio, in which
she outlines what she calls a "preposterous history."[13] The qualifier *preposterous* here does not refer exclusively to the outrageous or absurd, although
that sense is not insignificant. It also signifies a reversal of before and
after, where the past is reimagined from the position of the present; that
is, it sees in the art of the present a cause and creative source of the art of
the past. Once a historical work of art has been quoted or recast by a contemporary one, it does not remain the same. This view, Bal argues, is
emphatically different both from a naive presentism and a positivist historicism, both of which ignore the unbridgeable gap separating us from
the past.[14] Quite to the contrary, preposterous history takes this gap as its
point of departure and sets out to explore the particularities of a dialogue

between distinct historical moments. For my purposes here, it captures precisely the conspicuous superimposition of historical layers that so often marks director's opera. As I employ the term, it refers less to an academic method than to an aesthetic practice: the stagings I address here, in other words, are *doing* preposterous history on the stage. If they are to be properly understood, this endeavor must be taken seriously. In practice this means that I will attempt to construe the iconography of perversion in its relation both to the opera texts themselves and to their historical contexts.

Preposterous history also has a particular relation to the concept of the baroque. Bal uses phrases such as "baroque epistemology" and "baroque as historiography" to emphasize that the baroque itself is marked by what she calls a "heterochronic historical temporality."[15] The idea of the baroque is not only anachronistic at its roots, because the term stems from a classicist moment looking back (and down its nose) at the preceding century, creating in the process what we know as the baroque. It is also, even in its original moment, defined by a kind of delirious, multilayered coexistence of the present and the past, a "coevalness" or "shared time." Yet the word *shared*, she emphasizes, may suggest a more harmonious relationship than is appropriate: "Conflict and tension reside in the sharing as well. The idea of a 'contemporary baroque' is, then, a fundamentally baroque one and, hence, a tautology: baroque already entails contemporariness. 'Baroque' is always-already contemporary with the past, through a 'hallucinatory' relationship."[16] Put differently: in the contemporary baroque the intermingling of the moment of understanding and the moment of the understood, which hermeneutics has taught us to regard as a basic aspect of historical understanding, is embraced, affirmed, and flaunted to the point of hallucination. Nowhere is this more visible than in the heterochronic clashes between contemporary mise-en-scène and baroque opera. Although Sellars's stagings, fusing the Roman Empire with the foreign policy of the US in the Middle East, offer intriguing examples, Robert Carsen's Glyndebourne production of *Rinaldo* is perhaps the most instructive illustration of this point. This production marked the tercentenary of the premiere in 1711, which was a watershed in the history of opera: the young Handel had just arrived in London, and the explosive success of his first work for the Haymarket Theatre turned out to be the big breakthrough not only for him, personally, but for Italian opera in England. Carsen's production pays facetious homage to this historical significance: it begins, preposterously, with a history lesson.

The entire opera is played out in the imagination of a bullied schoolboy, who is dreaming up a story in which he acts as a heroic knight instead of the underdog. During the overture Gideon Davey's stage design presents the audience with a 1950s-style classroom, where the stern teacher (played by Brenda Rae, who will soon become the enchantress-dominatrix Armida) writes the topic of today's essay on the blackboard: "Were the first crusaders inspired by religious idealism or political revenge?" As the boy who will turn out to be the heroic knight Rinaldo (Sonia Prina) goes forward to sharpen his pen—a classic way of stalling the soporific task— his imagination suddenly explodes and the world around him is trans- formed: Goffredo's army of Crusaders enters the classroom, driving out teachers and bullies by the sword, and we see medieval cuirasses worn over school uniforms. Later, when Rinaldo sets out to recapture his beloved Almirena, who has been taken hostage by Armida and the Saracenes, the Glyndebourne staging sees him riding a bike through the sky in front of a giant moon—a visual quotation from Steven Spielberg's *E.T.* Throughout the opera a variety of other fantasies enter the story (not least the sexual ones, to which I will turn in a moment), often mediated through pop-culture imagery.

Such deliberately heterochronic imagery epitomizes the neobaroque, both as a loss of aesthetic totality and as Bal's notion of a preposterous history: elements from wildly disparate times, places, and sources join together in an entertaining and extravagant vision, which is quite up-front about its origin in the present moment and could not care less about val- ues of aesthetic coherence or historical accuracy. Whether or not one con- siders the production successful, however, it should be acknowledged that this anarchic assemblage resonates with the typical genesis of Italian baroque opera. *Rinaldo* itself is a particularly clear example. The first opera that Handel composed after his arrival in London in 1710, it had to be produced in a hurry.[17] Both text and music borrow generously from his older works, often with very little care for logic. In the words of Dean and Knapp, the librettist "is not afraid to mix his mythological metaphors": the historical setting is infused with images from fairy-tale, Christian, and classical sources.[18] Argante even borrows a whole aria, text and music, from the Cyclops in Handel's *Aci, Galatea and Polifemo* from 1708 ("Sibillar gli angui d'Aletto" [the hissing of Alecto's serpents]). Hence, we hear him singing of Alecto's snakes and the barking Scylla—preposterous indeed, coming from a Saracen commander in the eleventh century.

In the Glyndebourne *Rinaldo* Luca Pisaroni sings Argante's aria sporting an ensemble of chainmail, three-piece tweed, and schoolmaster's gown, topped off with turban and scimitar. This incongruity is a contemporary manifestation of the fortuitous overabundance that was part and parcel of baroque opera but that is often obscured by the anachronistic reverence, originating only in the late nineteenth century, with which the cultural practice of operagoing expects us to meet the works of the past. Similarly, the stage of the Stuttgart *Alcina* is scattered not only with antique furniture, elaborate golden frames, and worn-out wallpapers with baroque floral patterns but also with modern objects like lightbulbs and fluorescent tubes, constantly reminding us of the heterochronic clash of disparate historical moments. In the DVD version the camera shows us close-ups of these objects and others (not least an array of shoes, which will play an important part as the production's most prominently fetishized object—more of which later).

These productions, then, embody the neobaroque reading of baroque art, where the present is folded onto the past, each working with the most extravagant means available to their historical moment. They give a kind of pedagogical *exemplum* for the activity of interpreting irreverent stagings: the 2011 *Rinaldo* offers a preposterous history lesson, from which we can learn to regard the shifting interillumination of past and present moments as a productive source of operatic meaning. This notion makes the contemporary baroque more than a convenient historical starting point or case study. Rather, it becomes a paradigm of the way in which the productions discussed in this book stage historicity: they always present us with a particular configuration of present and past in the area of sex and power. In each one of them the contemporary iconography of perversion enters into a new constellation with a particular historical representation of eroticism, power, and violence. This is what raises the questions that I address: What happens when the visual codes of BDSM and fetishism intermingle with the past moment represented by the operatic text and its original context? What images of gender, sex, and power do the historical moments produce when mirrored in each other?

THE GENDER JUMBLE OF
THE CONTEMPORARY BAROQUE

The representation of gender and sexuality is a principal arena for the interplay between the specifically baroque and the specifically contemporary. At the beginning of the eighteenth century both male and female roles could still be sung by either men or women, as circumstances dictated, and the castrato voice, with its high register emerging from a male body, does not fit neatly into the binary models of representation that became increasingly dominant during and after the Enlightenment.[19] In their time the castrati were more typically thought of as male than as "ambiguously sexed," yet this did not prevent them from portraying female characters.[20] Conversely, male characters were sung by both castrati and women: in the five revivals of *Rinaldo* after the premiere of the 1711 season, for instance, all the male roles (even Argante) were at different times sung by castrati or women.[21] In addition, as Wendy Heller has shown, the libretti that Handel set were sometimes inherited from seventeenth-century Venetian opera, the carnivalesque ethos of which produced an even more flexible notion of gender than the one typical of the early eighteenth century.[22] This state of affairs has had a particular appeal on both gender-oriented researchers and opera directors in the last few decades, to the point of becoming a commonplace in both fields. When notions of gender performativity established themselves as core concepts of intellectual discourse in the 1990s, the complex configuration of gender in baroque opera seemed eminently open to reinterpretation in queer terms; Handel was even dubbed the "queerest of opera composers."[23] The catchphrase may seem a bit facile today, but both the Glyndebourne *Rinaldo* and the Stuttgart *Alcina* were very much born from this spirit: they purposefully superimpose new layers of gender performance on the early eighteenth-century norms of casting, which are reinterpreted from a present-day perspective as an anarchic gender jumble.

In *Alcina* this makes for a complicated addition to an already convoluted story. The opera's plot centers on the sorceress Alcina, who bewitches her lovers on an enchanted island and transforms them into rocks, trees, and beasts when she has tired of them. In Wieler and Morabito's staging the supernatural elements have been discarded and Alcina's extraordinary powers are placed entirely in the realm of sexual attraction. Among her present lovers we find Ruggiero, whose wife, Bradamante, comes to rescue him, disguised as a man called "Ricciardo." Meanwhile, Alcina's sister Morgana falls in love with this Ricciardo, which makes her lover, Alcina's general Oronte, mad with jealousy. Oronte tries to return the favor and make Ruggiero jealous, by suggesting that his beloved Alcina is not to be trusted. This happens in Oronte's first-act aria "Semplicetto! a donna credi?" (You young fool! Do you trust in women?), which serves well as an example of the confusion that arises. The scene features Oronte and Ruggiero, who are both unambiguously male characters in the plot. Ruggiero was originally sung by an alto castrato but is performed here by the British mezzo Alice Coote, who had her breakthrough in this Stuttgart production. Oronte, meanwhile, was sung by a tenor in eighteenth-century London and still is in Stuttgart: while delivering this aria, Rolf Romei performs a striptease presented in a stereotypically feminine body language. He lets his long hair out and caresses his own body while sensually ridding himself of his suit and shirt (he even smells his own shoes with relish as he takes them off), before crawling across the stage toward his interlocutor. Alice Coote's Ruggiero, meanwhile, adopts a masculine body language while he sings, sitting with spread legs and regarding him with disbelief, even distaste. There are several strip scenes like this—for instance, when "Ricciardo" (sung by Helene Schneiderman) reveals herself to actually be Bradamante, her three-piece suit gives way to a purple negligee. The striptease becomes an image for the elusiveness of gender, which cannot be definitively assigned to any of the bodies involved: as layer after layer is removed, it becomes clear that the tease itself lies in the fact that there is no "authentic" body to be uncovered but always only another layer of gender performance. Carsen's *Rinaldo*, meanwhile, seems to ascribe a kind of magical power to cross-dressing: when the Christian Magus—who is the boarding school's chemistry teacher—furnishes the Crusaders with the means to defeat the Saracens and liberate Almirena, what he actually does is to have them dress up as girls and arm themselves with bandy sticks.

It would be easy to read such antics as the symptoms of a narcissistic present, seeing only itself in any given historical moment. But both the Stuttgart *Alcina* and the Glyndebourne *Rinaldo* are marked by their own preposterous version of historicity: quite contrary to naive presentism, their effect depends on an awareness of historical distance. The flexible gender configuration of baroque casting and the turn-of-the-millennium attention to queer performativity are separated by several hundred years of a completely different and much more rigorous gender regime. Between those moments radical social changes occurred. Enlightenment and bourgeois values were established as the eighteenth century progressed, and the scientific discourse of the nineteenth century put an ever-stronger emphasis on policing and pathologizing sexual behaviors and identities that deviated from socially sanctioned norms.[24] The castrati fell out of favor, as their "brilliant vocal art . . . had started to cloud over with charges of aristocratic luxury, vanity, and decadence, charges that were inseparable from Enlightenment critiques of castration itself."[25] A similar fate befell the breeches part, with a few prominent exceptions, like Cherubino and Octavian, to prove the rule. Meanwhile, the long line of tragic operas that Clément read as obsessed with "the undoing of woman" evolved, supported by composers who, as Susan McClary has argued, made misogynist murder a musical necessity.[26] Under this paradigm it is not surprising that early eighteenth-century representations of gender were hard to swallow when attempts at reviving Handelian opera began in Germany of the 1920s and 1930s. The heroic male leads, even the ones originally sung by women rather than castrati, were thus transposed into a "normal" male range, a tradition that would be shaken off only in the late twentieth century, when the countertenor reemerged to play a central role in the baroque revival by reaching the castrato's register in falsetto.[27]

In other words, the gender structures of classical and romantic opera form the background against which directors like Carsen, Wieler, and Morabito produce their rereadings of Handel. Across this wide historical chasm director's opera regards the baroque and produces its preposterous history. The cultural concern with opera's volatile treatment of sex and gender cannot be reduced to a mere projection from a present-day perspective. In Handel's London, for instance, it was the cause of much controversy. The premiere of *Rinaldo* in 1711 was a major event. It was not only Handel's first opera in London but the first original Italian opera written for the London stage, and with its fifty-three performances during Handel's lifetime, it was vastly successful—not least because of the spectacular staging, which supposedly included a thunderstorm, a waterfall, a smoking dragon, and a flock of live sparrows.[28] But the appearance of Italian opera on the London stage also gave rise to a particular set of anxieties, which were more acutely felt in the British context than in the art form's native country. Italian opera, with its powerful women and castrati in lead roles, was perceived by many critics as a threat to British society and its ideals of masculinity and rationality, and consequently as politically dangerous.[29] Opera's representation of gender infused the genre with unsettling connotations of foreignness and debauchery. A wide variety of satirical pamphlets, which circulated in London at the time, suggest that its vocal seductions would corrupt men and women alike and elaborate at length on the sexual degeneracy that would inevitably result from the foreign import. For instance, a tract from the same year as *Rinaldo*'s first performance holds that the luxury of Italian opera has "changed our Natures" and "transform'd our Sexes," and in the end, the author basically fears that opera will turn London into a new Sodom: "The Ladies . . . seem to mistake their Interest a little in encouraging *Opera's;* for the more the Men are enervated and emasculated by the Softness of the *Italian* Musick, the less will they care for them, and the more for one another. There are some certain Pleasures which are mortal Enemies to their Pleasures, that past the *Alps* about the same time with the *Opera.*"[30]

The castrati, which were new to England at the time, were a particular cause for concern: they were paradoxically thought to be exceptionally virile and lecherous, at the same time as stories circulated to the effect that the mere voice of a castrato could turn women into hermaphrodites and men into effeminate sodomites.[31] Little wonder, then, that the crowds of London lined up to see and hear for themselves. In short: because questions of gender politics were far from unproblematic or unnoticeable in the operas' original context, but an issue equally charged with appeal and anxiety, it would be wrong to assume that the turn-of-the-millennium directors who draw attention to it are projecting a contemporary problem on a past where it did not exist. While the stagings I approach here do not aim to present that problem by recreating the opera as it was performed in its original context, they are not blind to the concerns of history. Instead, they insist that we attend to the interplay between early eighteenth-century questions of gender and those of our own age in a manner that simultaneously depends on and revolts against the modern gender binaries that were established in between. Is this approach to opera productive? Possibly. Is it perverse? Perhaps. Preposterous? Most definitely.

PLAYFUL POWER DYNAMICS AND NEOBAROQUE FETISHISM

Structures of gender are invariably intertwined with structures of power. Here, the iconography of perversion enters as a present-day lens through which the sexual power relations in operatic works may be reinterpreted. In what follows, I will focus on elements of kinkiness in the Handel productions by Carsen and Wieler/Morabito—which prominently feature rubber attire, bondage, caning, and fetishism—arguing that their function in the mise-en-scène is both to transform abstract and verbal notions of eroticized power into visible objects on the stage and to superimpose on the instability of gender relations a corresponding instability of eroticized power relations.

As the schoolboy's fantasy begins to run amok in Carsen's *Rinaldo*, his history teacher metamorphoses into a furious dominatrix. At this moment the iconography of perversion steps on stage: Brenda Rae rids herself of the schoolmistress's gown and mortar, exposing the Saracen sorceress Armida in high-heels, long black fingernails, and a skintight black rubber dress (fig. 2.1). Meanwhile, her furies constitute another allusion to British pop culture: when they entered with Argante, they were devout Muslim women, but now they strip off their burkas to become a band of wicked schoolgirls modeled on the Sixth-Form pupils of St Trinian's school (the setting of a series of 1950s and 1960s comedies about reckless juvenile-delinquent girls, based on a cartoon by Ronald Searle and later rebooted in movies of the 1980s and 2000s). Several reviewers also detected the influence of J. K. Rowling in the boarding-school world, and apropos the kinky furies one of them spoke of "Flogwarts": an "academy for trainee dominatrices."[32] What do these elements of contemporary kink mean in Handel's baroque opera?

Figure 2.1. "Horrifying furies!" Armida (Brenda Rae) wielding her cane in a rubber dress, summoning the furies of Flogwarts. *Rinaldo* (dir. Robert Carsen, Glyndebourne Festival Opera, 2011).

One way of interpreting the dominatrix persona in relation to both operatic performance and Handel's score is as a visualization of a specifically musical power: Armida's is an eminent example of the dominance of the female voice in opera. Musically, hers is far and away the most exciting part in this opera (and the only character that is even remotely rounded). It is the only role for which Handel drove his score into presto (in her entrance aria, "Furie terribili" [Horrifying furies] and "Ah! crudel" [Ah, cruel one]). It is also the highest vocal part (the only one that reaches to a high C, vertiginously attacked out of nowhere at the beginning of a phrase), which is important in a baroque context, where the agility of the high voice, regardless of its gender, was the prime focus of admiration.[33] Compared with Armida's musical fury, Almirena—the only other high female role—inevitably comes across as meek, however beautifully lyrical "Augelletti" (You little birds) and "Lascia ch'io pianga" (Let me weep).[34] In the Glyndebourne production Anett Fritsch's Almirena—wearing a gymslip, specs, and plaits—becomes the polar opposite of the sadistic Armida. Rae's powerful, edgy high register and fierce acting of the role emphasize the sorceress's function as the passionate engine of the opera. Here, Armida's sexually dominant behavior becomes a visual manifestation of the sensual allure of the soprano's voice, which towers above all other sounds in the room, and Rae's rendering of the role under Carsen's direction makes this point in an immediately effective way.

The school setting and the corporal punishment meted out by her cruel character, moreover, foregrounds the notion of discipline and thereby resonates with the bodily command required of an opera singer. As any singer knows, firework coloraturas like those of Armida demand that the vocal cords, articulators, and respiratory system be subject to a willed control that can only be achieved by extensive and rigorous training. The virtuoso singer develops a perfect control over his or her body. Another interpretation is that this bodily self-discipline is the internalization of a control exerted by others—such as the audience's insatiable demand for specific aural stimulation or the composer's demand for a perfect performance. The score can be thought of as a script for the behavior of the body, down to the tiniest muscular movements, its lines and bars even resembling an intricate system of bondage that forces the singing body to, move and breathe in a particular way to produce the desired sound. The ideas of contemporary directors add yet another layer to these restrictions. In the Glyndebourne *Rinaldo* Armida's kinky outfit highlights the notion of a strict bodily discipline not only metaphorically but, from the outlook of the singer, quite literally. Rae herself comments on the dress: "I didn't get to sing in it until a week before the show opened. . . . I'm running around all over the stage and I realize: I can't breathe . . . the way I normally can. It's okay in the slower moments, because you learn to . . . trust that rubber corset, because it will expand. But when you have to take a quick breath, it's trapping my ribs and my lungs so I don't get as much air as I normally would. So . . . every performance I get a little better, and I learn to love the rubber."[35] When Rae refers to this situation as a "very unique challenge," it is surely a euphemism, but in the performance captured on DVD, she does indeed appear to have become one with the material and mastered its physical restrictions, in terms of singing as well as acting. To "love the rubber," in other words, is to embrace the discipline that it symbolically betokens and physically demands.

The libretto offers another way of interpreting the iconography of perversion as it is deployed by Carsen. Giacomo Rossi's words consistently fuse the language of love and longing with that of war and violence, thus weaving the two main strands of the opera's plot together, as was very common in the early modern period. Cruelty and pain are repeatedly evoked as descriptions of erotic sentiment, as when Rinaldo uses the words "pena acerba e ria" (bitter and cruel punishment) to describe his yearnings for Almirena, or when Armida, beginning to desire Rinaldo, sings of how "mi serpe al cor un'amorosa pena" (a pang of love creeps into my heart). Those who withhold affection are "crudel" (cruel), and when rejected, Armida orders her furies to find "nova sorte di pena e di flagello" (a new kind of punishment and scourge), promising Rinaldo that "Al mio desio / Proverai la crudeltà" (You will the cruelty of my desire). All of these figures are part of a conventional rhetoric of erotic sentiment. Carsen's production reinterprets them as SM-themed allusions to an eros permeated by pain and cruelty. The baroque hyperboles that conflate love and pain are given physical shape in the contemporary visual codes of sexual power play, bondage, and fetishism. In other words, the boundary between the figurative and the literal is transgressed: just as Armida's musical power and vocal discipline, together with the potential sensuality of operatic singing, is made manifest in her dominatrix attire, so the libretto's rhetorical figures are literalized by the chains and bondage of the staging.

Fetishism plays an important part in the staging's creation of preposterous history. Charged with an unambiguously modern, post-Freudian view of sexuality, the fetishized objects on stage chafe demonstratively against the premodern work. More specifically, they seem to serve as a contemporary substitute for the magic that permeates the world of *Rinaldo*. Of course, the fetishist sorcery emanates most clearly from Armida. But it appears not only in the guise of the rubber dress: a number of characteristic objects are imbued with an erotic charge as the staging evolves. These objects serve as physical markers of a given position as top or bottom in the erotic power exchange. Armida's own regalia is the most striking example: in addition to her attire, she carries a slender cane, which she wields with relish throughout the opera, as a patently phallic marker of her sexual power. Less immediately obvious, perhaps, are two other objects that are employed in a similar fashion: the school-uniform tie and the classroom chair. Like the cane, they are props drawn from the world of the boarding school but put to use as symbols in an erotic power dynamic.

The use of these objects merits attention. First, consider the neckties: they carry with them connotations of discipline and uniformity, perhaps masculinity (although the girls at the boarding school wear them as well). They are repeatedly presented either as fetishized objects or as accessories of bondage, or both. When Armida's furies abduct Almirena, ties are used to bind and gag her. Next, when the schoolgirl sirens seduce Rinaldo in the second act, in order to lure him into Armida's claws as he attempts to rescue Almirena, they first caress their own ties as if they were an erogenous piece of clothing, and then they do the same with Rinaldo's. Once he is in Armida's realm—represented by the dormitory—the furies use their ties to secure his hands and feet to one of the beds, allowing for Armida to crawl lustfully over him while voicing her desire for the hero (who, in his own fantasy, ends up rejecting her) (fig. 2.2). Once she has untied him and her subsequent attempts have failed, she sulks: "Dunque i lacci d'un volto, / Tante gioie promesse . . . Forza n'avran per arrestar quel crudo?" (Is my own beauty and the promise of joys to come . . . not enough to hold that man?) The word *lacci* means "snares," which are of course metaphorical; she expected her face (or, rather, Almirena's, which she has just magically donned in order to trick Rinaldo) to be beautiful enough to bind him. Yet, because she tied him up literally a moment ago, *lacci* becomes a double entendre. In fact, there are several references in the text to Armida's "lacci indegni" (shameful snares), which are pushed toward the literal as Almirena is held captive. The onstage bondage culminates in the third act, as Rae's Armida keeps not only Rinaldo and Almirena but also Argante (who is in the doghouse after disclosing his desire for Almirena) blindfolded and in chains, in a dungeon of sorts. Like Armida's attempt at seducing the tied-down Rinaldo, the making-up of the Saracens includes an explicit eroticization of bondage, as Armida kisses and caresses her commander while his arms are still suspended from the ceiling.

The chair, meanwhile, serves as a signifier of powerlessness or submission. This is established even in the "realistic" boarding-school environment during the overture, while the obedient pupils are seated on their chairs and the harsh teachers walk around the room. Once the set is transformed by fantasies, these connotations enter into the erotic power dynamic. As the captive of the Saracens in the second act, Almirena sits on the chair in the dormitory with her hands bound behind her back (again,

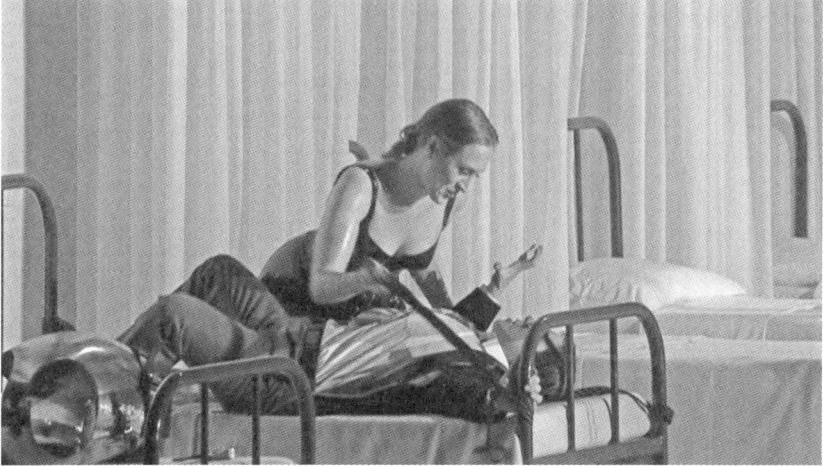

Figure 2.2. "I can offer you countless joys." Armida (Brenda Rae) trying to seduce Rinaldo (Sonia Prina) after her furies have tied him to a bed in the dormitory. *Rinaldo* (dir. Robert Carsen, Glyndebourne Festival Opera, 2011).

the school-uniform ties are used), while Argante is preparing to declare his love for her. Later in the same act, when Armida has summoned her furies—in order to come up with new kinds of punishment and scourge for Rinaldo—she has them lean over the chair one by one, to receive a thwack from her cane on their backsides (fig. 2.3). She is exercising her powers on her subordinates to compensate for the humiliation of Rinaldo's rejection, and the chair and the cane serve as the objective markers of her dominant position: they become fetishes entrusted with the task of signaling eroticized power.

The function of a fetish, however, is double-edged. On the one hand, it embodies and objectifies power, thus making it both visible and controllable. On the other, that power is simultaneously dissociated from the body of the person who claims it. It becomes a mere symbol. But that "mere" is not uncomplicated either. SM paraphernalia functions like classical insignia—the rod, the scepter, the emblems of military rank—in its ambiguous conferral of power. It bestows power performatively on its bearer. In that sense there is no "mere": the props *are* the power. But they also introduce a distance between the body of the bearer and the power he

Figure 2.3. "A new kind of punishment and scourge." Armida (Brenda Rae) caning her insubordinate furies one by one. *Rinaldo* (dir. Robert Carsen, Glyndebourne Festival Opera, 2011).

or she wields. They expose the fact that power is not really a natural part of their bearer but needs to be worn in the form of an external object that hides an original lack of power. In Lacanian terms this distance is the gap of symbolic castration: symbols of power—like Armida's cane in the present example—simultaneously guarantee the subject's power and point to the essential lack of it. Such phallic power is never fully possessed but must remain prosthetic, divorced from the organic body.[36] The chair and the necktie used for blindfold and bondage, conversely, are insignia of powerlessness: just as the cane (or the rod, or the scepter) invests its wielder with power without necessarily exerting it physically, so these props divest the submissive party of theirs.

On the one hand, this line of reasoning means that the power dynamics are nothing but theatrics. On the other hand, it may be argued that what we think of as "real" power also operates by asserting itself performatively. The significant difference, however, is that the latter kind of power does not allow for dynamic changes of position, for reversals of dominance and submission: it may be performatively constructed, but it constructs itself as irrevocable and unidirectional. In the externalized form of a fetishized prop, sexual dominance is always potentially subject to negotiation or even usurpation. Although this potential need not be realized—the wielder of the cane may hang on to it—it is consistently explored in Carsen's mise-en-scène of *Rinaldo*. Specifically, the fetishized objects allow Armida to enact the potential dissolution of her own power, while they let Almirena demonstrate that her submissive position is at least partially the effect of an active choice rather than external compulsion.

Almirena's role is that of the pure girl, in contrast to Armida's SM leanings. Her response to Argante's declaration of love is that the bondage is not conducive to erotic attraction: "In questi lacci avvolta / Non è il mio cor soggetto / D'un amoroso affetto" (wound up in these snares / my heart is not subject / to an amorous sentiment). After he has complied with her request and untied her, she gets up and delivers her heartrending ear-worm, "Lascia ch'io pianga." The aria's plea that she be allowed to weep is followed, in the B-section, by the notion that the pain itself will be able to break her fetters, by inspiring pity, and thus give her freedom ("Il duolo infranga / Queste ritorte, / De' miei martiri" [Let sorrow break these bonds that torment me]). During the da capo, however, she appears to hesitate and gradually approaches the chair again. Then, in the final bars, she slowly turns toward Argante and sits back down. To make the implications even clearer, she crosses her wrists behind the back of the chair, in the exact same position as when they were tied (further emphasized on the DVD version, directed by François Roussillon, which adds a close-up shot of her hands). By adopting the position of the bound prisoner, without the bondage actually being there, she clearly construes the position of submission as her own choice at this point. As a result, the A-section's patent tendency to seek consolation, even satisfaction, in powerlessness—"let me weep"—is reinterpreted as a voluntary return to the bonds she was in when Argante declared his love. When he, as an honorable Saracen (or a teacher who wants to keep his job), opens the door and offers her freedom, she is visibly frustrated—but leaves all the same. A similar moment of emotional confusion occurs in the third act, once she has been released from Armida's chains. She liberates herself from Rinaldo's embrace and walks over to the chains (looking over at Argante, who is still in fetters at this point), reflecting with an absent look on the pain that has passed:

Di quei strani accidenti	When I recall this strange
Se la serie ripiglio,	series of mishaps
Per dolor, per stupor, s'inarca il	My eyes grow wide with sorrow and
ciglio.	astonishment.
A sì crudeli eventi	Such cruel events
Ancor non so se dormi, o se sia	leave me unsure whether I am asleep or
desta.	awake.

Half of these recitativo lines originally belong to Goffredo but have been given to Almirena here, presumably to let her recall her bondage scene with Argante in the previous act. The hallucinatory events leave her uncertain about whether the erotic nightmare of captivity is still going on. Rinaldo, however, reassures her, and the moment is gone: if she has any submissive inclinations, they are effectively repressed.

Rae's Armida, too, uses the props of bondage and submission to act out an ambiguous position vis-à-vis Rinaldo, which is even more clearly split between erotic dominance and submission. Realizing that being tied up does not appeal to Rinaldo, she shifts to a submissive position in her second-act duet with him: she kneels on the chair, leaning forward over it, while avowing her faithfulness ("Fermati! Armida, son fedel" [Stay! I am your faithful Armida]). The steadfast hero, however, is not interested in taking the top position and leaves her alone in the dark dormitory, where she oscillates between utmost wrath and self-pity in "Ah! crudel!" This aria summons all the musical means of opera seria to dramatize the internal conflict that so often marks the genre's principal personae. The A section is a plaintive *largo* in G minor, in which we hear Armida praying for mercy from the cruel object of her affection. The contrast with the short B section is startling: it is a *presto* where the raging repetition of sixteenth notes in the strings is answered by breakneck coloratura figurations ("Al mio desio / Proverai la crudeltà"). Using the school-uniform ties and the chair once more, the staging maps the positions of dominance and submission over the da capo structure: as Rae launches into the *presto,* she clasps the school-uniform ties in her fists, but when she lapses back into the *largo,* she walks over to kneel by the chair, winding them around her own hands to indicate her own subjugation (fig. 2.4).

In the final act, after the cross-dressed schoolboys have defeated the furies and liberated the lovers, even her gender identity seems to be less

Figure 2.4. "Oh, cruel one, may my tears move you to pity!" Armida (Brenda Rae) in subspace, using the chair and necktie as props. *Rinaldo* (dir. Robert Carsen, Glyndebourne Festival Opera, 2011).

stable than one might expect. While hanging in chains from the ceiling, Argante accuses Armida of emasculating heroes (and being utterly power-less at the moment, he might well include himself in that category): "va', e non tentar d'effeminar gli eroi!" (go, and do not try to emasculate heroes!). Armida replies, while touching the dangling chains in which Rinaldo was recently trapped: "Ho un cor virile in petto, / Che sa emular la Gloria" (I have a manly heart in my breast / which knows how to imitate glory). The verb *emular*—meaning emulate or imitate—suggests that the glorification she desires is a matter of external appearance, which in Carsen's staging certainly implies the shackles she holds in her hands at this point. As the combination of a specifically masculine strength and sexual prowess suggested by "virile" is thus visually associated with the props of her personal dungeon, her taste for sexual domination becomes a gender-bending of sorts: beneath her rub-ber-wrapped bosom beats the heart of a man (of course, this also suggests an equation of masculinity and sexual domination, as if that joint were fixed enough to be the pivot around which gender identity turns).

In Wieler and Morabito's *Alcina* fetishism plays an equally important part. As mentioned above, the overture comes with close-ups of several pairs of shoes, and this theme is developed already in Alcina's first aria "Dì, cor mio" (Tell, dear heart), which centers on her love for her most recent catch, Ruggiero. Alcina, sung here by Catherine Naglestad, enters barefoot, in a very transparent black top, embracing Ruggiero, before picking up her high-heel shoes from the floor. While Ruggiero, trembling with desire, goes around the stage making passes at all present characters, male or female, Alcina carries her shoes around, clutching and caressing them as her coloraturas reach their climax and the word *sospirai* (sighed) is elaborated on over three bars. When she exits after her aria, Ruggiero remains seated on the stage, his gaze riveted on the shoe that he is still holding. As the production moves on, various types of footwear will be caressed, sniffed, polished, and generally admired not only by Ruggiero but also by Oronte and Morgana.

Why the shoe fetishism? Because it is, in one sense, an archetype of sexual perversion. When the term *fetishism* acquired its sexual connotations in the last decades of the nineteenth century, it also became a model for deviance in general. In the lineage of Richard Krafft-Ebing and Freud, where fetishism has an essential connection to masochism and remains intimately connected to the case of Sacher-Masoch himself, the shoe occupies a special place: Deleuze lists it as one of Sacher-Masoch's main objects of fetishism, and Krafft-Ebing states that, among his studied cases, those who feel an inexplicable desire for women's shoes are "simply innumerable."[37] Hartmut Böhme has argued that fetishism should be understood as part and parcel of modernity: no sooner had the Enlightenment banished myth and superstition in the name of reason, than it stole back into the heart of European society in the guise of fetishism.[38] In other words, the magic expelled from the rational world came to be channeled into specific, powerfully charged objects. Like the Glyndebourne *Rinaldo*, the Stuttgart *Alcina* uses this fact to do preposterous history: when the mythological tale is transposed into a contemporary setting, containing only faded remnants of the premodern world, Alcina's supernatural powers disappear and are replaced by modernity's fetishism. When the contemporary sorceress picks up her high-heel shoe as she first steps onto the stage, it takes on the displaced magic of a wand, granting her sexual power over whomever she pleases.

Like the chair or the necktie in Carsen's *Rinaldo*, the adoration of shoes is also used in the Stuttgart *Alcina* to signal one's utter powerlessness vis-à-vis the desired lover. As the multilayered gendering of sexual power play is further complicated, bondage and blindfolds are added to the shoe-and-foot fetishism. In the first-act aria "La bocca vaga" (Her lustful mouth) Coote's jealous Ruggiero warns Schneiderman's "Ricciardo" that the beautiful Alcina can never be his, unaware that the supposed rival is in fact his/her betrothed Bradamante disguised as a man. As the da capo arrives, however, s/he bends down over Bradamante-as-Ricciardo, who is lying on the floor in fear, as if leaning in for a kiss. While singing of Alcina's desirous mouth, the mouth of Coote's Ruggiero is pouring ornaments into Bradamante-as-Ricciardo's ears, and while singing about Alcina's dark eyes, s/he gazes deeply into those of his/her own betrothed—only to pull away with the conclusion "per te non è" (will not be yours). The ambiguity of Bradamante-as-Ricciardo's desire—which Ruggiero believes to be directed at Alcina, while it is actually directed at himself—is thus brought to the fore by the staging. Coote's Ruggiero continues to waver between teasing sensuality and assertive dominance, gently removing Ricciardo's tie and belt, as if intending to strip him of his/her shirt and trousers, only to use them instead to tie up his/her hands and feet in a rough manner (fig. 2.5). Finally, the victim is dragged to the corner of the stage and thrown on a pile of old, discarded objects, and Ruggiero takes off.

Next, Alcina's sister Morgana (Catriona Smith) enters to sing "Tornami a vagheggiar" (Come quickly back to court me), while Bradamante-as-Ricciardo is still in bondage on the floor. Morgana, who is equally unaware that there is a woman beneath the suit, takes advantage of the situation to extract a promise of fidelity. In the aria she then confesses her undivided love, and after kissing the one she believes to be Ricciardo, Morgana returns to the theme of shoe and foot fetishism: she sensually removes his/her shoe while her coloraturas reach their highest register on the phrase "te solo vuol' amar" (to love you alone) and clutches it to her chest before going on to arduously worship his/her feet (fig. 2.6). As the aria progresses, she unties her beloved, and they embrace, until, during the coloratura flights of the da capo, Bradamante-as-Ricciardo blindfolds her with the tie and uses the belt to lead her off, stage left. The objects that bind her, then, are the same that bound Bradamante-as-Ricciardo in the previous aria. In both cases the objects serve as objectifications of the erotic power relation between the characters on stage: when Bradamante-

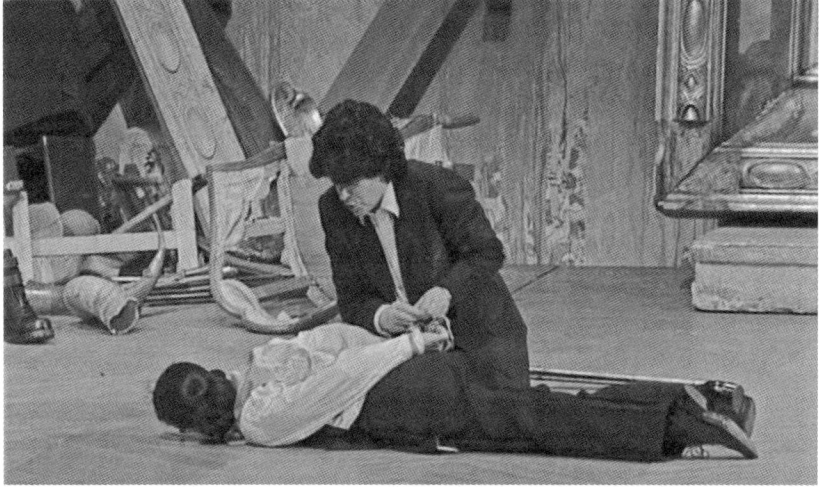

Figure 2.5. "Her lustful mouth will not be yours": Ruggiero (Alice Coote) tying up his girlfriend, disguised as Ricciardo (Helene Schneiderman), to keep him/her away from Alcina. *Alcina* (dir. Jossi Wieler/Sergio Morabito, Staatsoper Stuttgart, 1999).

Figure 2.6. "This faithful heart will love only you": Morgana (Catriona Smith) admiring the shoes of Ricciardo (Helene Schneiderman). *Alcina* (dir. Jossi Wieler/ Sergio Morabito, Staatsoper Stuttgart, 1999).

as-Ricciardo has his/her hands and feet bound, the tie and belt serve as physical symbols of the emotional ties of erotic love. Once Smith's Morgana voices her desire, they are transferred to her, and as they are used to blindfold her and lead her around, they become manifestations of her emotional delusion and disorientation.

Depending on whether one focuses on the performing body, the fictional diegesis, or the cross-gender masquerade within the fiction, the scenes can be said to play out between two men, two women, or one man and a woman. If the very impossibility of assigning a stable gender to any of the involved parties is what defines these scenes, the same can be said of the positions of dominance and submission. Just as in the Glyndebourne *Rinaldo,* because erotic power is invested in fetishized props, it can be transferred between the characters. The only constant in these scenes is the idea that the person who desires is powerless and that this powerlessness is given physical form in the allusions to bondage and fetishized objects. Yet even this notion is complicated by the multilayered masquerade. In "La bocca vaga" Bradamante-as-Ricciardo is in the underdog position, because he is in the shackles of desire, but the object of that desire is ambiguous: from Ruggiero's perspective it is Alcina's dark eyes and covetous mouth that ensnare Ricciardo, but from Bradamante's perspective it is her love for Ruggiero. In "Tornami a vagheggiar," meanwhile, the passivity of the dominant party undermines any straightforward coupling of power, agency, and initiative: when the necktie and the belt with which Morgana wishes to be blindfolded and led on is given to Bradamante-as-Ricciardo, the latter complies with an air of resignation. The desire represented in these scenes, in other words, cannot be defined as either heterosexual or homosexual, and neither erotic dominance nor agency and initiative can be identified as unambiguously masculine or feminine; intimations of erotic domination serve here to stage an emphatically polymorphous and unstable distribution of gender, power, and desire.

To sum up my argument thus far: in its heterochronic clash with the moment of baroque opera, the iconography of perversion plays with the possibility of letting abstract notions and rhetorical figures of opera—both the particular work and operatic performance in general—be taken literally and made manifest on stage. We have seen the materialization of a particular cluster of ideas that permeate the love relationships of opera seria. The props and gestures of SM serve to literalize the idea of erotic power. In relation to the plot they are manifestations of the emotional ties and power dynamics that shape the relations between lovers and rivals: those plagued by unrequited desire repeatedly find themselves in bondage or in a physically low position (kneeling, lying down). In relation to the rhetoric of the libretti, they are literal manifestations of the hyperboles of violence and domination used by the baroque imagination to represent erotic love: words like *pena, flagello,* and *lacci* suddenly appear before our eyes in the guise of chains and canes. In relation to the music they are manifestations both of the sensual—indeed, erotic—power of the virtuoso voice, and the extreme disciplining of the body that this vocal practice demands of the singer. The visual elements of SM thus consistently serve to push abstract notions of erotic power into the world of physical reality on stage. Often, sexual energy attaches to specific objects, charging them with the magical power of fetishes. One possible effect of this externalization, which seems to be particularly relevant to these productions, is that erotic power loses some of its essential connection to its subject: once it inheres in a fetishized object, it can migrate with that object from one party to another, coming across as inherently unstable. This mirrors the way in which the gender configuration of baroque opera is dealt with in these performances: erotic power, like gender identity, is represented as lacking a straightforward connection to the body of any given subject and is thus marked by reversibility and mutability. By locating erotic power in fetishes, the directors and performers are able to envision it as subject to playful perversions and performative renegotiations—a creative game of sexual dominance and submission for which the operatic stage then appears to be an eminently suited arena.

THE FRAMES OF SEXUAL FANTASY

There is no doubt that this emphasis on the playful and mutable can be productive, even necessary, for the understanding of stagings like the ones addressed in this chapter. But there is also a more troubling set of issues surrounding the relation between an erotic theater of domination and actual sexual abuse: the sinister realities outside the boundaries of the safe, sane, and consensual that frame the BDSM subculture (and opera as well). When opera turns its excessive gaze toward violence, molestation, and murder, it puts pressure on the frame that separates the theatrical fiction of the opera from what takes place in the real world. From this angle I will broach the topic in the final section of this chapter: both the Stuttgart *Alcina* and the Glyndebourne *Rinaldo,* in fact, dramatize the difficult relation between fantasy and reality on stage. They do this by establishing and then dissolving distinct levels of fiction. The device with which this dissolution is produced in *Rinaldo* and *Alcina* is a trademark both of the baroque and its revival in postmodern art and theory: the frame within the frame. I will dwell briefly on this device before I return to its relation to the question of eroticism, power, and violence.

To introduce the idea of the frame within the frame, here is a quotation within a quotation, where Heinrich Wölfflin speaks from Gilles Deleuze's *The Fold:* "The Gothic underlines the elements of construction, closed frames, airy filling; Baroque underlines matter: either the frame disappears totally, or else it remains, but, despite the rough sketch, it does not suffice to contain the mass that spills over and passes up above."[39] Deleuze goes on to elaborate on this spilling-over as characteristic of the baroque treatment of art and media:

> If the Baroque establishes a total art or a unity of the arts, it does so first of all in extension, each art tending to be . . . prolonged into the next art, which exceeds the one before. We have remarked that the Baroque often confines painting to retables, but it does so because the painting exceeds its frame and is realized in polychrome marble sculpture; and sculpture goes beyond itself by being achieved in architecture; and in turn, architecture discovers a frame in the façade, but the frame itself becomes detached from the inside, and establishes relations with the surroundings so as to realize architecture in the city planning. . . . We witness the prodigious development of a continuity in the arts, in breadth or in extension: an interlocking of frames of which each is exceeded by a matter that moves through it.[40]

If opera is often described as a quintessentially baroque creation, precisely because of its aspiration to a totality or unity of the arts, the Stuttgart and Glyndebourne productions exemplify the neobaroque visualization of excess and extension through a series of artistic media—of matter flowing through interlocked frames—which Deleuze describes. Here, the frames distinguish different levels of the diegesis on stage. They serve to separate, for instance, the main narrative from the fantasies, visions, and memories of the characters. When these boundaries are overstepped, we are faced with the figure of metalepsis.

The Stuttgart *Alcina*, to begin with, is a careful staging of precisely this aspect of the baroque. Throughout the opera, Anna Viebrock's stage set is dominated by an enormous golden, elaborately ornamented picture frame hanging on the wall that marks the far end of the downstage space. Through this frame, however, we can see a smaller upstage area, between the wall and the actual backdrop. What we have, then, is a two-part stage, divided by a frame. Crucially, the shape of that frame mirrors, and draws attention to, the other horizontal rectangles that frame our perception of the opera. First of all, there is the proscenium arch that marks the division between the theatrical fiction and the real world in which the audience find themselves (a function that had not yet been established in the early eighteenth century and thus is only visible from the contemporary perspective on the baroque). If we are watching a mediated transmission of the performance, further frames are added, such as the screen of a cinema or television, or the windows of our operating system if we are using a computer (as I am writing this, for instance, I am looking at the horizontal rectangle of my laptop screen, which contains in its turn a number of word-processor documents, dictionaries, and research articles, as well as a media player in which the Stuttgart opera proscenium arch can be seen to encompass the frame on the wall).

In Wieler and Morabito's *Alcina,* a lot of effort is put into exploring the different possible functions of the onstage frame. As Barbara Zuber has observed, its function does not let itself be pinned down: neither side of the frame can be unambiguously equated with the real world or the realm of magic and wonder.[41] Instead, it serves variously as a window into another room (when it simply shows us events going on upstage); a mirror (when characters on each side of the frame face each other, with synchronized movements); a photograph (when all the characters pose upstage for a wedding photo, facing the audience through the frame without moving, with Ruggiero and Bradamante as bride and groom in the middle); and a movie screen (when Ruggiero watches Alcina and Bradamante

Figure 2.7. Baroque framework: Anna Viebrock's stage set for *Alcina* (dir. Jossi Wieler/Sergio Morabito, Staatsoper Stuttgart, 1999).

dance through the frame, and the backdrop moves to the left while the couple move rightward, spinning, in order to suggest a panning camera). It is there to draw attention to mediated representation. Sometimes it appears to be a glass screen, as the singers place the palms of their hands against an imagined surface, creating a boundary out of thin air in the manner of a pantomime. At certain crucial moments, however, they step out of or into the frame, thus transgressing the carefully constructed limit of whichever medium it suggests (fig. 2.7). At these moments of metalepsis bodies are able to move between different levels of representation: between the photograph and the fictive reality outside it, between the film and the auditorium, between the mirrored world and the mirror world. Its function as a demarcation, not only between the different diegetic levels of the drama but also, by implication, between theatrical fiction and reality, is thrown into doubt. The overstepping of one horizontal rectangle, as it were, is enough to imply the possibility of overstepping all the other, analogous ones, including the proscenium or the computer screen.

The Glyndebourne *Rinaldo* uses a similar strategy to create a portal between the real world of the diegesis and the fantasies that lie beyond it.

Here, the stage set has a blackboard where the frame hung in *Alcina,* on a wall separating upstage from downstage. Starting out as a black-and-white surface of didactic discipline, it soon becomes the site of metalepsis. The blackboard is the cognitive frame that is dissolved by uncontainable imagination: through the blackboard, on which the history teacher writes the essay question in the allegro section of the overture, appears Goffredo's victorious army, as well as (later) the seductive sirens (who pull the hero into the realm of fantasy). The wall is mirrored by two others before and behind it, also with blackboards, suggesting a potentially endless succession of classrooms and imaginary spaces. The blackboards serve as the magic projection surfaces of fantastic vision, variously appearing as chalk writing, as animations, and as living bodies that repeatedly overstep the frame. Above all, it is through this frame that Armida the dominatrix emerges in her thrilling entrance aria "Furie terribili," brandishing her cane and embodying the conflation of educational discipline and erotic fantasy gone wild.

Before this transformation, however, the audience encounters both Armida and Rinaldo as their "real" selves: the harsh teacher and the bullied pupil. The very first thing that happens on stage, during the overture, is that Rinaldo is mercilessly humiliated by his classmates and then receives a savage beating by his teachers. The other pupils find a photograph of a girl (the Almirena-to-be) on his desk and proceed to lick it, rub it against their groins, tear it to pieces, and shove it into his mouth, while holding him down on the floor. When the two teachers enter the room, finding Rinaldo in a mess on the floor (along with a pack of cigarettes, for which Rinaldo also gets the blame), his situation turns even worse: they force him to bend over one of the benches, and he is held down while one of them (played by Brenda Rae, soon to be transformed into Armida) gives him a hard whipping on the buttocks with her cane (fig. 2.8). This scene serves as the original abuse on which the fantasy of Armida as a sexual sadist is modeled. In particular, the scene in which her furies are being caned in the dormitory is a direct parallel to this penalty. It is made very clear that the fantasy that plays out as the opera goes along is that of Rinaldo himself: he is alone in the classroom when the curtain rises, as well as in the final bars of the opera, when all the fantastical events have receded and reality restored. It is thus quite tempting to read the scene

Figure 2.8. A child is being beaten: Rinaldo (Sonia Prina) is given an unfair caning by his teachers (Luca Pisaroni and Brenda Rae). *Rinaldo* (dir. Robert Carsen, Glyndebourne Festival Opera, 2011).

along Freudian lines, as the provenance of masochistic fantasy—a child is being beaten, and the event leaves indelible marks on that individual's psychosexual makeup.[42]

Regardless of how one chooses to interpret the role of this scene, however, it deploys metalepsis in order to hint at a connection between the world of masochistic fantasy and the reality of corporal punishment, with the aid of the frame that is there in order to be overstepped. Since caning was employed in British schools from the late nineteenth century (when it gradually came to replace birching) up until the turn of the millennium, it is a fair assumption that many audience members at the premiere—especially those educated at elite schools—would have had firsthand experience of it.[43] It seems more than likely that Carsen intended this as an element of recognition for the (typically) socially privileged Glyndebourne audience. Despite its humor, the potentially disturbing undertones of this scene resound with particular clarity at this specific venue. When the opera of the contemporary baroque stages the overflow of excessive fantasy into the physical world, it dramatizes the relation between violence as actual abuse and as an element of erotic fantasy or role-play. As spectators we thus are urged to pay attention to the border between them, as well as its potential transgression.

The two figures that have been at the center of this chapter—hyperbole and metalepsis—both exemplify the baroque inclination for excess, and they are both reinterpreted by the iconography of perversion. Moreover, that iconography puts them in the service of what I introduced in the previous chapter as the *actuality effect*. When the hyperboles of the *Rinaldo* libretto (which insistently speak of love in terms of bondage, pain, and cruelty) are literalized by the SM imagery of Carsen's staging, this is an instance of what I described as a first-level actuality effect: in the fetishes the notion of erotic power ceases to be a mere figure of speech and takes the shape of physical objects. The metalepsis created with the aid of the blackboard, meanwhile, establishes a boundary between a sexual fantasy and a diegetic reality only in order to overstep it, which corresponds to the second level. These examples also illustrate how the actuality effect can serve different purposes and open up various potentialities of meaning. Thus, when the actuality effect is achieved by charging an object or prop with magic sexual power—as when both the Stuttgart *Alcina* and the Glyndebourne *Rinaldo* allude to fetishism—this seems to happen in order to suggest that this power is subject to negotiation or usurpation. When, as in the *Rinaldo* production, it is achieved by pointing to an overstepping of the boundary between a fantasy of eroticized power and the reality of the story, it simultaneously points to an analogous relation: that between the fantasy world of opera and the "real" reality in which the audience (and all of us) live and act. In this case the actuality effect makes a truly preposterous insinuation about opera: the boundary between theatrical representation—supposedly safe, sane, and consensual—and physical reality might be as volatile and permeable as the frames that are overstepped on the stage.

In the end Glyndebourne's boarding-school *Rinaldo* does not focus on the more disconcerting aspects of this idea but remains rather playful. It is most of all good theatrical fun, and with the gorgeous playing of the Orchestra of the Age of the Enlightenment under the baton of Ottavio Dantone and topped off by a cast of admirably agile voices, it is Handelian musical splendor at its best. But as we will see over the next chapters, the actuality effects that I have pointed to here insistently merge with representations of eroticized power, and the serious questions only hinted at here grow more prominent. What happens when we move on to more disturbing stagings, and the opera repertoire of the long nineteenth century, with the same set of issues in mind? What are the results when sexual domination is given a darker twist, by stagings that insist on broaching questions of real violence and abuse in a rather more aggressive manner, or when the visual codes of SM are being made to interact with operas created in a context marked by a harder policing of gender identity, stricter regimes of power, and unmitigated misogyny?

3 Schools of Libertinage

DON GIOVANNI WITH SADE

In the collaborations between W. A. Mozart and Lorenzo Da Ponte—threefold starting signal of the operatic core repertoire, fired amid the tumult of social upheaval and revolution—the entanglement of erotic desire with the distribution of power takes center stage. It is little wonder the iconography of perversion features frequently in recent stagings of *Le nozze di Figaro* (1786), *Don Giovanni* (1787) or *Così fan tutte* (1790). In these operas, however, present-day mise-en-scène encounters a configuration of sexuality and gender miles apart from the Handelian opera seria discussed in the previous chapter. By the end of the eighteenth century, the casting customs that allowed both men and women to sing roles of any gender had yielded to a more regulative focus on sexual difference, which also shaped the scores and libretti. The way was already being paved for what has been called nineteenth-century opera's "shrine to heterosex," where love affairs between tenor and soprano voices would become a normative core.[1] In that century above all *Don Giovanni* came to be regarded as a sort of paradigm of opera itself. It exerted a profound influence not only on the composers of Romanticism and beyond but also on thinkers and authors who returned the favor: the writings of E. T. A. Hoffmann, Søren Kierkegaard, and others came to have a lasting impact on the reception history of this opera.[2] *Don Giovanni* has retained its hold over audiences to this day and is among the repertoire staples most frequently subjected to makeovers by director's opera, not least in versions for cinema and television.[3] Its current topicality is hard to miss: since the explosion of the Me Too movement in the autumn of 2017, few performance reviews fail to connect Giovanni to present-day abusers of power and privilege, and productions from 2018 and 2019 regularly held this forth as a selling point: "our #metoo modern-dress production will demonstrate just how relevant this 231 year old opera still is."[4]

The hornet's nest of sexual violence that drones beneath the opera's comical surface, however, has been growing increasingly audible for several decades. As Richard Will notes, there has been a general tendency to move away from a traditional idealization of Giovanni on stage: while midcentury versions show Giovanni as "far more charming than calculating, and scarcely violent," he "grew more wicked in the 1980s and 1990s," and in the last decades he has "continued his moral descent" and "run a gamut of depravity."[5] From a performance-centered perspective there is no one "correct" way of staging the characters and the events, either philologically or morally. Yet the moral question of sexuality, power, and violence permeates every single scene of the opera, and any directorial decision will refract and reflect it. In his essay from the colloquy "Sexual Violence in Opera," Will outlines the way in which the performances of *Don Giovanni* have "at once undermined and reinforced modern rape culture."[6] For instance, once Giovanni appears as a ruthless rapist rather than a gentleman philanderer, to what extent are his actions to be understood in relation to social inequalities of class and gender? To make Giovanni a vehicle for social critique may help the spectators "recognize a real-world system of oppression whose beneficiaries include the generally white, affluent institution of opera itself," yet at the same time, the very act of "exposing the rot that makes a Don Giovanni inevitable" also "diverts attention from his personal agency as a predator, and the agency he robs from his prey."[7] Another issue is what level of initiative or consent to ascribe to the female characters in the events of the drama. In stagings by Ruth Berghaus and others, their willing acts of infidelity have aimed at resistance and empowerment, "liberating them from bourgeois femininity"—a reading that simultaneously risks mitigating the malice of Giovanni's own behavior: "if consenting women cleanse the story of rape, they also introduce one of the most familiar and debasing stereotypes of rape culture, lying women."[8] The most obvious and contested question in this regard is the offstage encounter between Donna Anna and Giovanni in the first act, after which she accuses him of assaulting her in her bedroom.[9] As Will notes, doubting her account is tantamount to "upending the moral compass of the entire story," yet this interpretation seems to exert an irresistible pull on contemporary directors: "of the twenty-odd stage versions released on video since 2000 more than half depict Donna Anna as either vacillating about Don Giovanni or conspiring with him outright."[10] Perhaps 2017 was the turning point after which this portrayal of Anna is no longer possible, and Don Giovanni must be held accountable.[11]

This chapter does not center on Donnas Anna or Elvira, the noblewomen of Giovanni's own social circles, but on Zerlina. She is the country girl whose wedding celebrations Giovanni crashes in the first act, while instructing Leporello to distract her fiancé, Masetto, with a lavish party to make sure she can be ensnared without interruptions. Her soubrette persona has something elusive about it: she seems to be in motion, less readily classifiable than the nobility and servants around her. As Theodor W. Adorno maintained, she is a character in between historical moments: the peasant girl who is no longer a shepherdess but not yet a *citoyenne*. (Adorno also joins the long rank of commentators who imply that the opera's women owe Giovanni gratitude for his predations: "For where would her grace and loveliness have been had not the half-powerless noble on his flight through the opera only just awakened them.")[12] Berthold Hoeckner notes that she "stands between epochs because she stands musically between classes"; and unlike a *mezzo carattere* combining *buffa* and *seria*, she "is not torn apart by generic opposites but bridges the gap instead in her fleeting appearance."[13] Unlike Donna Anna, moreover, Zerlina initially expresses ambivalence about her feelings toward Giovanni.

Her undecidability stems from the fact that her principal numbers outline a character in the process of becoming, which contrasts sharply against Giovanni's static obsession and refusal to change. In their duet "Là ci darem la mano" (There we will hold hands) her musical persona is indecisive, her phrases relying heavily on repetitions of his. By contrast, in the two arias she sings to Masetto—"Batti, batti" (Beat, beat) and "Vedrai carino" (You will see, my dear)—she appeases her hurting boyfriend with considerable rhetorical flair. Finally, in the duet "Per queste tue manine" (By these little hands), which was written for the Vienna premiere in 1788 (and is often left out of present-day productions), we see a different and very aggressive Zerlina exacting her revenge on Leporello. Because these numbers are tightly interwoven musically, moreover, they encourage a reading of the narrative as one of becoming, easily distinguishable in the overall action. The two duets that form the outer parts of this story are each other's counterparts as male-female dynamics of seduction and antagonism respectively. Midway between these two pairs, Giovanni's attempted rape of Zerlina in the first-act finale stands as a traumatic peripeteia: the moment of her offstage scream is the most musically tumultuous moment in the first act, abruptly ending any affection she may have held vis-à-vis Giovanni.[14] As several observers have pointed out, moreover, the musical structure of "Batti, batti" and "Vedrai carino" are modeled on that of "Là ci darem": just like Giovanni's initial attempt at seduction, Zerlina's success in coaxing and consoling Masetto are performed by a change of meter ("Batti, batti") and of rhythmic gesture ("Vedrai carino") in the final part of the arias.[15] Zerlina, as it were, appears to learn from Giovanni's musical rhetoric.

If hers is a story about coming of age and exploring sexuality, it is also shot through with stark images of violence, not necessarily less troubling because they are presented in such a charmingly untroubled vocal persona. When she sings "Batti, Batti," which will be my central point of focus in the following, Giovanni's plans of seducing her have been thwarted. The jealous Masetto confronts her with accusations of infidelity, and she replies in a sweet F major:

Batti, batti, o bel Masetto,	Beat, beat, o beautiful Masetto,
la tua povera Zerlina;	your poor Zerlina;
Starò qui come agnellina	I shall stand here like a little lamb
le tue botte ad aspettar.	and await your blows.
Lascerò straziarmi il crine,	I shall let you pull my hair out,
lascerò cavarmi gli occhi,	I shall let you tear my eyes out,

| e le care tue manine | and your dear hands |
| lieta poi saprò baciar. | then gladly I shall kiss. |

Ah, lo vedo, non hai core!	Ah, I see you do not have the heart!
Pace, pace, o vita mia,	Peace, peace, o my darling,
In contenti ed allegria	In contentment and joy
notte e dì vogliam passar.	we shall pass day and night.

This is a comical aria sung by a predominantly comical character, and its imagery illustrates the continuation of the hyperbolic imagery addressed in the previous chapter. But how does the light lyrical mood of the aria relate to the stark violence contained in its literal stratum? What are we to make today of the rhetorical intertwining of *botte* and *baci*, of abuse and eroticism? The standard answer—still the one most often suggested on stage and probably not far from authorial intention—is that it is an ace display of tongue-in-cheek cajolery. Zerlina is in full control, knowing all along that she will get her way in the end and that she certainly will not be subjected to the brutality about which she is singing.[16] Even so, streaks of darkness shine through her scintillating wit, because the threat of real violence lies right behind it; otherwise, the text would not only make no sense but could never have been written in the first place.

Contemporary productions frequently attempt to make this sinister backdrop visible. A watershed production in this regard was Peter Sellars's blaxploitation version, which premiered in 1987 and was released as a film three years later: here, the story is set in the streets of South Bronx, and during the preceding recitativo we hear how Zerlina is beaten up off stage by her boyfriend.[17] Another notable example is Martin Kušej's 2006 staging from Salzburg, which silhouettes Zerlina's aria against an anonymous crowd of battered women, moving slowly, wincing and touching their hurting faces, arms, legs, and torsos. As Zerlina proceeds to the happy ending of her tune, a wall slides in front of this unsettling background, a cover-up demonstratively reminding the spectators of the forgetfulness needed to make light of her words. The two stagings I discuss in this chapter take another approach, no less fraught with uncomfortable questions: Calixto Bieito and Claus Guth interpret Zerlina's plea in this aria neither as a chucklesome ploy nor as a codependent abidance by abuse but as an expression of an ambiguous fascination with the dynamics of power and powerlessness. Bieito's Barcelona version places the emphasis on sexual violence, whereas, in Salzburg, Guth gives precedence to consensual power exchanges. Both productions, however, create variations on what I have called the actuality effect: figurative language and hyperbolic fantasy crystallize here into something more palpable, more real.

CONTEMPORARY SADE: HYPERBOLIC VIOLENCE
IN BIEITO'S *DON GIOVANNI*

"The creation of this Zerlina," says Spanish-Argentinian mezzo Marisa Martins, "was enormously gratifying."[18] A strong believer in opera as teamwork, Martins considers it essential to respect each other's roles and always starts out from believing in the director's vision: "I do not question it, I do not think about if I agree or not, I simply work hard to empathize with what the director proposes." "Bieito," she stresses, "does not underestimate at any time the interpretive capacity of the singer, he treats us as actors and his demands on us correspond to that. But he also gives deeply psychological tools to go out and defend the character as he conceives it. I went on stage totally convinced of this Zerlina." Martins sang the role at the Gran Teatre del Liceu in Barcelona, where Bieito's *Don Giovanni* traveled after its premiere at the London Coliseum in 2001 and where the recording released on DVD was made in December of 2002. Like Bieito's *Un ballo in maschera* (2000), which also played in both Barcelona and London, and his first productions for the Komische Oper in Berlin (the aforementioned *Entführung* in 2004 and *Madama Butterfly* in 2005), his *Don Giovanni* caused an immense uproar and helped lay the ground for his notoriety as the bad boy of director's opera. In the UK it was pilloried by critics, who called it a "crude, anti-musical farrago," a "coke-fuelled fellatio fest," and "a new nadir in the vulgar abuse of a masterpiece," opinions that the revival conductor David Parry attributed to critics being "weird," "prissy," and unable to "see beyond the surface" to the "very serious examination of the piece."[19] Bieito's *Don Giovanni*—just as his *Entführung*—was one of those productions that came to take on a symbolic function in the infected debate about directorial license in opera, arguably at the price of obscuring its strengths and weaknesses alike.[20]

The staging actually contains little of the pornographic imagery that was to pervade the Komische Oper *Entführung* a couple of years later. The cruelty, however, is a common denominator. Its atmosphere is thick with violence, and the source from which it radiates is Giovanni himself, sung in Barcelona by Polish baritone Wojtek Drabowicz. The murder of the Commendatore—here a senior gangster performed by Anatoly Kocherga—is just the beginning: throughout the opera he obsessively abuses and batters everyone around him. Elvira (Véronique Gens) arrives with her face patched up, and when she draws a gun at the sight of Giovanni, it is clear who has beaten her. Later, he subjects both Leporello (Kwangchul Youn) and Masetto (Felipe Bou) to assaults with sexual undertones. If half of the production's shock value lies in its violence, the other half lies in its no less brutal ugliness. The scenery is a deserted nocturnal cityscape (which specifies the unnamed "Spanish town" of the libretto as the Olympic Port in Barcelona) full of litter, junk food, drugs, and violence; Martin Scorsese and Quentin Tarantino are frequently mentioned as cinematic points of reference.[21] The class differences of the drama have faded from view: Giovanni is a small-time pusher, Leporello a drug-addict football fan in a Barça jacket, and the others seem to belong roughly to the same circles. The design hinges on garish images of consumerism—the consumption of merchandise, the consumption of fast food, the consumption of human bodies—all of which, ultimately, implicates and undermines the cultural consumption of opera as a marker of "high" taste.[22]

In the light of these aesthetics Giovanni's battle cry, "Viva la libertà" (long live liberty), is subjected to an overdetermination emblematic of this production and its way of doing preposterous history. With its raw violence and deliberately tacky imagery, the staging adds to the prerevolutionary pathos of *libertà* a ring of the contemporary neoliberalist credo that has allowed free-market capitalism to run amok in all areas of contemporary life, commodifying human sexuality in general and the female body in particular (in the second act, this point is hammered home as Giovanni winds up a crowd of dancing clockwork Barbie dolls). Furthermore, its eroticized violence amplifies the note of libertinism inherent in the call for freedom to the point where it acquires a Sadean ring. The ghost of the marquis—who was locked up in the Bastille while

Figure 3.1. "You lying tramp!" An abusive Masetto (Felipe Bou) grabbing Zerlina (Marisa Martins) by the throat. *Don Giovanni* (dir. Calixto Bieito, Gran Teatre del Liceu, 2002).

Mozart wrote this opera, secretly penning his fantasies of murder and mutilation—haunts the Barcelona production. In the end I will argue that Bieito's Giovanni can be understood as a kind of Sadean neolibertine, whose commitment to the principle of destruction and violence overrides his commitment to pleasure, to passion, even to his own life.

Zerlina is represented here as irresistibly drawn to Giovanni's violence and authority. Rather than a masochistic desire to be passively *subjected* to power and violence, I would argue, she displays a desire to actively *partake* of it—to be able to wield it herself. When Giovanni first meets Zerlina and Masetto—their party is translated from merry peasantry to an inebriated white-trash club crowd, the bride and groom apparently having rummaged through secondhand stores for gaudy wedding wear—Bieito foregrounds the violence that surrounds her and the fact that her position is one of extreme vulnerability. Masetto, who is as inflamed with jealousy at Giovanni's attempt to seduce Zerlina as he is frustrated at his own lack of Giovanni's power, grabs her by the throat, retaining his grip as she struggles to break free (fig. 3.1). This gesture will be given a different meaning later on, but at this point his violent behavior is a desperate attempt to hold on to what he considers an asset in danger of being expropriated by a rival.

Zerlina's resulting sense of powerlessness is the weak spot on which Giovanni is to focus his attack in the following duet. Normally, his tactic is based on class difference: "he does not just tell her that she is beautiful," as Joachim Kaiser puts it, "but gives her clearly to understand that she is of a mettle above her station."[23] Bieito has erased class from the equation, however, and Zerlina is titillated by power in the more direct form of violence. As Giovanni sings the words "Là ci darem la mano" for the second time, he extends his hands to her. But rather than the affection signaled by the offer of an empty hand, he offers her two tokens of power: the right one is holding a gun, the left one two credit cards. Zerlina rejects the money but grabs the firearm. As a result, her "vorrei e non vorrei" (I would like to and I wouldn't) is interpreted not as a general hesitation about whether to yield to his seduction but as a specific choice between violence and wealth: this I do want, and this I do not. Her object of choice is eroticized not only by the duet's seduction theme but also by Martins's gestures. After grabbing the gun with both hands and pointing it in the direction of the audience, she wraps her hand around the barrel, gently stroking it back and forth, lyrically panting "mi trema un poco il cor" (my heart is trembling a little). The gun is treated as a sexual fetish and worshipped as a substitute phallus. Like the fetishized objects in the stagings of *Rinaldo* and *Alcina,* the role of the gun is to represent the passing of power from one character to another: it is first drawn by Elvira, then snatched by Giovanni, who lends it to Zerlina.

When the lovers reconvene in the recitative preceding "Batti, batti," Bieito focuses on the power struggle between them. At her line "Vien qui, sfogati, ammazzami, fa tutto di me quel che ti piace" (Come here, blow off your steam, destroy me, do to me anything that you like), she grabs hold of his wrists, forcing them into violent movements. Rhetorically asking him to maltreat her, she appears to guide his hands in toward that end, thus preparing the power transactions that are about to be articulated in "Batti, batti": the dominant role is projected on him, but she claims the prerogative of defining it. After a brief but tumultuous struggle, he gets hold of her wrists on "che ti piace." As, during the ritardando phrase "ma poi, Masetto mio, ma poi fa pace" (but then, my Masetto, make peace), the recitativo reaches a brief but tense standstill around the dominant major

Figure 3.2. Masetto (Felipe Bou) and Zerlina (Marisa Martins) in a power equilibrium before "Batti, batti." *Don Giovanni* (dir. Calixto Bieito, Gran Teatre del Liceu, 2002).

of the subsequent aria, so do Masetto and Zerlina: they are almost immobile, his hands clasping both of her wrists (fig. 3.2). Yet both their bodies are obviously still vying for control, as if they were two forces in equilibrium. While the musical tension dissolves onto the F major tonic with the descending opening phrase of the aria, however, the physical tension remains: barring a slight flurry before the repeat of the first stanza, as if to confirm that they are still struggling, they remain thus poised until the music moves into the contrasting C major section. At this point the physical tension is finally released, and she is pushed away, ending up on the billiard table, where she sings the second stanza of the text.

When the reprise returns to F major and the original exhortation "Batti, batti," a ribald Zerlina reclines on the billiard table. She spreads her legs and pulls her skirt up to reveal laced silk stockings, while beckoning him in a come-hitherly manner (fig. 3.3). Zerlina's "aspettar" comes to mean "expect" rather than "wait": it is not a promise of patient endurance but a challenge to his machismo. As the superimposition of sexual invitation on the libretto's verbal exhortation to violence eventually provokes his arousal, at her final "aspettar" he rushes across the stage and throws him-

Figure 3.3. "Beat me, beat me!" Zerlina (Marisa Martins) beckoning her boyfriend. *Don Giovanni* (dir. Calixto Bieito, Gran Teatre del Liceu, 2002).

self violently on her, grabbing her by the throat and holding her down with his left hand, while unbuttoning his trousers and reaching up under her dress with his right (fig. 3.4). At first glance this throttling repeats exactly what happened earlier. Then, it was Giovanni who challenged Masetto. Having been assigned the role of a commodity threatened by misappropriation, Zerlina could show no sign of initiative or agency and Masetto's behavior was simply that of a jealous and abusive boyfriend. This time, however, the gesture has altogether different implications because Zerlina has gained a rhetorical agency that potentially changes the economy of power. To explain how, I will need to retrace the development of her words and music between these two moments when Bieito has Masetto grab her by the throat.

In her first confrontation with Masetto (in the recitative preceding his aria "Ho capito, Signor, sì" [Yes, My Lord, I understand]), Zerlina's discourse was limited to a vacuous repetition of Giovanni's lines. As the seducer told Masetto that "la Zerlina è in man d'un cavalier" (Zerlina is in the hands of a gentleman), she echoed: "Va'! non temere. Nelle mani son io d'un cavaliere" (Go, don't worry! I am in the hands of a gentleman).

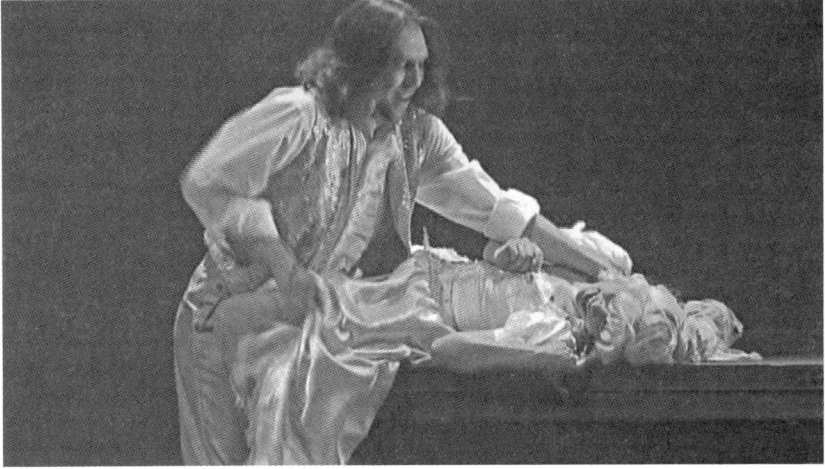

Figure 3.4. Again, Masetto (Felipe Bou) grabbing Zerlina (Marisa Martins) by the throat. *Don Giovanni* (dir. Calixto Bieito, Gran Teatre del Liceu, 2002).

Irrespective of whether one understands her iteration as a naive belief in Giovanni's honor or as a sarcasm thrown in Masetto's face, Zerlina cannot be accredited with any extraordinary gifts of eloquence here.[24] As she addresses Masetto in "Batti, batti," however, her rhetorical skills appear to have gone through a significant transformation.

When he does not resort to violence, Giovanni relies on rhetoric. From Elvira's description of his deceitful adulation in the second scene ("A forza d'arte, / di giuramenti e di lusinghe arrivi / a sedurre il cor mio" [With artifice, oaths, and flattery you managed to seduce my heart]), via the seduction of Zerlina in "Là ci darem," to the canzonetta with which he serenades Elvira's maid in the second act, his forte lies in his ability to conjure up and control libidinal energy by words and music alike. In *Don Giovanni* the female characters, too, have access to ample rhetorical means (as is also shown by Donna Anna's deployment of *hypotyposis* for visualizing the events leading up to her father's murder, as she recounts them to Don Ottavio).[25] Unlike Anna, Zerlina is structurally subordinate in a double sense: to both Giovanni and Masetto as a female but also to Giovanni as the peasant to an aristocrat. Yet, as Brown-Montesano points out, in "Batti, batti" "Zerlina always maintains actual control."[26] Her role in this scene is active rather than passive. She takes as her point of departure the very vulnerability that results from being lodged in a triangular constellation between two men and transforms it, by a rhetorical sleight of hand, into an asset to her own empowerment.[27]

Zerlina puts her trust in hyperbole: the list of violent acts in her two first stanzas are, precisely, intended to draw attention to their own exaggerated quality. Their persuasive efficacy depends on the stepwise intensification. By gradually blowing the chastisement out of all proportion, Zerlina seeks to manipulate Masetto into realizing the minute dimensions of her misdemeanor and thus forgive her for the act of infidelity that she was on the verge of committing but never actually went through with. This is Zerlina's version of the hyperbolic gambit. Normally, it plays out as comedy, since it makes Masetto's jealousy seem absurd, and any discomfort with the violence suggested by the aria's imagery is thus eclipsed by lighthearted wit. But Bieito's production does something completely different. Doing away with any subtlety about the sexual innuendo, it turns Zerlina's aria into a declaration of masochistic submissiveness. The intention behind her rhetoric remains exaggeration—nothing suggests that Martins's Zerlina wants her boyfriend to tear out her eyes—but instead of appeasing him by revealing her innocence, her hyperboles are meant to arouse him by revealing her kinkiness. Figural language, however, is a dangerous game: it always depends on context. Surrounded by Bieito's graphic violence, the reassuring figurativity of Zerlina's submissiveness is called into question. When her hyperboles are articulated as masochistic desire and pushed into the realm of the erotic, the literal register of her discourse is suddenly turned into an uncomfortable possibility.

We left Zerlina and Masetto at the moment before the aria's third stanza, his left hand on her throat and his right one fumbling with his trousers, as the music was about to pass into its final, pastoral section in six-eight time. Here, she shows herself an apt pupil to Giovanni: this time change echoes the one in "Là ci darem," in both cases signaling the moment when rhetoric has persuaded its addressee to yield. In other words, this is where Zerlina would normally have managed to convince Masetto of the triviality of her misbehavior and bring the aria to an end in loving reconciliation. In Bieito's production, however, there is no restoration of harmony between the lovers in this scene, only utter defeat for Masetto. When he progresses in his sexual approaches and buries his face in her cleavage, she reaches the final phrase of the aria's gavotte section: "Ah, lo vedo, non hai core" (Ah, I see you do not have the heart), which is the turning point of the aria. At this moment Zerlina's rhetorical trick is made manifest in a simple but effective way: because Bieito has staged Zerlina's hyperbole as sexual invitation, Masetto's failure to deliver equals impotence. It is not the heart he lacks but the balls. During the ritardando leading up to the fermata, this displacement endows the trill figures of the violins with a distinctly mocking quality, as if the music were echoing Zerlina's spiteful allusion to his sexual inadequacy. As the music comes to a halt on a grand pause, Masetto discontinues his advances and falls motionless, his face still hidden in the bosom of her dress. During the final section of the aria he stands before her, silently moping, while she unfurls the sleeves of his shirt, ties his hair up with a ribbon, and puts his jacket back on—all the time caressing him and singing cheerfully about how all will be well. The violence that he would otherwise deploy—his two attempts at choking her underscore the parallelism—has been disarmed: Masetto is, at this moment, nothing but a sulky child, forgiven and consoled by his mother.

Bieito's staging of this scene, then, construes the dynamic between the two lovers as a struggle for power, far removed from the affectionate wheedling to which her words are often reduced. Channeling the force of the sexualized brutality that surrounds her into a rhetorical blow against Masetto, Zerlina shatters for a moment his ability to exercise that brutality. Her hyperboles turn her appeal into an actual demand for a stereotypically masculine power. Being just as entrenched in the gendered power structure as she is, he has little choice but to recognize the validity of this appeal. At the same time, however, the rhetorical inflation confers on that demand a proportion that makes it impossible to live up to. It is her masochistic discourse that defines the expectations against which his masculinity is measured, and precisely because of its hyperbolic nature, that masculinity is one that he cannot deliver.

Importantly, her hyperboles depend on the trope of the fragmented female body. As Giovanni sets out to seduce her in the recitativo preceding "Là ci darem," he zeroes in on distinct parts of her anatomy in order to praise them: "Vi par che un onest'uomo, un nobil cavalier, com'io mi vanto, possa soffrir che quel visetto d'oro, quel viso inzuccherato da un bifolcaccio vil sia strapazzato? . . . Voi non siete fatta per esser paesana. Un'altra sorte vi procuran quegli occhi bricconcelli, quei labretti sì belli, quelle dituccie candide e odorose, parmi toccar giuncata e fiutar rose." (Do you think that an honest man, a noble gentleman, which I consider myself to be, can suffer this precious little face, this sweet visage to be mistreated by a common lout? . . . You are not born to be a countrywoman. Those mischievous eyes hold a different fate in store for you, those beautiful lips, those snow-white, fragrant little fingers, which seem like touching cream and sniffing roses.) He begins, then, by singling out her face (and given the generally brutal atmosphere of Bieito's staging, his ambiguous observation suggests that her face *will* be mistreated). Then, as the recitativo repeats the same unaltered melodic morsel three times, he isolates her eyes, her lips, and her fingers as objects of praise. In so doing, Giovanni mobilizes a lyrical tradition with centuries if not millennia under its belt. From Petrarch's Laura via French Blason poetry and Shakespeare's Dark Lady to Baudelaire's passerby, male poetic fantasy has continuously depicted the female body by way of a separation of her body parts from each other.[28]

In "Batti, batti" Zerlina internalizes this fetishistic perspective on the female body, adding the element of violence. She rhetorically asks not only to be beaten but to be torn apart: to have her eyes and hair removed from her body. She articulates herself as a dispersed, or dispersible, set of objects. Eyes and hair (as well as the lips, which are brought into the picture by the promise of her kiss) are of course classical attributes of feminine beauty, while the beating hands betoken control and action.

If the Barcelona Masetto is unable to respond to Zerlina's rhetoric and thus loses their power struggle, Giovanni is a different matter. In Bieito's production the finale of the first act takes place in the same bar as "Batti, batti." The characters, binging on booze and assorted substances, dress up in masquerade gear: Leporello dons a giant sombrero, Ottavio (somewhat ironically) a muscular superman suit, and the humiliated Masetto a red clown's wig with a bald crown. Zerlina and Giovanni, both so intoxicated they can barely stand, are tied together with a ribbon by the wrists. While they dance and flirt, she licks the cocaine from his fingers. Suddenly, at the line "Vieni con me, mia vita" (Come with me, my dear), Giovanni throws her over his shoulder and carries her off behind the bar stage right, from

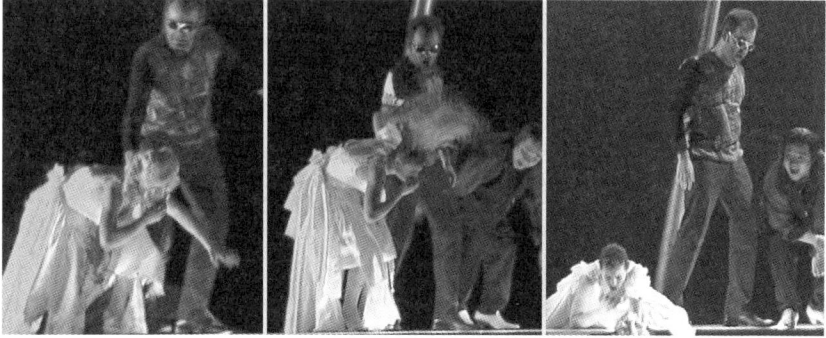

Figure 3.5. "Here is the scoundrel!" Don Giovanni (Wojtek Drabowicz) tearing off Zerlina's (Marisa Martins) wig. *Don Giovanni* (dir. Calixto Bieito, Gran Teatre del Liceu, 2002).

where we hear her desperate cries for help above the harmonically chaotic orchestra. When they reappear, he is holding her by the neck and drags her up onto the bar, as if putting her on display: her face has been battered, she presses her hands against her mouth, and the front of her white dress is soaked in blood. Then, as he sings "Ecco il birbo che t'ha offesa" (Here is the scoundrel who wronged you), Giovanni shoves his fist into her blonde hair—which has been identifiable as a wig all along—and triumphantly tears it off her head (fig. 3.5).

This is a pivotal moment in Bieito's staging of the first act. The words "Ecco il birbo che t'ha offesa" usually address Zerlina and refer to Leporello, whom Giovanni is trying to scapegoat. Bieito stages the situation quite differently: "il birbo," at this moment, is patently meant to refer to Zerlina herself. "Ecco," exclamation of disclosure, purports to reveal *her* as the scoundrel. The wronged "you" of the line, in view of what has happened in the preceding scenes, can thus be no one but Masetto. Since the word *birbo* refers to a male person, this reading of the line upsets the conventional distribution of gender. With its golden curls Zerlina's wig is stereotypically feminine, while the hair revealed beneath it is cut short and, by comparison, bespeaks androgyny or boyishness. Giovanni's act of pulling her wig off and calling out "Ecco il birbo," then, is tantamount to undermining her gender identity: he claims to unmask her (remember that they are at a masquerade) to reveal the inauthentic nature of her femininity, while simultaneously consolidating the authenticity of his own masculine power. Taking command of rhetoric in order to acquire sexual power, Zerlina has entered into a male territory. As punishment, she is now ceremonially stripped of her femininity.[29] Giovanni's humiliation of Zerlina in this scene, as it were, becomes the mirror image of his emasculation of Masetto, performed by proxy in "Batti, batti."

This moment in the finale produces a disturbing version of the first level of the actuality effect: Giovanni picks up the exact terms of Zerlina's violent rhetoric and pushes them into physical reality. Just as she sang in "Batti, batti," her hair (albeit a wig) has now been torn off her head, while the blood flowing from her mouth testifies to the grim materialization of her own intertwinement of *botti* and *baci*. By taking her hyperboles literally, Giovanni transforms the lyrical fragmentation of the female body into actual violence. If this rhetoric fetishizes a set of stereotypically admired body parts (hands, eyes, lips, hair, breasts), it can be understood as a counterpart to the fetishism that charges certain chosen props with an eroticized power. But whereas the fetishized prop (like the gun in this production) can be disconnected from the body of its owner—thus diverting the fear of castration that psychoanalysis suspects behind fetishistic desire into the more harmless letting-go of an external object—the disconnection of a fetishized body part always suggests dismemberment. It is this suggestion that Bieito's rendering of the first-act finale literalizes through Giovanni's violence against Zerlina: when the fetishization of a body part becomes the locus of the actuality effect, the symbolic gap is revealed as a literal cut, ultimately dehumanizing and mutilating its victim.

In Bieito's staging, the result is not just sadistic but, in a more precise sense, Sadean. The preposterous history that it produces can be understood as a conflation of the libertinage of Giovanni with that of Marquis de Sade, under the sign of a contemporary kitsch aesthetic. Apropos the attempted rape of Zerlina, one fictionalized version of Sade delivers the following instructions for its mise-en-scène: "*As to Zerlina, the charming peasant girl, be sure during the party at the end of the first act we see Giovanni with her. Don't leave the scene to the audience's imagination. Perhaps you could have a dungeon represented onstage, where he could do to her what he pleases. . . . Let the world see it, accompany the acts by pretty music, but be sure to shock, because through shock you gain social approval.*

(As an aside, this is a point I have made in my novel The 120 Days of Sodom. *Perhaps Maestro Mozart would consider this book as the basis for an opera. It would be an honor to rework it as a libretto, although its length may be an impediment.)*"[30] This advice on operatic stagecraft is imparted by the marquis in the novel *Imagining Don Giovanni* (and Casanova reads the passage aloud to a riveted Mozart). The book may not be the most graceful piece of prose, but the fact that the above passage saw the light of day in the same year (2001) as Bieito's staging seems fitting: the letter almost reads as a program for the production. Bieito stages Mozart as if Zerlina's rhetoric of clawed-out eyes and torn-off hair resonated with the endless and limitless violence of *The 120 Days of Sodom, or the School of Libertinage* ("they cut off her ears, they burn the inside of her nose, they put out her eyes by letting molten sealing wax trickle into them, they score her skull all around, they hang her up by her hair with stones attached to her feet so that she falls and the top of her skull is pulled off").[31] As we have already seen, moreover, the director's preference for Sadean imagery is not restricted to his *Don Giovanni:* his *Entführung* abounded with scenes of sexual mutilation—not just during "Martern aller Arten" but also, for instance, in the scene in which Osmin sinks his teeth into a prostitute while performing cunnilingus—which echo the countless descriptions of knife-torture and severed nipples and clitorises in *120 Days of Sodom.*

While Bieito's *Entführung* thus takes the bestial acts to even further extremes than his *Don Giovanni,* the latter opera is nevertheless more closely linked to the core beliefs of the Sadean universe. Its protagonist echoes the contemporaneous discourse of Enlightenment libertinage in general and Sade in particular, who advocates absolute transgression in the name of the authenticity vis-à-vis nature and autonomy vis-à-vis morality. In the words of Charles Ford, "Giovanni's exploits . . . are justified by what Sade referred to as the perpetually destructive agitation of a *malfaisant* nature."[32] Bieito's staging makes this point precisely by adding a brutality that is mostly absent from Mozart's opera—at least on a surface level—but that marks every page of Sade. In his account of masochism Gilles Deleuze contrasts Sade's impulse to make violence explicit and shocking with Masoch's preference for suggestion and suspense: while Masoch's descriptions always "bear the stamp of decency," Sade's are "obscene in themselves" because he "cannot do without this provocative element."[33] Neither, as we have seen, can Bieito. Importantly, this obscenity of description in Sade is a direct function of his commitment to negation. What the Sadean libertine seeks is an act of pure negation. That is, a transgression that does not have to rely on transgressing human law and negating "second nature" but defies even the ideal realm of the "primary nature."[34] Yet his actual acts of destruction can only take place in the world of experience, directed against individuals, and thus amount only to partial rather than absolute negation: "Hence the rage and despair of the sadistic hero when he realizes how paltry his own crimes are in relation to the idea which he can only reach through the omnipotence of reasoning. He dreams of a universal, impersonal crime."[35] Attempting to approach this dream, the libertine must resort to an acceleration and condensation of personal crime, that is, violence against other human beings. In Deleuze's reading this is "the meaning of repetitiveness in Sade's writing and of the monotony of sadism."[36] An unfinished work, the story of *The 120 Days of Sodom* gradually dissolves into a mere catalogue of gruesome violence. From Deleuze's perspective the fact that the savage acts of the libertines are finally just sketched out and numbered rather than narrated reveals Sade's main priority: multiplying the victims and their suffering to suggest the idea of an absolute negation. Furthermore, the will to reach beyond the petty sin against second nature means that these acts have to be committed in cold blood because if they were grounded in libidinal impulses, they would remain hopelessly tied to the personal.[37] In the end, paradoxically, the commitment to absolute destruction thus overrides any individual pleasure for the libertine and becomes a principle of duty.[38]

This is the point where a resonance can be found between Sade's thought and *Don Giovanni*, which is amplified by Bieito's mise-en-scène: just as the Sadean libertine is driven by the idea of the Crime that would transcend all his individual crimes, so Giovanni is eternally propelled by the idea of Conquest that would transcend all his individual conquests. In Slavoj Žižek's words, it is as if "next to and other than women who embody different qualities satisfying different needs, existed, furthermore, *the* Woman, the individual incarnation of the feminine kingdom—*this* is the woman who, according to Lacan, 'doesn't exist,' which is why Don Giovanni is condemned to eternal flight from one woman to another." As a result, "the ultimate driving force of Don Giovanni's conquest is not passion but *adding to the list,* as is openly ascertained in the . . . 'champagne aria.'"[39] From this perspective Giovanni's catalogue of conquests is analogous to Sade's list of bestial sexual acts: both are aimed at conjuring up an ideal that can only be obtained through its incessant accumulation, next to which all other concerns must yield. The difference is the degree of (explicit) violence involved, which is precisely what is added by Bieito. Ultimately, sexual gratification, although seemingly the root of Giovanni's obsession, is overtaken by its underlying principle. Drawing on Žižek's reading, Mladen Dolar has captured this perspective on Giovanni in words that smack of Sadean negation (although neither writer explicitly makes the connection with Sade in this context): "By following so uncompromisingly the pleasure principle that he refuses to renounce, he takes this principle to an extreme, to an ethical attitude in whose name he finally is willing to die. . . . This ethical attitude indicates an absolute autonomy of the subject in rebellion against the existing order, its moral principles and religious arguments. . . . Whereas *Figaro* ends in the spirit of *liberté, égalité, fraternité,* for Don Giovanni *liberté* is placed beyond and in opposition to *égalité* and *fraternité,* in a zone where pure liberty coincides with pure evil."[40] Such is the Giovanni put on stage by Bieito. Like the endless accumulation of conquests, his repeated refusal to repent—the nine iterations of his "no"—takes aim at a greater defiance, which values the credo of transgression even at the expense of his own life. In Barcelona Giovanni is not dragged to hell by the stone guest. Instead, the bloody Commendatore emerges from the trunk of his car (possibly as a drug-induced hallucination) only to suffer a second death at the hands of Giovanni, who thus stubbornly repeats his crime from the opening scene. He dies himself to the *lieto fine* music of the final scene, tied to a chair and slain by those whom he has wronged: Leporello, Anna, Ottavio, Masetto, and Zerlina each take turns stabbing Giovanni with a knife and finally cut his throat. In this staging, the other characters graduate *summa cum laude* from the Don's school of neolibertinage: while Giovanni as individual perishes, Giovanni as Sadean principle—the absolute commitment to violence— triumphs to the sound of the jubilant D major finale.

The stark contrast between the mood of the music and the acts it accompanies raises the question of what attitude Bieito's staging as a whole takes vis-à-vis the violent world it depicts. It can hardly be accused of sugarcoating the sexual violence by portraying Giovanni as gentleman seducer. Yet the protagonist in this opera is strangely difficult to safeguard from glorification. No matter how openly a production flaunts his evil, he still claims the position of the antihero, and the ideals he represents tend to make the opera's most lasting impression. When Bieito inflects those ideals toward a Sadean celebration of violence, he dives so deeply into the nihilism he endeavors to expose that the production itself has difficulties washing its hands of the violence laid bare. The interpretative choice of regarding it as a critique rather than an endorsement remains open—it is even quite clearly the intention—but when the sadistic acts reach a certain level, they threaten to hollow out the opera's moral stance to the point of collapse. If a reading of *Don Giovanni* that makes light of Zerlina's vulnerability risks becoming deaf to the echoes of violence that resound in her arias, Bieito's blaring amplification of those echoes risks drowning her out entirely.

OUT OF THE WOODS: ZERLINA'S EXPLORATIONS IN CLAUS GUTH'S *DON GIOVANNI*

There is little in the Barcelona *Don Giovanni* to suggest BDSM in the sense of a mutually agreed-upon scenario among the characters. Giovanni, Zerlina, and Masetto are not consenting subjects in pursuit of sexual satisfaction; rather, they inhabit a neo-Sadean world where sex is only a means to the higher end of excessive violence and absolute power. If Bieito's staging can be thought of in relation to SM, it is thus not as a scenic representation of it but as a staged ritual analogous to it, performed by the singers—in that sense, it is an enacted scenario of eroticized power where everyone participates of their own accord and nobody gets hurt for real. Claus Guth's 2008 staging for the Salzburg Festival, by contrast, alludes explicitly to BDSM-style play among the characters in the drama: here, Zerlina's relation to the two male rivals starts out as an exploration of the pleasures afforded by the consensual exchange of eroticized power. The original class hierarchies have again been eradicated at the expense of the characters' individual trajectories.

Like so many of the stagings discussed in this book, Guth's *Don Giovanni* split critics into booers and applauders when it first premiered.

Gradually, however, the cheers grew louder, and the production took on an almost iconic character. After having been recorded during its first Salzburg summer and released on DVD via EuroArts in 2010, it was exported both to the Dutch National Opera and to the Berliner Staatsoper, where it was revived as late as the 2019–20 season. Although this *Don Giovanni* shares the bleakness of Bieito's reading, it is more compelling visually: the drama is set in a misty, nocturnal pine forest (designed by Christian Schmidt), which revolves on stage throughout the two acts. It is a *selva oscura* where Giovanni—superbly acted on the DVD by Christopher Maltman—has lost sight of his pathway and wanders aimlessly with his fellow characters. A bus shelter, where he waits with Erwin Schrott's Leporello for a ride that never comes, serves to underscore the isolated character of the location and lend the two characters an air of Beckett's Vladimir and Estragon. But the most distinctive trait of Guth's interpretation is to have Maltman's Giovanni shot in the belly by the Commendatore (again portrayed by Anatoly Kocherga) in an extended slow-motion fight during the overture. As a result, he is plagued by an open wound during the whole opera, twitching at dissonant passages and relying on various drugs to keep him going while he tries to squeeze the last bitter drops of pleasure out of life.

The triangular constellations surrounding Zerlina—whose ghost-white wedding gown contrasts sharply with the gloomy woods and the men in black—are even more closely knit in Guth's production than in Bieito's. All of Zerlina's numbers, sung with great lyrical luster by Ekaterina Siurina, are set up to mirror one another visually as they do musically.[41] For starters, they take place in the same clearing in the forest (to emphasize this fact, Alex Esposito's Masetto finds in "Batti, batti" a high-heel shoe left there by Zerlina during "Là ci darem," which inflames his jealousy). From one of the trees hangs a swing, openly bespeaking play. A prop for Zerlina's pseudo-innocent girlishness, its back-and-forth movements also serve as sexual innuendo and evoke a make-believe age difference. In the recitativo before "Là ci darem" Giovanni sets it in motion, gently pushing the small of Zerlina's back. Later, in "Batti, batti," she has learned how to gain momentum herself. The erotic interplay in the second of these numbers is also presented as a more-or-less precise reproduction of the first, with Zerlina having learned from Giovanni how to take initiative. As Giovanni

Figure 3.6. Swinging in the forest: Don Giovanni (Christopher Maltman) and Zerlina (Ekaterina Siurina) playing around during "La ci darem." *Don Giovanni* (dir. Claus Guth, Salzburger Festspiele, 2008).

begins the duet, he is lying on his back on the ground below Zerlina, who is still on the swing, resting her feet on his chest (fig. 3.6); in "Batti, batti" she replays the same scene, placing Masetto in the same submissive position beneath her feet. Similarly, during the final section of "Là ci darem," Giovanni picks up a fern leaf and tickles her arms, face, and breasts; while in "Batti, batti" she does the same with Masetto's legs and crotch. This production, then, makes more markedly visible the mirrorlike symmetry between Zerlina's two main numbers in the first act by repeating the same erotic power exchange in the same sylvan spot. If Bieito's staging of "Là ci darem" suggests that Giovanni infuses Zerlina with the desire for power and the means to attain it in "Batti, batti," Guth even more manifestly represents their relationship as that of tutor and pupil: Giovanni teaches her, by playing the submissive role, how to explore and enjoy the dominant aspects of her own sexuality. It is as if he were advising her on how to spice up her marriage with a little light kink. Although complex in its implications, this reading resounds with the same notion as Adorno's dubious justification of Giovanni: should Zerlina not actually be thankful to the nobleman for awakening her charms?

Figures 3.7–8. Zerlina (Ekaterina Siurina) tying up and blindfolding Masetto (Alex Esposito) during "Batti, batti." *Don Giovanni* (dir. Claus Guth, Salzburger Festspiele, 2008).

Zerlina also adds a few creative elements of her own to Giovanni's game, however: singing the second stanza, she gently shoves a shocked Masetto against the trunk of a tree and ties him up with her bridal veil (fig. 3.7). As he breaks loose, she goes on to blindfold him with his own bowtie, before pushing him to the ground and placing herself in the swing above him (fig. 3.8). As she jumps off of the swing, she seats herself on top of him and tears open his shirt to caress his chest, the back-and-forth movement of the swing is transposed (back) from the register of child's play into the lovemaking that it hinted at in the first place. Her affirmation of their love in the concluding phrases of the aria's pastoral section—"sì, sì, sì, sì, sì, sì, sì, sì, sì"—becomes an ecstatic climax, as she bestrides her fiancé with her eyes closed and arms raised. When the aria comes to a halt on the final cadence, he bites her arm, keeping it between his teeth until they break out in a common fit of laughter (fig. 3.9). It is clear from Masetto's initial overacted looks of disbelief that this kind of sexual behavior is a new element in their love life, inspired by Giovanni's intrusion into it (although he does not find it unpleasant, once his surprise has receded). Her visual restaging of the duet with Giovanni, however, also seems to suggest that she is not entirely present: just as much as she returns to her fiancé, she

Figure 3.9. Coming to power: Zerlina (Ekaterina Siurina) singing "sì" to Masetto (Alex Esposito). *Don Giovanni* (dir. Claus Guth, Salzburger Festspiele, 2008).

goes through with the interrupted infidelity. The staging has her simultaneously make love to Masetto and to her fantasy image of Giovanni.

In its allusions to light bondage and BDSM, Guth's staging of "Batti, batti" creates a gap between the words and the stage action on two distinct levels: on the one hand, between the verbally evoked acts of violence and the actions and objects that serve as visual signs of power; on the other hand, between Zerlina's rhetorical position of submission and her dominant behavior. Although she is following Giovanni's example, it is Zerlina who is the agent behind this gap: through her own actions and initiatives a space is created for the exploration and articulation of her sexual subjectivity.

To begin with the former level, the violence of the words is disproportionate not primarily in relation to a reasonable punishment for her supposed infidelity but in relation to the power that we actually see performed on the stage. When Zerlina blindfolds Masetto, for instance, that action takes on the role of referent for the phrase "lascerò cavarmi gli occhi" (I shall let you tear my eyes out): they both signify bereavement of vision, and those subjected to such bereavement become powerless, blind objects of the gaze rather than beholding subjects. The blindfold, however, interprets this bereavement not as an irreversible act of violence but as a piece of playacting that can be interrupted at any point. Similarly, the threat of physical force implied by the submissive rhetoric of the aria is construed as Zerlina's playful control over Masetto's body: her pushes would clearly have been too gentle to control Masetto's body had he not willingly submitted to them, just as the bridal-veil bondage is much too loose to restrict his movements (on the DVD recording Siurina even fails to tie it properly at the first attempt and has to pick it up again after it has fallen off). Like the fetishized props in the Handel productions, the blindfold and the bondage are not physical enforcers of power here but mere symbols of it, the efficacy of which depends on a convention to which both parties willingly subscribe. Masetto's bite, similarly, is an intimation of pain, a piece of playacting within the play. The characters both appear to know it is, and their infatuated giggling is the result of a relocation of their emotional tension into the framework of a game where it can be released into sexual satisfaction.

In one sense Guth's staging thus mitigates the violence that Bieito's version amplifies, by displaying on stage possible referents for Zerlina's words that are far less severe than their literal meaning. This treatment of her rhetorical figures corresponds to the first-level actuality effect that I pointed to in *Rinaldo* and *Alcina:* just as the chains, rubber, and shoe fetishisms in those productions are visual manifestations of the rhetoric of violent erotic sentiment, so Zerlina's props become visual manifestations of the power dynamics implied in the libretto. Guth does not let her rhetoric break out into violence here but rather confirms its status as hyperbole. By moving the hyperboles into the sphere of consensual BDSM, this staging acknowledges the eroticized violence of the libretto, while giving it a form that may be controlled by the participants. Again, when the eroticized power is located in objects rather than in the body itself—applying a blindfold rather than in gouging someone's eyes out—it becomes the potential subject of playful negotiation rather than something irreversible and violent. Siurina's Zerlina, too, enrolls in Giovanni's school of libertinage, but the model is consensual BDSM, not Sadean brutality.[42]

This observation brings me to the second discrepancy between the stage action and the words in Guth's staging: the reversal between Zerlina's verbal submission and her enacted dominance. On her verbal acceptance of a submissive position Guth superimposes an active-dominant Zerlina and a passive-submissive Masetto, thus redistributing the parameters of agency, initiative, and power articulated on the surface level of the text. One way of expressing this dissonance is that it makes manifest the fact that Zerlina's rhetorical proficiency gave her the upper hand in this scene all along. Her verbal initiative takes physical shape, revealing the hyperbolic challenge that defeated Masetto in Bieito's staging as a game of symbols. There, he was faced with an excessive demand on his masculine power, which effectively emasculated him; here, Zerlina herself claims that power but makes clear that it depends on symbolic objects and actions rather than brute virility. By transferring the dominant position to herself, and by disclosing the hyperboles precisely as hyperboles, she deprives both of their threatening proportions. The dissonance between the dominant Zerlina seen and the submissive Zerlina heard, then, can be said simply to expose the ambiguous power structure that inhered in her words in the first place: the rhetorical articulation of the submissive position was already a result of her symbolic agency and initiative, both means and expression of empowerment.

In combination with the playfulness and pleasure evoked by this scene, moreover, the superimposition of submissive and dominant tendencies in one person amounts to a questioning of the very idea of a fixed sexual identity. Zerlina's simultaneous inhabiting—in parallel semiotic systems—of "top" and "bottom" positions gives her sexuality a fluid character that belies a rigid definition in terms of either inclination. One might say that she embodies the operatic version of switching: dominance and submission are cast less as fixed identities than as roles to be negotiated, (ex)changed, and developed depending on the shifting desires of the participants—a practice that has become increasingly encouraged, even idealized, in parts of contemporary BDSM subculture.[43] In contrast to large-scale social power structures, a scene like the one enacted between Zerlina and Masetto allows for the self-construction of a subject that is not tied to a single sexual identity but may oscillate between or simultaneously incorporate a number of different ones. The power exchange, then, is staged by Guth as a means of resolving the tension between the lovers into a volatile pleasure, which is the very opposite of what happened in Bieito's staging of the same aria. There, Zerlina's aim was neither sexual satisfaction nor reconciliation: sex was the means, power the end. Here, the power exchange exists only to serve the end of pleasure for both parties. The clearing in which "Batti, batti" takes place becomes a visualization of the space of the safe, sane, and consensual: it is a neatly delineated arena in the surrounding darkness, a dimly lit stage-upon-the-stage for the performance of Zerlina's fluid sexual identity as a combination of submissive and dominant behavior.

What about the sexual violence to which Zerlina is subjected? To be sure, it still lurks in the woods. After first having met, Zerlina and Giovanni are so impatient to leave the stage together that Esposito's Masetto is left to finish "Ho capito, Signor, sì" by himself. Unable to vent his anger to the absent traitors, he hangs Zerlina's bridal veil in a tree and beats it with a stick. When he is once more overcome by jealousy after "Batti, batti," he threatens her with the same weapon and—just as his Barcelona counterpart—grabs her hard by the throat, thus taking a step from fantasies of violence toward their realization. Giovanni's attempted rape of Zerlina, however, is nowhere to be seen. Like Bieito, Guth employs the dramatic climax of the music in the first-act finale to stage a breach of the border between representation and reality. Zerlina's offstage scream again gives the occasion for an actuality effect, revealing as real the violence that was thought to be a mere fantasy but not as violence done to her. In an ingenious rereading of the scene, Guth has her scream not because she is abused but because she has discovered Giovanni's bullet wound, the blood of which is suddenly all over her (the Lammermoorian image of red blood on a white wedding gown is too thrilling to resist for Guth and Bieito alike).

The scene is patently about Zerlina's perspective. Her scream and the orchestral tumult tell of the shocking revelation of Giovanni's wound *to her:* she does not know that the wound has been there since Giovanni's initial battle with the Commendatore. Having accepted the "top" role vis-à-vis Giovanni in "Là ci darem," and repeated and developed it with bondage and hyperboles of violence in "Batti, batti" (in which she was as much making love to her idea of Giovanni as to her fiancé), the domination that she imagined only as a sexual fantasy suddenly seems to her as if she had inflicted a mortal wound on the submissive part—not in a straightforwardly causal manner, of course, since Giovanni's wound is "actually" inflicted by the Oedipal father figure of the Commendatore. The point is that Zerlina's discovery of the wound coincides with her decision to physically consummate her relation with Giovanni, which follows on her learning from him how the sexual game is to be played. Guth's staging of her second-act aria "Vedrai carino" has her still preoccupied with this discovery. While supposedly promising to heal Masetto's battered body with the balm of her love, she ignores her boyfriend altogether, leaving him lying in the shadows outside the spotlight. Instead, she focuses on Giovanni's blood on her dress, suggesting that it is indeed his body to which she would deliver the remedy. She has forgotten all about Masetto, and the erotic allusions of the aria become a compassionate-masturbatory fantasy about Giovanni.

As the second act progresses, Zerlina continues along the lines of sexual domination, eventually crossing the limits of that which began as a game. In Guth's staging, her story has a scene that picks up the imagery established in "Là ci darem" and "Batti, batti." Unlike the Barcelona production—and most other contemporary productions—the Salzburg one includes the duet No. 21a, "Per queste tue manine," which Mozart added for the Vienna premiere. In this number we encounter a very different Zerlina, who ties up and threatens to kill Leporello. Identifying herself as a tiger, a lion, an asp, she sets out to give patriarchy its just deserts. The fact that the duet is a kind of counterpiece to "Batti, batti" is clearly suggested in Da Ponte's libretto: as a frightened Leporello asks in the preceding recitativo "dunque cavar mi vuoi . . ." (so you want to tear off my . . .), Zerlina retorts "i capelli, la testa, il cor e gli occhi" (hair, head, heart, and eyes), in an explicit inversion of the violence that she evoked in "Batti, batti." The rhetoric of poetic dismemberment is thus directed away from her own body, against his, as is the beating: "o Dei, che botte" (Oh Lord, what blows). Conversely, the hands that would supposedly have done the beating in "Batti, batti," and were therefore submissively adored, are now hers.[44] Leporello begs:

Per queste tue manine,	By these little hands,
candide e tenerelle,	snow-white and tender,
per questa fresca pelle,	by this pristine skin,
abbi pietà di me!	have mercy on me!

Guth stages the scene as a continuation of Zerlina's development in the first act, employing the same visual motifs: it takes place in the same clearing and with similar allusions to violent sexuality. Here, too, Zerlina is entrusted with a gun, with which she now threatens Leporello. She kicks him in the groin and shoves him to the ground before demanding his hands in order to fetter them. And this time she does it properly; unlike the bridal veil that tied Masetto, these knots do not come off easily, perhaps because they are fastened to the libretto; in the following recitativo he is still struggling with them: "Se potessi liberarmi coi denti" (if I could free myself with my teeth). (At the same time, Schrott's rather muscular Leporello has to struggle a bit in order to appear coerced by Siurina's Zerlina.) Since Guth has already introduced the bondage theme together with the rhetorical *botte* in "Batti, batti," her tying him up becomes in this staging a direct resumption of her dominant behavior in the first act. What was then a light erotic game has now become real violence, in another instance of the actuality effect on what I called the second level: Zerlina's dominance was first established as a fantasy role-play but then breaks out into the "reality" of the diegesis. Sitting on top of him, exactly as she did with Giovanni and Masetto, and ripping his shirt open, she draws blood by carving what appears to be a Z for Zerlina on his chest with a sharp stick. Inscribing this Zorroesque mark, the blood of which might be taken to suggest a less severe version of Giovanni's wound, is an act of branding, confirming her status as proprietor of his body.[45] At this point, then, Zerlina is very far from being a docile commodity in a male economy. Yet, because she still acts as Giovanni's pupil, her agency is not self-evident either.

The swing is now broken, dangling from its rope. With this rope—the remains of that which once attested to the playfulness of the erotic interaction—she ties a noose that she places around Leporello's neck: "Così cogli uomini, così si fa" (That is how men should be dealt with). She has, once more, picked up Giovanni's lesson and "realized," from the sight of his wound, that death and murder are simply the way in which men should be treated. Since her interest in Masetto's wounds during "Vedrai carino" was moderate at best, her violence in "Per queste tue manine" now seems less explicable as revenge for his suffering. Instead, it becomes a direct continuation of the erotic game initiated by Giovanni, which has escalated beyond what is definable as consensual play. As her dominant behavior is redirected against Leporello (whose identity is already mixed up with his master's anyway), it also takes leave of its playground origins and passes from a representation of an enacted power exchange to a rep-

resentation of actual violence. The servant's life is saved in this staging by
the intervention of Masetto at the end of the number, who carries a kick-
ing and screaming Zerlina off stage. Notably, this gesture undercuts any
empowerment previously suggested by the staging. It is her fiancé who, by
simply lifting her up and moving her out of the clearing, decides where the
line should be drawn. As a result, the sequence of dominant roles that she
has tried out ends, rather disappointingly, with a childlike tantrum. This
infantilization of Zerlina is all the more tangible after Guth's upending of
the first-act finale: by erasing Giovanni's violation, the staging also suggests that her fury is groundless and exaggerated.

Insofar as the progression from "La cì darem" to "Batti, batti" (and
onward to "Vedrai carino" and "Per queste tue manine") is a narrative of
Zerlina's subjective progress—of her loss of innocence or the development
of her sexuality—Guth's allusions to BDSM give that narrative a different
reading from the typical Freudian story of subject formation: it is staged
as a series of performative actions that may be seen as the actual sites and
moments of her becoming, rather than the digging-out of a preexisting
psychological character from Mozart and Da Ponte's score. She is struggling to be the free agent of her own becoming—a "free agent" because she
is empowered both in the aforementioned terms of rhetorical prowess and
in her choice to reverse the image of her own torn-out eyes by depriving
Masetto of his eyesight, and "struggling" because this process of subjec-
tivation is nevertheless fueled by the Oedipal figure of Giovanni. In "Batti,
batti" the bondage props serve her as a way of containing the hyperbolic
signification, preventing its meaning from running amok into the realm of
the literal. They give her the freedom to move ad libitum between—even
superimpose in words and actions—contradictory positions of dominance
and submission. By staging her *jouissance* as the result of actively chosen
roles and theatrical playing, she is able to create, in "Batti, batti," a space
for the articulation of her nascent sexual subject. That space, however, is
retrospectively invaded by real violence, the presence of which she is suddenly aware, and by Masetto, who repeals the dominant position that she
takes vis-à-vis Leporello by dragging her off the stage. As opposed to the
Barcelona staging, the real violence is not directed at her but at Giovanni
(in the first-act finale) and Leporello (in "Per queste tue manine"). Zerlina
thus never receives the severe punishment she did in Bieito's version. Even

so, both Guth and Bieito clearly confer power and agency on her character only in order to take it back, and it is not self-evident that these stagings are on her side.

If *Don Giovanni* came to constitute an operatic paradigm for subsequent generations, its projection of musical and verbal hyperboles on sexual power relations is part of that constitution. It holds on to the baroque legacy of hyperbolic rhetoric but surrounds it with a stricter regime of gender and social power, which intensifies the undercurrents of violence below the lighthearted wit. The excessiveness of the figures—such as the ones evoked by Zerlina—is meant to be obvious, thus preempting the possibility of taking them literally. Yet attempts to restrict signification and guarantee consensus about meaning are never failsafe. The Barcelona staging of Zerlina's story is an exposition of the risks involved, where the literalized misreading of her rhetoric ends up striking ruthlessly against her own body. The Salzburg staging, by contrast, frames the same problem with explicit reference to consensual BDSM: Zerlina's and Masetto's interplay is a game of light bondage, equally enjoyed by both participants. But just as the literal encroaches on the figurative in Bieito's staging, so the (diegetically) real violence, in the shape of Giovanni's wound, bleeds into the circle of the safe, sane, and consensual.

These two productions, with different means and emphasis, thus produce their own versions of the actuality effect. First, they draw our attention to the existence of a firm boundary, within which eroticization of power and violence is only a performance of signs. Second, they subject that boundary to different kinds of pressure, evoking its perforation or even dissolution. The relevance of this effect exceeds the theatrical spaces of the Gran Teatre del Liceu and the Haus für Mozart, as it points to what I take to be the core problematic of the nexus of opera and SM. By breaking the boundaries between the figural and the literal, between play and reality, it points to the permeability of an analogous boundary: that between enacted violence and actual violence. Hyperbole—in opera and BDSM just as anywhere else—relies on a contingent basis that allows its participants to safely distinguish exaggerated theatrics from reasonable reality. If that partition starts dissolving, however, the power and violence enlisted for aesthetic or erotic pleasure can no longer be contained, and the game is no longer just a game. From such a perspective these two operatic schools of libertinage teach a lesson on the representation of violence in a broader sense: do not trust too wholeheartedly in the fictiveness of the cruelty. As spectators at the opera house, we know that the blood on Zerlina's dress—whether it is her own or Giovanni's—has not come from a human body. But in the stagings by Bieito and Guth the transgression enacted within the perimeter of the safe, sane, and consensual deliberately evokes the transgression of that perimeter itself, suggesting the instability of the very limits by which we circumscribe and define operatic performance. This is the ultimate aim of the actuality effect: for a fleeting moment the exaggerations of opera may seem less exaggerated and the violence portrayed less safely consigned to the onstage make-believe. As a consequence, these stagings also expose themselves to the risk that they are participating in the wrongdoings that they are attempting to portray. The question with which the actuality effect presents us—spectators, listeners, fans, voyeurs—could perhaps be phrased thus: is this vision of a dissolving boundary a disturbing dream from which the applause awakes us, or is it—even more disturbingly—a moment of revelation that is merely covered up again by the fall of the curtain and the restoration of a safe boundary that it represents?

4 In-House Allegories

ENACTMENT AND ACTUALITY IN
PARSIFAL AND *TOSCA*

The boundary between opera's fantasies and its physical reality appears to exert a magnetic attraction on directors and dramaturges. The stagings that I have discussed so far have all used the visual codes of SM and fetishism precisely to enact various breaches of that boundary, giving rise to the actuality effect. In this chapter I will attend to a particular metaoperatic development of that effect, which turns the characters of the story world into the laborers of opera. In these stagings it is fictional singers, conductors, producers, and stage designers who act out the drama of power and eroticism. As the operatic fiction incorporates elements of operatic reality, the production shades into an allegory of the site in which it is staged. While still enlisting the imagery of SM, the actuality effect here approaches its third level: it takes aim at the boundary that separates the role from the singing body that inhabits it, the plot persona from the performer, and the space of the fiction from the space of the performance.

Both sides of that boundary are haunted by the nexus of power, violence, and sexuality. The productions I discuss in this chapter turn their attention to the power structures built into their own home and use the iconography of perversion to pose uncomfortable questions about the eroticism that flows through those structures. As a workplace, the opera house is itself a structure defined by rigorous hierarchies and not seldom home to gender inequality and sexual harassment. When the Me Too movement exploded during the autumn of 2017, it came as no surprise that opera was profoundly implicated. In Sweden, for instance, seven hundred opera singers—including international stars like Katarina Dalayman, Anna Larsson, Anne Sofie von Otter, and Nina Stemme—signed an open letter testifying to experiences of abuse and harassment in the opera world.[1] The (unnamed) perpetrators were without exception men in positions of power, most of them conductors and directors. Victims, meanwhile, were primarily but not exclusively women. The countertenor David Daniels and his husband, conductor Scott Walter, were accused by a male singer of drugging and raping him in connection with a performance of Handel's *Xerxes*.[2] The most prestigious opera house in the United States even fired its favorite conductor after an investigation found credible evidence of repeated sexual misconduct by James Levine both before and during his forty-year position as music director at the Met, and later the allegations against Plácido Domingo led to a spate of cancellations.[3] At the opera, dramas of sex, power, and violence are thus realized on stage by singers, conductors, directors, dramaturges, producers, and designers who may themselves be entangled in pernicious hierarchies. In the face of such discouraging realities, the iconography of perversion seems to ask to what extent operatic performance is actually a safe, sane, and consensual activity. How firm is the border that separates enacted operatic fantasies from actual abuse of power? Can opera put its own house in order by confronting such issues on stage, or does the theatrical foregrounding of the problem merely contribute to its perpetuation?

The operas through which I approach these questions here are, at least seemingly, the strangest bedfellows: *Parsifal* and *Tosca*. If the German *Bühnenweihfestspiel* endeavors to expel everyday life from the opera house altogether, the Italian *verismo* puts it squarely in the spotlight; if Wagner's faux-Catholic rituals demand that the audience forget actual ecclesiastical practice altogether, the procession of Puccini's Te Deum walks onto the stage straight out of the basilica of Sant'Andrea della Valle; if *Parsifal* insists on the absolute banishment of the outside world in the name of reverent attention, *Tosca* insists with equal force on the constant intermingling of theatrical spectacle and external reality. These differences, however, also mean that they are both concerned with the same questions of immersion and estrangement and of acting and actuality. Moreover, both are marked by fin de siècle perspectives on gender and power, and both display a profoundly ambiguous attitude toward sexual desire: their plots condemn and punish those who are slaves to their sexual impulses, yet their musical and scenic representation of those impulses constitutes the seductive core of both dramas (as well as the centerpieces of their three-act structures). As we will see, contemporaneous critics—sexologists, psychiatrists, cultural theorists—were quick to lambast both Wagner and Puccini for their depravity. Last but not least, they both hail from an era when singers lost much of the status they had had during the bel-canto era: in the last decades of the century their role was reduced from cocreators to interpreters, serving more or less faithfully the composer and the work.[4]

When contemporary director's opera creates preposterous history with these works, the fin de siècle views on sexuality, pathology, and opera are placed at the forefront. In what follows, I will first attend to a 2011 production of *Parsifal* from La Monnaie in Brussels—the first opera taken on by the celebrated avant-garde theater director and visual artist Romeo Castellucci—and then to two stagings of *Tosca:* one from Nederlandse Opera, directed by Nikolaus Lehnhoff in 1998, and one from Opernhaus Zürich, directed by Robert Carsen in 2009. I will argue that Friedrich Nietzsche, Leopold von Sacher-Masoch, and other turn-of-the-century writers can be understood as the sounding boards behind these productions, serving, together with the iconography of perversion, to amplify opera's overtones of sadomasochism. In the final part of the chapter I will listen to the thoughts of some aficionados of BDSM and opera, respectively. Their accounts suggest that these two practices share a particular fascination with the pushing of limits and crossing of boundaries, which finds expression in the actuality effect. They both enact violations that supposedly remain within the limits of the safe, sane, and consensual. At the same time, however, both repeatedly point to the difficulties of maintaining a clear border toward the violence that lies outside those limits, prompting the question of whether the risk of violation itself forms part of their magnetism.

CASTELLUCCI CONTRA WAGNER:
PARSIFAL AT LA MONNAIE

No other composer divides audiences as thoroughly as Richard Wagner. Still today, his music seems to be a repulsive invasion to his deprecators and sublime bliss to his admirers. Both the cultic adoration and the aversion can be traced back to Wagner's own time. In the last decades of the nineteenth century his work became the focal topic of a discourse that suspected modern music of being both perverse and pathological, and its representation of sexuality was at the core of the problem.[5] No doubt, the tendency of Wagner's plots to idealize erotic relations that flew in the face of bourgeois sexual morals contributed to such worries, as did his fetishistic fascination with rose fragrance and pink silk undergarments.[6] In addition to these factors, however, nineteenth-century listeners testified to the experience of Wagnerian music itself as intensely sensual. Drawing on the composer's writings, as well as the reception of his stage works, Laurence Dreyfus has argued in *Wagner and the Erotic Impulse* that Wagnerian drama was radically new in that the very sound of the music was both intended and perceived as an erotic stimulus: "Wagner distinguishes himself from his operatic predecessors who, for all their wonderful music, observe sexual desire from a safer aesthetic distance. If one thinks of suggestive scenes in, say, *Poppea, Dido, Don Giovanni, Le Comte Ory, Norma,* or *La Traviata,* the dramatic effect depends on listeners' belief in a character's libido, though the music can scarcely be said to fuel an audience's libidinal drives."[7] In their attempts at defining this audible libido it is striking how Wagner's contemporaries took recourse to images of violence and violation, domination and submission. In a rapt letter to Wagner from 17 February 1860, Charles Baudelaire describes his listening experience in terms unambiguously allusive to erotic submission: he feels "swept up and subjugated" and goes on to state, "I frequently experienced a rather odd emotion, which could be described as the pride and joy of comprehension, of allowing myself to be penetrated and invaded—a truly sensual pleasure."[8] Many were less inclined than Baudelaire to submit to a Wagnerian invasion, of course. After attending a performance of *Tristan,* Clara Schumann wrote in her diary: "It was the most repulsive thing I have ever seen or heard in my life. To be forced to see and listen to such sexual frenzy the whole evening, in which every feeling of decency is violated and by which not just the public but even musicians seem to be enchanted—that is the saddest thing I have experienced in my entire artistic life."[9] In J. L. Klein's *Geschichte des Dramas* one reads about Wagner's "dissolute corybantic caterwauling," "ear scalpels," and "diabolic cheers of lust as the instrumental clamor of hell triumphs over the soulful music of Christ."[10] I mentioned in my first chapter formulations like "slap-in-the-face orchestral accompaniment" (Klein) and "the erotic flagellation music of the Liszt-Wagner school" (Hanslick), but they bear repeating.[11] Also, on the topic of aural violence, one should not neglect André Gill's famous caricature in *L'Eclipse* from 1869, which shows Wagner drawing blood from a giant ear by driving an eighth-note into it with a hammer.

Among the critics of Wagner's eroticism, however, none was more influential than the philosopher who was once his most eloquent apologist: Friedrich Nietzsche. In the Brussels *Parsifal* from 2011 his vitriolic attacks—published in *The Case of Wagner* and *Nietzsche contra Wagner*—are mobilized in a staging of the very work that was the prime target of his reproof. Romeo Castellucci's mise-en-scène introduces Nietzsche as a towering presence as soon as the work begins. During the prelude, the first thing the audience sees—at the climax of the *Glauben*-motif's winding imitations—is an image of aural intrusion: a giant live snake, suspended in midair, against the backdrop of an enormous projection of Gustav Schultze's famous photograph of Nietzsche, around whose ear it is coiling itself. By giving Wagner's music the physical form of the Edenic seducer, slithering into the head of the philosopher who called *Parsifal* a work of "secret poison concoction against the precondition of life," Castellucci visualizes the sexual connotations that form a central part both of the Nietzschean critique and of the nineteenth-century discourse on pathological music.[12] The toxic qualities of Wagnerian eroticism are stated clearly enough by the serpent (despite its being impersonated by a nonvenomous albino python), which returns, carried by Anna Larsson's Kundry, in the seduction scene of the second act. When Nietzsche vented his hatred against "the disgusting sexuality of Wagnerian music," he was not attacking sexuality as such but, on the contrary, defending the precondition of life against Wagner's concoctions.[13] To Nietzsche, it was specifically the Christian interpretation of sex as sinful knowledge that handed

Parsifal over to poisonous perversion. This view of sexuality is epitomized precisely by the tempter reptile. Castellucci's serpent thus functions simultaneously as a symbol of sexuality as viewed from the perspective of Christian morality and as a visual embodiment of Wagner's music, even as it smoothly penetrates the ears of the audience.

Castellucci's staging, mystifying in its richness of strange detail, lets the drama progress from a pitch-black forest in the first act—where the grail knights are a camouflage-clad army at war—to a populated present-day society in the last. In the final scene of redemption a large, anonymous crowd embarks on a communal wandering. What is most striking about this crowd is its normality: individuals wander on in everyday clothing— jeans, T-shirts, skirts, and chinos—as if to deliberately undercut the ritual separation from the ordinary world demanded by the idea of the *Bühnenweihfestspiel*. Not even Gurnemanz and Parsifal stand out very much, even though they do not always walk in the same direction as the crowd. The principal effect of this curiously pedestrian scene is its contrast with the second act. The diatonic splendor of the ending is conflated with the quotidian and ordinary, emphasizing the half-diminished harmonies and creeping chromaticism of the middle act as the deviant underside to that normality. As a result, Klingsor's music, and its somber black-mass variation on Tristanesque eroticism, is highlighted as the drama's epicenter of perversion. This hellish realm of sin and seduction turned out to be the most controversial part of the production, while also leaving a palpable mark on contemporary staging: "I think Castellucci was a real genius in the second act," says Anna Larsson. "It was a masterpiece, really. And it has had a resonance in the whole world of opera; you see a lot of directors trying to imitate precisely this act of the Brussels *Parsifal*, putting writing on the back wall and hanging chandeliers askew, trying to grasp what it was that made it so awesome."[14]

Before the second act begins, the spectators are treated to an abundance of toxicological trivia: the effects of hydrofluoric acid, beryllium bromide, hydrazine anhydrous, and sulfur mustards are all described in detailed texts. Penetrating the body through skin contact or inhalation, the acids and gases cause lethal damage to lungs, liver, eyes, kidneys, and the central nervous system. In most cases the horrifying effects of the toxins are noticeable only after a certain delay ("contaminated areas may appear completely normal, so victims can unknowingly receive high dosages"). Keeping Castellucci's initial evocation of Nietzsche in mind, with the snake coiling around his ear, it is not difficult to see in these descriptions an elaboration on the harmful bodily effects that the philosopher ascribed to Wagner's music. The fact that the audience at the opera is not experiencing any symptoms while listening does not mean that they have not been contaminated. Of the music in *Parsifal* Nietzsche writes: "Drink, O my friends, the philters of this art! Nowhere will you find a more agreeable way of enervating your spirit, of forgetting your manhood under a rosebush."[15] Wagner's venom may feel perfectly pleasant, but in the end, says Nietzsche, it is inherently harmful to your sexual self—especially if you are a man, allowing it to undermine your masculinity.

As the curtain rises, we see the stage through a transparent white gauze. The large room is bathed in cold light, the air seems misty—suggesting the presence of the lethal fumes—and across the floor the naked bodies of the flower girls are strewn, as in death or heavy sleep. Midstage, a strange apparition faces us. Raised on a small podium stands Icelandic bass baritone Tómas Tómasson, the production's Klingsor. Or rather, there stand two and a half Klingsors: behind Tómasson stands another one, his double, and to his left, an extra arm is hovering in the air, presumably as an image of his self-imposed castration (fig. 4.1). Klingsor is in tails, with a baton in his right hand, and just before the climax of the *Zauberschloss* prelude, he starts conducting the music that we hear: stiffly, awkwardly, mimicked in his every movement by his double standing behind him on the podium (while the severed arm remains still, impotent). What we see is the source of Wagnerian music, visualized in Nietzsche's terms as a "first-rate poison for the nerves," with the "double quality of a narcotic that both intoxicates and spreads a *fog*."[16] In a hallucinatory vision of the sorcerer as opera conductor, the reality of the musicmaking—the physical labor that Wagner took such pains to make invisible in his *Festspielhaus*—becomes part of the drama. This is the Castellucci production's version of the actuality effect: the work of operatic performance is made manifest on stage, as if the fictional world of *Parsifal* had partly given way to a distorted version of the opera house itself.

In this opera house sexual perversion reigns. Klingsor's troupe of seducers, the flower girls that are both scent and song, are tied up in elaborate

Figure 4.1. The Wagnerian *Kapellmeister:* Klingsor (Tómas Tómasson) conducting the prelude to act 2. *Parsifal* (dir. Romeo Castellucci, La Monnaie, 2011).

patterns and meticulously controlled by their chemist-conductor. As he instructs "Auf denn, ans Werk" (So rise, do your work), his double gets off the podium and puts on a protective apron before he starts dragging their limp bodies together stage left. Klingsor himself soon joins in, donning another apron and leaving his baton hovering above the podium. Together they arrange the girls, fastening their tied-up bodies to ropes hanging from the ceiling and raising them up into the toxic air (fig. 4.2). The restraints are of a very particular kind, namely the Japanese bondage technique known as *shibari* or, sometimes, *kinbaku*. It is a highly aestheticized practice, the roots of which run deeply into Japanese cultural history.[17] It reached Western culture in the 1990s as a practice at the intersection of a growing BDSM community and an increasing interest in all things Japanese, from karaoke to anime. On the Brussels stage it is combined with contortionists, who also play the roles of the flower girls: their bodies are bent out of shape and positioned together in the most impossible constellations. Much as the shibari artists, they come across less as human bodies than unsettlingly body-like objects.

The constellation of allusions in this scene is a very particular superimposition of specific moments in the spirit of preposterous history. The idea

Figure 4.2. "Arise then! To work!" Klingsor (Tómas Tómasson) with members of the production's shibari troupe (Gala Moody, Frances D'Ath, Jorgos Fokianos, and Dasnyia Sommer). *Parsifal* (dir. Romeo Castellucci, La Monnaie, 2011).

of flower cultivation as the expression of an erotically infused version of aesthetic refinement was a recurrent topic in fin de siècle culture, as exemplified by the protagonist's obsession with orchids in Huysmans's *À Rebours* from 1884 or, even more to the point, Octave Mirbeau's 1899 *Jardin des Supplices,* where tortured bodies are collected and displayed for aesthetic appreciation in a carefully cultivated Chinese garden.[18] In this extreme form the ideal of art for art's sake dehumanizes the Other into an object of beauty, whose pain serves only to intensify the pleasure of the spectator. In Castellucci's reinterpretation of *Parsifal* Klingsor's magic garden can be seen as an operatic counterpart to Mirbeau's torture garden: the mise-en-scène not only picks up the aestheticized and eroticized practice of sophisticated torture, which turns the suffering human body into an object of detached appreciation, but also provides a contemporary visualization of the erotically inclined orientalism of the fin de siècle, which is integral to the seductive powers of Kundry as well as the flower girls. The effect is striking in its contrast to the semichildish seductresses often seen in stagings of this scene. Larsson formulates Castellucci's ambition thus: "he wants the audience to feel that Klingsor's castle is a cabinet of horrors, and that the flower girls are not some happy, sweet whores with whom Parsifal gets to enjoy himself. They suffer tremendously."[19]

In this nightmarish vision the garden of bondage is also a site of operatic performance, within the fiction itself: the erotic laboratory of Klingsor the *Kapellmeister* is littered with visual traces of an opera house. After Kundry's failed seduction, he returns once more to the podium. The baton is in his hand, and as he starts conducting again, it even takes on the role of the spear itself, that catalyst of Amfortas's fall and redemption: "Dich bann' ich mit dem rechten Wehr" (I cast you out with the proper weapon). As his castle comes crashing down, the lights go out, and the lit onstage chandelier—another phantom of the opera, returning to haunt the auditorium after having been banished by Wagner himself—comes loose, the act closing with the striking image of its swinging back and forth in the darkness.

By placing a sadistic Klingsor on a podium and having him conduct the music we actually hear, as well as the chemical experiments with the flower-girls-in-bondage, Castellucci suggests an affiliation between practices of sexual domination and the Wagnerian art. Ultimately, it is Wagner who is aspiring to complete control over the bodies in the opera house: the ones that are seen and heard, as well as those that look and listen. Alongside Nietzsche this notion is indebted to Max Nordau, the Jewish intellectual who invented the concept of "degenerate art" that would later be instrumentalized by the Hitler regime. In Nordau's view Wagner was more degenerate than all other degenerates put together. Apropos some of the most scandalous scenes—among them "the entire second act of *Parsifal,* in the scene between the hero and the flower-girls, and then between him and Kundry in Klingsor's magic garden"—he exclaims with amazement: "How unperverted must wives and maidens be when they are in a state of mind to witness these pieces without blushing crimson, and sinking into the earth for shame!" He went on to diagnose Wagner himself as a sexual sadist: "With Wagner amorous excitement assumes the form of mad delirium. The lovers in his pieces behave like tom-cats gone mad, rolling in contortions and convulsions over a root of valerian. They reflect a state of mind in the poet which is well known to the professional expert. It is a form of Sadism. It is the love of those degenerates who, in sexual transport, become like wild beasts. Wagner suffered from 'erotic madness,'

which leads coarse natures to murder for lust, and inspires 'higher degenerates' with works like *Die Walküre, Siegfried,* and *Tristan und Isolde."*[20]

While Nordau's diatribe lacks entirely the biting humor of Nietzsche's
attacks on Wagner, it makes sense to see the Brussels Klingsor as just such
a "higher degenerate," who stylizes his beastly sexual impulses into art.
Castellucci's interpretation can be traced back to the intersection of Nordau's
image of Wagner as sadist and Nietzsche's of Wagner as sorcerer: "Ah, this
old magician! This Klingsor of all Klingsors! How he thus wages war against
us!"[21] The highest-ranking officer in this war is the *Kapellmeister,* whose
domination is unsurpassed: "Never has obedience been better, never has
commanding. Wagnerian conductors in particular are worthy of an age that
posterity will call one day, with awed respect, *the classical age of war."*[22] The
idea of a military hierarchy also appears to have entered Castellucci's staging; not only are the grail knights modern-day soldiers, but by the end of the
second act, the flower girls also carry automatic rifles. The commander in
chief is Wagner, whose general is the conductor leading the orchestra, and
the chemical-musical war is waged on "us," the audience, who will show up
as the civilian crowd in the third act.

Showing this hierarchy on stage, however, is also a way of deconstructing its hegemony: once its image is framed by the imagination of so recu-
sant a stage director as Castellucci, musical authority can no longer be
self-evident but becomes a matter of ritualized negotiation. Castellucci
thematizes the multilayered dynamics of that authority, making it visible
on stage in subtle ways. For one thing, the music of the second act is actually set in motion before Klingsor's arms—as if the music were conducting
him rather than the other way around—making clear that Hartmut
Haenchen is there conducting before Klingsor, and Wagner before
Haenchen. Klingsor's assistant, who follows his every motion at the
podium, is another instance, suggesting a potentially endless concatena-
tion of conductors and conductees. The Wagnerian *Kapellmeister*—or,
ultimately, Wagner himself—can no longer remain the unquestioned ruler
of opera once he is implicitly pulled inside its theatrical space. By making
visible the musical chain of command as an infinite deferral—in which
everyone shares the anxiety of phallic lack embodied by Klingsor's severed
arm—the staging undermines the very idea of a position of supreme
power, whether inhabited by the director, conductor, or composer.

Yet a gendered hierarchy may remain. In the professional world of classical music the unquestionable authority of the conductor—still predominantly male—is more or less taken for granted as a condition for the aesthetic excellence of the end product. It is worth noting that the Kundry of the Brussels production has been one of the voices that insistently point to the consequences of such assumptions. Apropos the Me Too movement, Anna Larsson has commented: "The conductors' reign is simply dangerous for young women.... That damn genius cult is dangerous, because you give them carte blanche professionally and create an environment where they can take advantage of their elevated position."[23] This is precisely what Castellucci puts on stage: Klingsor as a sexual predator whose misconduct is made possible by the magic of his conducting, and against him Kundry as the dramatic female voice raised in performance, which overpowers any other. Opera, as visualized in Castellucci's staging of *Parsifal,* is the ceremonial enactment and eroticization of this very struggle. The sorcerer and the seductress find their correlates in the male conductor and the female singer. When Kundry does not want to play along in his scheme of seduction, Klingsor retorts: "Wohl willst du, denn du mußt" (You do want to, because you must). Today, even more than when this production premiered, it is perhaps inevitable that we hear this line, uttered by a conductor character making an indecent proposal, in relation to testimonies of sexual harassment of singers. In Larsson's words: "As a soloist, you are very vulnerable.... The single most important thing is that the conductor likes you. To first accept an invitation to a restaurant, but then decline coming along to the hotel may mean that you will never work with that conductor again."[24] Larsson also recounts several stories from female colleagues: one conductor spreads the word about a singer's lack of talent after having had his advances turned down; another locks the door for private "rehearsals"; a third offers "wolf massages," where he undresses and bites female colleagues—and victims who testify to their experiences find their careers threatened. It is a system that fosters "men with extreme power," who have "the right to fire a singer from a production 'for artistic reasons' at any time during rehearsals."[25] It is this system and its abuse at the hands of a sadistic conductor that Castellucci evokes in the second act of *Parsifal.*

The power struggle continues in the pivotal seduction scene. Here, Castellucci assigns to Parsifal the role of the listener and spectator, who

Figure 4.3. "You want to, because you must." One of Klingsor's emissaries (Tamara Bacci) forcing Kundry (Anna Larsson) to open her mouth in song. *Parsifal* (dir. Romeo Castellucci, La Monnaie, 2011).

serves as the audience's onstage delegate. He makes his entrance like Perseus approaching Medusa, carrying a mirror as a shield against the sensory impressions of female evil: instead of seeing her, he will make her see herself. If Parsifal is sent out on the mission to be the audience member who resists seduction, Klingsor, in turn, has sent forth not only Kundry but also a dancer to make sure she follows orders: one of the flower girls—another body double of sorts—dances by her side as she sings to Parsifal. Their limbs move in synchronized gestures, and the flower girl forces Kundry's mouth open in silent song, until the latter manages to slowly push her arm away (fig. 4.3). The *Kapellmeister* is wielding his baton by proxy, forcing Kundry to seduce—you want to sing because you must sing. The snake, still cast as the symbol of eroticized music, is coiled around her arm.

The crucial moment of Kundry's kiss sets off one of Castellucci's most interesting ideas. After the failed seduction the actuality effect is used to subvert with great precision the Wagnerian ideology of immersion: the mezzo-soprano herself suddenly becomes visible through the character she represents. During Parsifal's compassionate vision of Amfortas—

Figure 4.4. The writing is on the wall: Kundry (Anna Larsson) watches as Parsifal (Andrew Richards) is liberating a flower maiden from her bondage. *Parsifal* (dir. Romeo Castellucci, La Monnaie, 2011).

whose projected specter suddenly grows from out of Parsifal's body and falls to the floor to copulate with a projection of Kundry[26]—the seductress goes to the back wall and writes, in big black block letters, a name: "ANNA." Soon after, she adds three words, presenting us with the unwieldy and perplexing phrase "ANNA. ME. NOW. TIED." (fig. 4.4). Kundry's character is, implicitly but quintessentially, a singer. As Michel Poizat puts it in *The Angel's Cry:* "Kundry *is* The Voice, the epitome of the vocal object."[27] She seduces siren style, and her failure to seduce can only be a vocal one. A crisis of this kind makes visible the individual whose voice is bound, subjugated, and forced to its own limits by the authority of the composer's score and the conductor who interprets it. Kundry's vocal failure is ascribed to "Anna," and it is this failure that lets the singer appear through the cracks in the role. This "Anna," of course, cannot be equated with the actual Anna Larsson (whose performance here is, quite to the contrary, a patent vocal triumph). At the same time, the borders are sufficiently blurred to remind the spectators of the power dynamics between the actual singers and the composer, conductor, or director who works by controlling their bodies on stage. In short, Larsson is playing the part of herself in an operatic cameo role, which receives additional weight from the fact that she is an eloquent spokesperson of female singers against the hegemony of conductors and the sexual misconduct that it makes possible.

To recognize the radical anti-Wagnerism of this stage strategy—and the paradoxical Wagnerism of the terms in which it is couched—one must turn to the composer's own statements on the matter. Unquestioned immersion was, for Wagner, a *sine qua non* of aesthetic excellence: "Strictly speaking, art ceases to be art at the moment when it enters our reflective consciousness as art."[28] This phrase comes from "Über Schauspieler und Sänger" (On actors and singers), an 1872 essay in which Wagner formulated his view of the ideal stage actor. Notably, it is dedicated to Wilhelmine Schröder-Devrient, the soprano whose acting and appearance made such an impression on the young Wagner that the old man—during the rehearsals for the premiere of *Parsifal* in 1882—was still imagining her as the perfect Kundry in the seduction scene.[29] Perhaps his imagination was also fueled by the pornographic novel *From the Memoirs of a Singer*, published in the 1860s, which Schröder-Devrient was claimed to have authored.[30] Be that as it may, on stage she was, according to Wagner, "entirely and exclusively that other being whom she was portraying."[31] This is the core of what Wagner demands of an actor: a state wherein he (or she) has "fully replaced their own self with that of the portrayed individual."[32] The violent force *(Gewaltsamkeit)* of this state can be grasped, Wagner continues, "when one considers that a completely immaterial imagination here commands *(beherrscht)* his person down to every muscle of his body."[33] This imagination, of course, is Wagner's own. In a radically Cartesian division of labor, the actor's body is under the unconditional control of the composer's spirit. Wagner insists on speaking of this phenomenon as a transaction of power: "Here, all rivalry for rank ceases, and all submission *(Unterordnung)* disappears, because it is voluntary. The power of the poet over the actor is limitless as soon as the former, in his work, presents the latter with the right model, and its rightness can only be recognized when the actor, in his attempts to appropriate that model, is capable of completely abandoning his own self."[34]

In the 2011 Brussels seduction scene Anna-as-Kundry refuses to submit to this limitless power. Instead of abandoning her own self, she makes it manifest. She rebels against the absolute Wagnerian power from the inside, and she does so by the unmistakably Wagnerian act of significant naming: "ANNA. ME." If she serves Klingsor and Wagner by attempting to sing and seduce, she is nevertheless, by the very act of acknowledging her bondage, attempting to break free. In an image of the liberation for which she longs, Parsifal gently frees one of the flower girls from her shibari bondage in the same scene. But soon afterward, the other girls arrive to restore Klingsor's order: naked but for the heavy firearms they carry, they cover up the name "ANNA" with a huge white screen, leaving only "ME. NOW. TIED." The conductor's army does Wagner's work and hides the individual singer in order to preserve the illusion. She has to wait until the third act for her liberation: there, she marches with the masses in her civilian clothes and no longer has to sing at the command of Wagner-Klingsor (except for the one word *dienen* [serve], which, disconnected as it is from her vocal profusion in the first two acts, comes across here as a continuation of her fragmented writings on the wall).

As I suggested above, the anonymous crowd that dominates the stage during the third act is an emblem of a faceless normality. They are the crowd leaving the opera, having survived Klingsor's chemical warfare together with the onstage spectator Parsifal. Understood as a redemption brought about by assimilation into the masses, this image would lump opera and sexual deviance together as the psychopathological other of that normality—as the necessary evils of the second act, overcome at the moment of redemption. Yet this polarization does not hold: the Wagnerian music, at its most beautiful, is still in the air. As Parsifal returns to redeem Amfortas, the snake—which has been cast as the physical manifestation of Wagner's music all along—makes a final appearance. Crucially, this happens at the line "Die Wunde schließt der Speer nur, der sie Schlug" (Only the spear that made the wound will heal it), when a member of the crowd holds it up with both arms. The snake is the spear, and both are the music: while Castellucci's staging casts operatic music as a slithering perversion in the hands Klingsor, it nevertheless retains its role as the primary agent of Wagnerian redemption. In effect, this means that the troublesome purity of the grail realm is undercut: Wagner's serpent sound is raised as the object for adoration, instead of the spear and the grail. Music's redemptive power penetrates the dividing walls of *Parsifal*, slithering from

Klingsor's opera out into the ordinary world. Consequently, Kundry's uneasy oscillation between normality and perversion, between singer and role, does not turn her into the abject element that must be expelled in the name of purity. Rather, it elevates her to a paradigm of redemption. The strategy of letting her live—more rule than exception in contemporary productions—thus makes perfect sense in this one: it is precisely as the bodily transmitter of music that Kundry the singer can finally achieve redemption without extinction. The sexually perverted *Kapellmeister* and his mezzo-soprano character also become redeemers redeemed, perhaps suggesting in the process that perversion cannot be completely exorcized from normality.[35] And if the wound is healed only by the spear that smote it, this *Parsifal* seems to ask, must not the harmful power structures of opera be remedied—and remediated—by opera itself, in the very act of stage performance?

LITTLE DEATH, BIG DEATH: *TOSCA*, SACHER-MASOCH, AND THE PLEASURE OF VOCAL PENETRATION

In Castellucci's staging of *Parsifal* the breakdown of the boundary between the opera singer and her role under the pressure of an eroticized power results from an imaginative and idiosyncratic stage interpretation, subtly interwoven with the words and music. In what has justly been referred to as Puccini's "most self-consciously 'theatrical' opera," by contrast, that same breakdown is a key concern (and rather less subtle).[36] Long before Joseph Kerman dubbed it a "shabby little shocker," *Tosca* was chastised for its perversity and tasteless sensationalism, and the opera's continuous appeal to audiences worldwide has certainly aggravated the gall of many critics.[37] One of the opera's more acrimonious detractors was Italian music critic Fausto Torrefranca. His 1912 monograph *Giacomo Puccini e l'opera internazionale* was a vitalist-nationalist-chauvinist attack on fin de siècle decadence, replete with metaphors of sickness, effeminacy, and impotence—not unlike the concerns of Nietzsche's late tracts on Wagner, albeit lacking both their stylistic flair and critical acumen.[38] From the perspective of the present book, the following sentence from Torrefranca stands out: "*Tosca* might appear to be realistic, but it is not: even the excess of reality . . . is a sort of Romanticism: this, too, is sublime, in the sense that it goes beyond the safe and sane conscience of art."[39] The anachronistic echo of the catchphrase "safe, sane, and consensual" is perhaps less random than it may appear: if there is a *locus classicus* of operatic sadomasochism, it is the second act of *Tosca*. Baron Scarpia's ruthless torture of Mario Cavaradossi is carefully intertwined with his attempt to take advantage of Floria Tosca, and he makes abundantly clear that the abuse and violence to which he subjects the two lovers is key to his own arousal. Equally important, however, is the heroine's profession. The fact that Tosca is an opera diva places the oscillation between singer and role at the center of the drama: like Anna Larsson in the Brussels *Parsifal,* the lead soprano is always, to some extent, playing a fictional version of herself.

This state of affairs is a symptom of the excess of reality that, in Torrefranca's view, transgresses the confines of art. Although inscribed into score and libretto rather than added by the mise-en-scène, it corresponds exactly to the actuality effect that has marked the productions I have discussed so far. It is typical of its time: the upsurge of characters who are professional performers and the presence of a "real" diegetic sound world in the score—bells, choirs, diegetic music—are hallmarks of Italian *verismo*. They can be understood as a response to a growing discomfort with opera's basic lack of verisimilitude, aimed at furnishing it with a naturalistic motivation.[40] These elements, however, are made to blend and blur with the conventional elements of opera. The realistic sounds function less as a pretext for the unrealistic ones than as reminders of an "outside" into which the latter can erupt: from Tosca's role as a fictional soprano, embodied by a real live one, to the lethal mock-mock execution of Cavaradossi, the line between acting and actuality is repeatedly drawn only to be dissolved. The drama as a whole unfolds between those events and emotions that are feigned and those that are—in one sense or another—real. Indeed, the appeal of the opera seems to lie precisely in the actuality effect that disrupts the border between them.

Recent years have given us several productions that visualize these disruptions with the iconography of perversion, spotlighting Scarpia's sadomasochistic inclinations. Luc Bondy's 2009 production from the Met, later revived both at the Bayerische Staatsoper in 2010 and at La Scala in 2015, belabored the baron's lubricity in every thinkable way. For instance, during his second-act aria, three prostitutes crawled over him and gave him fellatio while he sang the phrase "Ha più forte sapore la conquista violenta che il mellifluo consenso" (There's a stronger flavor in violent conquest than in mellifluous consent), thereby making it an expression of a man who is too used to getting anything he asks for and turns to violence in an attempt at thrilling his desensitized numbness into arousal. The same Scarpia wielded a riding crop to showcase his authority in fetishist fashion. The riding crop, always an effective symbol of SM leanings, also figured in Nikolaus Lehnhoff's 1998 staging from the Nederlandse Opera, where Bryn Terfel's Scarpia used it to alternately caress and lightly slap the faces of Spoletta and the Sacristan. Lehnhoff's staging amplifies the opera's undertones of perversion—not least in the setting of the second act, which he describes as "a subterranean dungeon" and "a carnal lair," in which an "oversized turbine propeller in the wall symbolizes a bestial torture chamber, where sadistic rituals are taking place."[41] The question of Scarpia's sadist inclination is an important one that is too often taken for granted by critics.[42] There is, of course, much that motivates the label: the pleasure he takes in torturing Cavaradossi (physically) and Tosca (psychologically) is patently sadistic, as is his preference for violent conquest over soft consent. The question of who is the subject of the "conquista violenta," however, is less straightforward than one might initially believe. As the iconic poster intimates—with Tosca leaning over the recumbent Scarpia, ritually placing a crucifix on his chest—much of Scarpia's character may be read within a masochistic framework, which casts Tosca in the dominant role.

Throughout the second act Scarpia is strongly focused on triggering Tosca's hatred: her revulsion is essential to his arousal. At the moment when he has offered the sordid bargain for Mario's liberty, he sings: "Come tu m'odii! . . . Così, così ti voglio!" (How you hate me! That is how I want you!).[43] The fact that he craves Tosca's contempt to achieve sexual gratification might imply that his fantasies are less top than bottom. When she replies, "Non toccarmi, demonio! T'odio, t'odio, abbietto, vile!" (Do not touch me, fiend! I hate you, I hate you! Despicable, coward!), he confirms his confusion of aggression and love: "Che importa?! Spasimi d'ira, spasimi d'amore!" (What does it matter?! Spasms of wrath or spasms of passion!). The constitution to which Scarpia thus gives voice here lies close to Žižek's Lacanian understanding of masochism as aimed at producing repulsion in the Other by putting one's desire on display: "while he [the masochist] seems to offer himself as the instrument of the Other's *jouissance,* he effectively discloses his own desire to the Other and thus gives rise to anxiety in the Other—for Lacan, the true object of anxiety is precisely the (over)proximity of the Other's desire."[44]

This is exactly what Scarpia does: he forces Tosca to look at his own desire, while masking it as acquiescence to hers. When he dreams of Tosca's eyes, what he imagines is not a compliant gaze but a triumphant one, which languishes in amorous convulsions (which he sees as tantamount to spams of wrath anyway): "Ah di quegli occhi vittoriosi veder la fiamma illanguidir con spasimo d'amor" (Ah, to see the flame of victorious eyes pine with the spasms of love). At one point, his longing to be subjected to those eyes even approaches the idea of penetration: "Quel tuo pianto era lava ai sensi miei e il tuo sguardo che odio in me dardeggiava mie brame inferociva!" (That weeping of yours was like lava to my senses and your gaze, shooting darts of hatred into me, inflamed my desire!). These lines, which associate the desire for the Other's revulsion with the desire to be a pierced object of the gaze, point subtly forward to the moment when Tosca stabs him to death. Hence, they form another instance of the actuality effect operating by literalization (that is, on the first level): at a given moment opera's hyperbolic rhetoric violently bursts into the sphere of the literal. The figurative description of her hatred entering his body is soon to take physical form in the dagger that she thrusts into his breast.

Most influential post-Freudian readings of masochism—including Lacan, Deleuze, and Žižek—agree on the notion that the masochist always remains in complete control of the scenario but uses that control to play the part of the submissive.[45] Scarpia, of course, does call the shots in the second act—at least until he is stabbed (and, as the idea of the piercing darts of hatred inflaming his desire suggests, perhaps even then). Nevertheless, he repeatedly assumes a subservient posture. When Tosca finally realizes that she has no way out, the baron presents the result as an agreement to which *he* yields: "Cedo—A misero prezzo / tu, a me una vita, io, a te chieggo un istante!" (I yield—at a meager price / you ask of me a life, I of you an instant!). Lehnhoff's staging discreetly emphasizes the elements of enacted submission in Scarpia's role by having him kneel in front of Tosca at several key moments; for example, as Terfel's Scarpia sings

Figure 4.5. "I yield at a meager price." Scarpia (Bryn Terfel) kneeling before a repulsed Tosca (Catherine Malfitano). *Tosca* (dir. Nikolaus Lehnhoff, Nederlandse Opera, 1998).

"Cedo," he kneels on the floor before her, and as he sings "Come tu m'odii!" he kneels on the divan (fig. 4.5).

Another vital element in the psychosexual makeup of the masochist, as it is commonly understood by psychoanalysis, is fetishism. Deleuze, who in his influential reading of Sacher-Masoch argues that the sadist and the masochist are absolutely separate and incompatible entities—the former operating by institution and instruction, the latter by pact and persuasion— even goes as far as claiming that "there can be no masochism without fetishism in the primary sense."[46] This primary sense, which derives from Freud, is the denial of female lack. On this view fetishism is the disavowal of castration, assigning to a given object (the fetish) the role of a female phallus, which is there to ward off the fear of castration by taking the place of the supposedly missing part. As a result, the fetish is charged with a profusion of erotic energy, and the male masochist may yield to the phallic power invested in the woman, who is no longer marred by lack. In this Freudian narrative (which has been taken apart on a regular basis ever since its first appearance) some objects take on the fetishistic function more readily than others: drawing on Sacher-Masoch's life and work as the paradigm, Deleuze places shoes and furs at the top of the list of the masochist's sexual obsessions.[47]

In Lehnhoff's mise-en-scène both of those objects are patently fore-grounded as fetishes. When Catherine Malfitano's Tosca enters the stage in the second act, she is descending the stairs to Scarpia's dungeon almost completely covered behind a wall running along the stairs: we see only her high heels treading the steps (and the DVD recording assists the fetishistic impulse by zooming in on the footwear). The fur fetish, meanwhile, is even more pronounced. Once she becomes fully visible, we see Tosca wrapped in a thick, lavish fur coat—an accessory as natural to an opera diva as to a Sacher-Masoch heroine. At Scarpia's first appearance in the same act, moreover, we find him reclining on his divan with a cat on his lap, which he is caressing as he sings (Terfel even holds the poor creature up in front of his face while shouting that Cavaradossi and Angelotti will hang) (fig. 4.6). In the director's words the cat scene is there to "foreshadow the las-civious gratification for which he has selected Tosca."[48] Here, too, we see the mise-en-scène playing with the visual manifestation of the libretto's verbal imagery: "Agil qual leopardo ti avvinghiasti all'amante; Ah! In quell'istante t'ho giurata mia!" (Agile as a leopard, you clung to your lover. Ah, at that moment I swore that you would be mine!) In Scarpia's erotic imagination the domesticated cat has metamorphosed into a ferocious predator, and at that very instant, he knows he must have her. After listen-ing to "Vissi d'arte," finally, he picks up the fur coat that Tosca has left lying on the stairs, stroking it and sniffing it with intense delight (fig. 4.7).

Indeed, it is hard not to see in this predilection of Terfel's Scarpia a direct allusion to Sacher-Masoch and *Venus im Pelz,* where the protago-nist, Severin, elaborates endlessly on the sensual pleasure of soft, lush furs (and of being despised, hurt, and humiliated by the woman wearing them). What is more, the transformation from pussycat to predator subtly permeates Sacher-Masoch's novella: the first thing we learn about Wanda is that she is the owner of a ball of yarn, endlessly played with by a kitten, and once she has made Severin's acquaintance, she summarizes his predi-lection for animal furs with the remark that "a woman in furs is nothing more than a large cat."[49] As Severin gradually manages to turn her into the ruthless tyrant he desires, she draws blood with her teeth while they are making love, and he starts feeling "like a mouse held captive by a

Figures 4.6–7. Venus in furs: Scarpia (Bryn Terfel) as fetishist with feline preferences. *Tosca* (dir. Nikolaus Lehnhoff, Nederlandse Opera, 1998).

beautiful cat who plays with it daintily, and at any moment is ready to tear it to pieces."[50] And sure enough, in his dreamlike visions and verbal imagery she soon metamorphoses into a sharp-clawed she-bear, as well as a fierce lioness.[51] Even if Tosca's eyes are dark and fiery, while Wanda's are green and cold, and even if Scarpia's methods are more violent than Severin's, the baron's penchant for furry predators in Lehnhoff's production evokes the fetishist analogy and emphasizes the basic desire of both men to foster the contempt of the Other while kneeling at her feet. The amalgamation of fin de siècle fetishism and contemporary SM imagery is the Amsterdam *Tosca*'s version of preposterous history.

Scarpia, however, arguably has one fixation that is even stronger than shoes and furs: the soprano voice. His desire for Tosca is indissociable from the fact that she is an opera singer. Few stagings bring forth this aspect as consistently as Robert Carsen's 2009 production from the Opernhaus Zurich, starring Emily Magee as the diva and Thomas Hampson as the baron. Carsen, always prone to stage-on-the-stage solutions, situates all three acts in an opera house: the church of Sant'Andrea della Valle becomes the auditorium, the Palazzo Farnese becomes a backstage area, and the

Castel Sant'Angelo becomes the stage itself but seen from the wings, at an angle, so that we may discern the darkness of a second auditorium beyond a set of footlights stage left. Tosca, of course, remains the great opera diva, while Cavaradossi is a stagehand decorating the auditorium and Scarpia a managing director of sorts—the impresario, dramaturge, and producer all at once.

This rendering spotlights the fact that Scarpia, like any masochist in the original sense, takes on the responsibility of directing the scene that kindles his lust. During the second act the score has him constantly giving orders about entrances and exits and about what is to be seen and heard on stage. He opens the window when he wants to hear the music playing outside and closes it when he has had enough of the cantata, just as he opens the door to the torture chamber when he wants the screams of Cavaradossi to be heard on stage. His attention, of course, is directed above all at Tosca's performance. Before her arrival he listens in anticipation through the window: "Alla cantata ancor manca la Diva, e strimpellan gavotte" (The Diva is still missing from the cantata, and they're strumming gavottes). On one level he means that the Diva is not yet heard in the instrumental gavotte, but on another he implies that she is also eagerly awaited in the dramatic scene that he himself is arranging. Later, when Tosca is horrified by Cavaradossi's suffering, he cruelly observes: "Mai Tosca alla scena più tragica fu!" (Never was Tosca more tragic on the stage!). When proposing the bargain for the painter's life, he emphasizes again that it is a diva he wants: "Già mi struggea l'amor della diva! Ma poc'anzi ti mirai qual non ti vidi mai!" (I was already consumed by desire for the diva! But just now I saw you like I never saw you before!). The pain of the lovers is nothing but an element in a theatrical performance to him, a kind of foreplay aimed less at learning Angelotti's hiding place than at inflaming his own desire. In the end his carefully arranged operatic scene is above all a means of triggering extreme vocal emissions from Tosca.

If fetishism is understood as the disavowal of lack, the soprano voice is the ultimate maternal phallus: emerging from the cavities of the female body, it cuts through all other sonic resources of the operatic machine and pours into the body of the listener. When Carsen turns Scarpia into an opera producer, he emphasizes that he is above all a voice fetishist, who craves this vocal penetration. From this perspective Scarpia could be said to epitomize the opera fan described by Poizat in *The Angel's Cry*, obsessively chasing the moment of *jouissance* that can be delivered only by the high female voice when it transcends meaning and, for a brief moment, turns into a pure vocal object.[52] Or, to cite a memorable formulation along the same lines from Lawrence Kramer's *After the Lovedeath:* "To be caught up by the opera *is* to find bliss in pain and humiliation, to drown in the honey of the breast; it is to be blissfully penetrated, and that not by a mere penis, but by that for which the penis itself can only substitute, the phallus."[53] In the end, is not Scarpia's elaborate scheme of torture and violence designed precisely to deliver such vocal-erotic enjoyment? In the opening aria of the second act, as he muses on how he devours and discards the objects of his desire, the baron notes that God created different beauties and different wines, concluding that "Io vo' gustar quanto più posso dell'opra divina!" (I want to savor as much as possible of God's creation!). The "opra divina" that he wants to taste is, on a literal level, the divine creation of woman, but given his insistence on calling Tosca "la Diva," we may assume that he is also expressing his desire to indulge in divine opera.

The operatic *jouissance* of which Poizat writes is always situated at the climactic moment of an aria, where the soprano voice takes flight and soars into angelic heights. In Puccini's opera the best example of such a moment is certainly Tosca's grand aria "Vissi d'arte," which stands out as a song act, preceded by silence and (typically) followed by applause.[54] Carsen's staging makes the most of that quality. Turning it into Tosca's private, backstage performance for Scarpia, Carsen places Emily Magee's Tosca in a defined downstage spotlight, while Hampson's Scarpia, behind her, is lit by another one. In an inordinately slow rendering of the aria, Magee stands almost motionless, raising her glove-clad hands before her at the top notes to mimic the most stereotypically melodramatic gestures of opera acting. It is almost as if her posture were modeled on Degas's famous painting *Singer with a Glove:* in addition to performing an aria, she is parodically performing the performance of an opera diva. Meanwhile, Scarpia watches and listens intensely, pressing against an upstage brick wall (fig. 4.8). He has a serious expression, bespeaking melancholy, perhaps even dread. For the duration of this aria Hampson lets go of the condescending irony that otherwise dominates his rendering of the role. This change is very clearly highlighted, and one way of construing it

Figure 4.8. "I lived for art." Tosca (Emily Magee) performing performance, while Scarpia (Thomas Hampson) listens. *Tosca* (dir. Robert Carsen, Opernhaus Zürich, 2009).

would be as Scarpia's premonition of his imminent death at Tosca's hands. Yet however struck he is by the performance that he has managed to extract from her, he will not let on: in the silence after the aria he regains control of himself and rewards her only with a smirk and a sarcastically listless applause.

It is the nature of the climactic vocal performance to be transient. Like the quest of the opera fan in Poizat's essay, Scarpia's search must always go on, since the attained goal never lasts for more than an orgasmic moment: "La cosa bramata perseguo, me ne sazio e via la getto . . . volto a nuova esca" (I pursue that which I desire, satisfy myself and throw it away . . . then turn to a new prey). Yet the fantasy of a final fulfillment remains, and that finality can only be achieved in death. Correspondingly, the heart of an interpretation of Scarpia as a masochist would have to be the moment when Tosca thrusts the dagger into his body. If he is indeed producer and director of the whole scenario, we must ask whether he does not, in some sense, actually want to expire in Tosca's arms. Is his death not the climax toward which his mise-en-scène has been directed all along? From Poizat's perspective the longing for operatic *jouissance* coincides with the longing for death. Both mark the ecstatic moment of escape from the symbolic order: "To identify with the lost vocal object is to become loss oneself, to become supreme purification, to *be* silence; in other words, to die. Death becomes the only possible locus of return to that initial real that has not yet been elaborated by the symbolic."[55] To Poizat death is thus the end point of the quest for pure voice. To Sacher-Masoch, similarly, it is the ultimate stage of the masochistic fantasy. In *Venus in Furs* Severin signs a contract to the effect that Wanda has the right to kill him if she so desires, and he even points her dagger at his own breast.[56] Though it never occurs, the notion of his death is repeatedly evoked as the ultimate consequence of her absolute power over him: "She draws a little dagger, and at the glint of its blade I am seized with terror, convinced that she is about to kill me. But she laughs and cuts the ropes that bind me."[57]

Tosca, as we know, is not as merciful: with the punch line "Questo è il bacio di Tosca" (This is the kiss of Tosca), she gives her adversary what he deserves. The kiss thus becomes the metaphorical expression that is immediately literalized in a lethal actuality effect. Yet if Tosca and Scarpia cross the line that Severin and Wanda only play with, Carsen's situating of the story in the opera house muddies the distinction: the bodies on stage are constantly poised between characters and singers, and every event is half playacting, half reality. Scarpia's death is also a mock death, a *petite mort*. Magee's Tosca straddles Hampson's Scarpia after the stabbing, and as he dies, lying on his back, he is still caressing her face while moaning softly. Meanwhile, she is singing from the top of her lungs right into his ear, delivering the vocal penetration that he has desired all along. This, indeed, is the kiss of Tosca: the sound flowing from her mouth. The knife with which she stabs him is only an objectification of that voice, which is what really pierces him at the climactic moment. Hence, as he expires in Carsen's production, he does so with a smile on his face—not in agony but in sensual bliss (fig. 4.9).

Insofar as one finds this interpretation convincing, *Tosca* seems to align itself very neatly with the account of opera given in *The Angel's Cry*. Yet in one important respect it resists Poizat's account of the quest for operatic *jouissance,* which may explain the fact that he devotes virtually no attention to this opera, despite its affinity with his topic. In the drama of Tosca and Scarpia the trajectory toward a heavenly disembodied voice and the

Figure 4.9. "This is the kiss of Tosca." Scarpia (Thomas Hampson) dying the little death with Tosca's (Emily Magee) chest voice in his ear. *Tosca* (dir. Robert Carsen, Opernhaus Zürich, 2009).

silence beyond it, which is crucial to Poizat, is completely reversed. Tosca's most operatic moments in the second act outline a progression from absence to presence, not the other way around. They do not soar upward so much as fall to the earth. First, Scarpia listens for Tosca but finds only her silence, underscored by the gavotte. Next, he hears her through the window, as a voice with no physical presence, performing the cantata about vocal aspiration to divine transcendence: "Sale, ascende l'uman cantico, varca spazi, varca cieli, a te giunge o re dei re" (The human voice rises and ascends, traversing space, traversing heavens, to reach you, oh King of Kings). Eventually, she performs her grand aria in his immediate presence. The final climax, however, arrives with their actual body contact, when her voice is not metaphysical but, on the contrary, so physical that it hurts. The stratospheric high notes—a C in the cantata, a B-flat in "Vissi"—are gone; during his orgasmic death itself Tosca is yelling as much as singing, and mostly in her lower register. For Scarpia to be sexually gratified, the disembodied voice is essential as foreplay. But the real ecstasy coincides with the other end of the vocal spectrum: the rough howls of the chest voice. Indeed, this may be Scarpia's most remarkably deviant desire: he perverts the operatic norm—to be spiritually penetrated by a gradually immaterialized vocal object—by turning it into its opposite, the longing to be physically penetrated by a voice that has taken the material form of a sharp object. At the finale of the second act the border between enactment and actuality, with which the opera plays throughout, is thus placed between the little death and the big one. The dissolution of this border coincides with the orgasmic dissolution of the subject, and the dramatic apex of the Tosca-Scarpia interplay thus already tells us what Cavaradossi's death at the end of the third will confirm: the score places these disruptions at the most climactic points in the drama, thus marking the violation of the boundary between the safely acted and the dangerously actual as the ultimate means of achieving ecstasy.

EDGE PLAY: OPERA, BDSM, AND THE LIMITS OF THE THEATRICAL SPACE

In *Tosca* the actuality effect is perhaps closer to the core of the drama than in any other opera of the repertoire. It consistently evokes a distinction among different layers of representation solely for the thrill of dissolving it, and the point at which the representation or fantasy breaks out into reality is always one of pain and cruelty, even death. The excitement of seeing and hearing boundaries being thus pushed and violated, all within the safe frame of the stage, has turned out to hold a lasting appeal for operagoers. There is an important analogy to be drawn here with the way in which practitioners of contemporary BDSM conceptualize their actions and desires. The concept of the safe, sane, and consensual has been crucial to the BDSM community, serving internal as well as external purposes: on the one hand, it has come to define what is acceptable behavior within the community, and, on the other hand, it has allowed that community to gain widespread acceptance. As recent ethnographic work has shown, however, reality is considerably more complicated than what the official slogan may suggest.

First, it is highly questionable whether the BDSM scene can create a space that is isolated from gendered power structures in the way that its practitioners and advocates have so often imagined. Thus, for instance,

Margot Weiss argues in *Techniques of Pleasure* that the contemporary BDSM scene is intrinsically tied to capitalist ideology—not least as a result of the expanding market of BDSM gear and the central role played by commodity consumption in the identity of practitioners—and codefined by the hierarchies of gender, race, and class from which it purports to liberate itself. According to Weiss, BDSM is instead best described in terms of sexuality circuits, the power of which flow back and forth across the supposedly firm boundaries of the safe, sane, and consensual play space. Second, many practitioners conceptualize their habits and desires in ways that clearly challenge the idea of the safe, sane, and consensual. Thus sociologists like Staci Newmahr and Robin Bauer suggest that BDSM may be understood as a kind of "edgework": their interviews show that those engaged in BDSM typically perceive it as a field of activities where deliberate risk-taking and challenging of one's personal boundaries constitute an objective in their own right.[58] From this perspective it should come as no surprise that the self-implemented control mechanisms of the BDSM community—which may include, for instance, trained and certified "dungeon monitors," whose task is to make sure that the activities at a given gathering do not violate a particular set of safety guidelines—are perceived by some practitioners as incompatible with what they see as the core of BDSM.[59] In the words of BDSM activist and historian Alison Moore, from whose speech at a Sydney Leather Pride Week Weiss quotes the following: "For me the whole beauty of SM play is that it doesn't always make sense, that it does take us outside of our 'safety-zone,' that it is frightening; it taps into the purest essence of sex which is ultimately chaotic, chthonic, exhilarating, exuberant, a dizzying abyss, an electrifying scream. . . . There is no political slogan to describe this."[60] Certain practitioners even pursue activities that deliberately target the borders of the safe, sane, and consensual, in so-called *edge play*. While this term sometimes refers simply to the testing of one's individual limits, it is more typically used for scenarios that include extremely dangerous activities and props, such as branding, fire, knives, electricity, or asphyxiation. Even for experienced and careful practitioners the risks involved in such behavior are severe: "Breath play to me is asking to kill someone," says one of Weiss's interviewees, adding, "I've lost several friends to breath play."[61] A lethal outcome is admittedly a very drastic example, and the willingness to take such risks is in no way representative for the BDSM scene (breath play, Weiss notes, is widely prohibited in the community).[62] Even so, the very existence of a concept such as "edge play" shows both that the supposedly firm borders of sexual power play are liable to be drawn into the theatrical space that they were created to contain and that certain practitioners find that notion enticing in itself.

What has this got to do with opera? Whether understood as sadist or masochist, Scarpia is of course a ruthless tyrant and deaf to any safe word, but the actors and the audience themselves are never at risk. It is only for the *characters* that the border between make-believe and real violence breaks down, and no one actually gets hurt, even though everyone dies. After all, opera always remains squarely within the confines of the safe, sane, and consensual. Or does it? "There's a lot of power games that happen," says a soprano I interview. "I was in this situation where I was doing rehearsals and the guy kept whispering in my ear what he wanted to do to me, in what position. He was obviously trying to screw up my singing." Or another memory, from the same singer: "I'm singing Tosca and the Cavaradossi runs to me and sticks his tongue in my mouth when I'm supposed to be singing." Stories about transgressions at the opera house have been circulating since long before the autumn of 2017, of course; only they were often heard in a very different light. In fact, opera lore teems with anecdotes playing along the edge of actual abuse and violence. To mention a handful, which, like the story of *Tosca,* involve blades: Singing Desdemona in Rossini's *Otello,* Maria Malibran was reputedly told by her father and voice teacher, who was doing the title role, that he would stab her to death for real if her singing did not meet his standards (Rossini's version, unlike Verdi's, uses a knife for the murder).[63] Christa Ludwig recounts how Jon Vickers, singing Don José to her Carmen, once stabbed her with such rage that he drew blood, even though the knife was just a stage prop: "I still bear the scar to this day."[64] Naturally, similar stories abound with reference to *Tosca,* especially involving Maria Callas. Franco Zeffirelli, who directed the famous Covent Garden performances with Callas and Tito Gobbi in 1964, supposedly conceived of the Tosca-Scarpia interplay in analogy with Callas's relationship with the magnate Aristotle Onassis, who is said to have beaten her on a regular basis.[65] As biographer David Bret puts it: "It was no secret that in *his* lovemaking, Onassis enjoyed aggression, and Maria once admitted, albeit jokingly, that she would have loved to have seen the expression on his face, had she suddenly drawn a dagger!"[66] During one of the rehearsals, the blade of Tosca's knife failed to retract, and, like Vickers, Callas stabbed so violently that Gobbi started bleeding, "gasped a horrified 'My God,' and continued with the scene."[67] Although they may make us snicker, such stories have a discomfiting subtext: they bring opera's predilection for actuality effects—here on the third level—too close to lived tragedy and actual violence, while also suggesting that this subtext itself holds a fascination that contributes to their endless retelling—verbally or in the guise of staged opera.

Tito Gobbi gives us another *Tosca* anecdote. Gobbi, who sang a peerless Scarpia (and his cartoonish evil-eyebrow acting does nothing to diminish this achievement), was also the stage director for numerous productions of *Tosca*. Musing on his relationship with this signature role, the retired Gobbi tells the following story:

> One illustrious colleague refused for years to perform Tosca with me because she could not overcome the indignation and revulsion which I, as Scarpia, aroused in her. Finally I persuaded her; we studied the opera together, and I took charge of the production, the better to be a support to her. The first night arrived and everything went smoothly until the death of Scarpia—"È morto . . . or gli perdono . . ." ("He is dead . . . now I pardon him . . ."). Then suddenly, as she saw the *open eyes* of the dead man, she gave me a look of utter horror and, trembling and screaming, she ran from the stage, leaving me alone and in agony, without candles or crucifix, still and helpless before a stupefied audience, which was stunned by this totally unfamiliar finale to Act II.[68]

From Gobbi's perspective it is not difficult to understand the point of relating this event. The story is meant to illustrate his ability to inhabit his role so perfectly that even his coacting soprano falls prey to the illusion. Reminiscing about his collaboration with Callas, for instance, he includes her in a similar boast: "With Maria it was not playing but living; we were Tosca and Scarpia and felt completely free on stage on the strength of a perfect understanding."[69] But what of the perspective of the other, unnamed soprano, who apparently felt less comfortable than Callas? She is not available to interview, but if we assume for a moment that Gobbi's anecdote is actually an accurate description of what happened, what does it tell us? Her behavior is something quite extraordinary. If it is difficult for an audience to get up and leave because the performance is too disturbing, for the prima donna to do so is almost unthinkable. One must wonder what really lies behind her reaction, and Gobbi's genius as an actor does not quite suffice as an explanation. As the one who coaxes her into something that she is reluctant to do, and who is not only her presumably senior colleague but also her mentor and stage director, Gobbi's position is obviously one of authority and power. It is not hard to imagine that the pleasure he takes in playing the part of the predator—and this pleasure shines through clearly enough in his account—might easily approach sexual harassment. Considered from this angle, the anecdote suddenly becomes rather less amusing.

My point is not, however, to throw speculative accusations at Gobbi from a post–Me Too perspective. The temptation to project an opera's narrative on the real people performing it may no doubt lead to unwarranted conclusions. Take, for instance, the flower girls in the Brussels *Parsifal*. In the fiction they are divested of any agency: they are visualized as tortured targets who have no choice but to participate in their master's nasty opera-within-the-opera. But what about the actual performers, whose bodies are undeniably put on display as the potential objects of scopophilic pleasure? The bondage scenes were performed by Jorgos Fokianos (Klingsor's double), Gala Moody, Frances D'Ath, and Dasnyia Sommer, who was also responsible for the choreography. Sommer is a classically trained dancer and choreographer who also teaches workshops in shibari, and together with D'Ath she regularly incorporates rope bondage into contemporary dance performance.[70] In the rehearsals of this scene it was they who called the shots, not Castellucci. Anna Larsson recalls: "They had to demonstrate to the team what they could do, to Romeo and to the others. So they had to show and explain how long they could hang in certain positions. Because it is pretty dangerous too, a lot of what they do. But we—the others who were involved—we were struck by seeing that these girls took such pleasure in hanging there. That they thought it was such a great kick, this pain. And how they challenged themselves to hang longer."[71] Regardless of how one construes the meaning of the production and the kind of gaze it invites, imagining the female performers themselves as exploited victims caught in the perverse snares of a male director would thus be too simple. Like many objections to consensual SM, such a critique could only be leveled at the expense of the participants' own perspective, since it implicitly claims that they do not know what is best for them.

The stagings and anecdotes discussed in this chapter show that opera—which, like any cultural performance, is embedded in a social world full of inequalities and asymmetric power structures—points obsessively and with relish to the dissolution of its own boundaries. It is simply unable to resist playing with the edges of its own theatrical space. If, as I have argued, the productions' surfeit of fetishized objects, riding crops, whips, ropes, and chains is underlaid by a structural analogy between opera and consensual, eroticized power exchanges, the actuality effect offers a specific interpretation of a that analogy. Its essence, as it emerges from the mise-en-scènes I have highlighted here, does not lie merely in the visualization of opera as an erotic power exchange but in the specific way these two practices relate to the limits of their own play space. They enact violations inside the limits of the safe, sane, and consensual, yet those enactments themselves repeatedly point to the difficulties of maintaining a firm border toward the real cruelty that lies outside those limits, thereby implying that the fantasy of violating them is an integral part of their appeal. Condensed into formulaic proportions, this is what the actuality effect reveals: the fascination with the violation of boundaries *within* the theatrical space depends on the fact that it evokes the violation of the boundaries *surrounding* the theatrical space.

The examples given in the present chapter suggest that these violations can be either disturbing or compelling, or both. They can give us oneiric allegories of the opera as a workplace—the world of professional singers, conductors, and directors—portraying it as replete with hierarchies and power structures through which undercurrents of violence and eroticism are surging (as when *Kapellmeister* Klingsor ties up his flower girls or when Scarpia the producer preys on his star soprano). Anecdotes about the dissolution of the theatrical space circulate and fascinate widely, but in the wake of the Me Too movement their affinity with abusive behavior is impossible to ignore (as when Scarpia's assaults on Tosca mingle with the interrelation between an inexperienced soprano and her instructor, director, and coperformer, or with the personal tragedies of Callas). Ultimately, the issues raised by these examples point back at ourselves and our role as spectators and listeners. It is we, the audience, who constitute the raison d'être of conductors, directors, and singers. When Klingsor conducts his choir of tied-up bodies, we are there to watch and listen, and when Scarpia directs his scene of physical and psychological torture, he does so for our pleasure. Does the audience not come to the opera house to hear extreme suffering voiced in stylized, high-pitched cries? Does the control exerted by conductors, choreographers, and directors over the performing bodies warrant the analogy with ropes and fetters, and if so, does that bondage form part of the pleasure of an operatic performance? If the answer to these questions is yes, what does that make the opera lover?

5 More or Less Human

WOZZECK, LULU, AND THE SOPRANO CONDUCTOR

One of the most widespread tropes about operatic singing centers on its intrinsic humanness. In a basic sense opera's dependence on the human body marks it as specific to our species. More specifically, it makes extreme use of that body in order to maximize vocal power and timbre, arguably pushing its physical limits to form an acoustic outline of sorts. From there, devotion to the art form has beaten a path to less rather self-evident ideas, such as the operatic voice being expressive of an essential humanity or subjectivity. Recent work on voice has done much to uncover the cultural, ethnic, and racial biases of such conventional wisdom.[1] Voice, Martha Feldman summarizes, is "not a universal index of the liberal subject, not therefore an unambiguous sign of 'humanity,' not a singular marker of identity. . . . Voice guarantees humanness at the same time as it calls it into question, delineates the human as it challenges it."[2] Operatic singing, then, can neither be taken as a marker of a panhuman essence nor be entirely detached from the notion of humanness. Here, I will not venture into posthumanist territory by questioning the divide between the human and the nonhuman.[3] While many of the assumptions that cluster around humanness have been critiqued for good reason, the basic category, as we will see, remains central to the examples I address. Specifically, the

BDSM-influenced scenes dealt with in this chapter use opera to perform a role-play that gestures *outside* the category of the human. Their meaning depends on the boundaries of the human and its culturally created power dynamics, which are simultaneously mobilized, problematized, and invested with an erotic charge.

The authors of the volume *Different Loving: The World of Sexual Dominance and Submission*—a five-hundred-page compendium of SM practices based on extensive interviews from the early 1990s—list three types of fantasies under the heading of "Depersonalization": "first, behaving and being treated like an animal; second, the fantasy of being an inanimate object, such as a piece of furniture; and third, institutional scenarios in which the submissive is treated like a prisoner, a hospital patient, or a reform-school student—in other words, someone whose rights have been revoked by an omnipotent, impersonal, and usually heartless system."[4] Such scenarios share with all BDSM an eroticization of power and powerlessness, but they put the aspect of dehumanization at the center. Playing the part of an obedient beast, an inanimate object, or the captive of a totalitarian system, the submissive is stripped of agency, initiative, and dignity habitually—though by no means unproblematically—associated with human beings. These scenarios tend to cast the nonhuman as the subhuman, ascribing, for instance, to the animal not only unbridled lust but also a supposedly justifiable subservience to human domination. Taking its cue from such sexual fantasies, this chapter will consider opera as a stage for humans role-playing the nonhuman and the subhuman but also the superhuman and the panhuman. By approaching these positions not as natural necessities but in terms of role-play, I hope to clarify their functions on the opera stage without either bringing along the metaphysical baggage of "humanity" or leaving behind its physical dependence on the human body.

The main examples are drawn from performances of Alban Berg's operas. That eroticized performances of depersonalization have found their way to *Wozzeck* (premiered in 1925) and *Lulu* (premiered as an unfinished work in 1937) is not surprising. Not only is the notion of dehumanization an insistently recurrent element in conceptualizations of modernity and modernism—which was already clearly formulated at the time when Berg's works were composed[5]—but both operas explicitly dramatize their respective protagonists' gradual loss of human worth. In the story of *Wozzeck,* based on Georg Büchner's unfinished play from 1836–37, this process is a result of desperate poverty. To provide for his girlfriend Marie and their illegitimate son, Wozzeck submits to humiliating treatments by his superiors, while his peers beat him and Marie cheats on him. Driven to the edge of insanity, he finally murders her in a fit of jealousy. In *Lulu,* based on Frank Wedekind's plays *The Earth Spirit* (1895) and *Pandora's Box* (1904), the process is more complex. Lulu, a social parvenu on the rise through serial marriage, is desired by everyone who surrounds her, but her husbands and lovers die one by one. In the second half of the opera she gradually loses her status and becomes a prostitute in London, where she ends up being murdered by Jack the Ripper. Lulu's dehumanization takes the form of a fitful struggle, through which she attempts to gain power over her lovers and to retain her own agency. Her character is often described by critics as a blank surface onto which the erotic fantasies and desires of her lovers are projected, as if her very existence were conjured up by the seedy dreams of patriarchal society. From this perspective she is not a person at all but a figment of the fin de siècle imagination: a mythical ur-woman turned nightmare as the trail of dead lovers extends ever farther behind her. But what is so troubling about Berg's opera is precisely the insistent suspicion that this false narrative is wrapped around a human being in order to justify the violence against her.

The end point of such dehumanization is death, which comes to Wozzeck and Marie, as well as to Lulu and her lovers. Ultimately, the fantasy of the subperson or the inanimate object reverts to a literal loss of life. Although death is the extreme antithesis of safe BDSM practice, psychoanalytic thought always suspects its presence in the unconscious darkness beyond the perimeter of the play space: "the aim is ecstasy, the fantasy is death," to quote once more Susan Sontag's summary of the sadomasochistic master scenario.[6] Representing a gradual loss of humanness ending in murder, the BDSM depersonalization scenarios stage a particular version of the actuality effect. As visual elements in contemporary mise-en-scène, performances of the obedient beast and the inanimate object can be said to represent stages of depersonalization, foreshadowing its final mutation into death. Crucially, (representations of) safely enacted scenarios are established prior to their metamorphosis into (representations of) real violence. In the productions I address here, not just the singers but the *characters* are thus involved in playacting their own depersonalization as part of a game of erotic dominance and submission *before* the boundaries of that game are crossed and they suffer the lethal consequences of the actuality effect.

The visual codes of BDSM are closer to Berg's operas than to any others I have discussed. In the 1920s, Berlin had seen a veritable explosion of the prostitution, pornography, and sexual recklessness dealt with in *Lulu*. This was where the music of *Wozzeck* and *Lulu* was first heard: the Staatsoper was the site of the *Wozzeck* premiere in 1925, and Berg kept envisioning the same for *Lulu* even after the Nazis' rise to power, relishing the projected scandal.[7] But the disasters of German politics and the composer's death in 1935 prevented its performance in any other form than the suite of five symphonic pieces, premiered at the Staatsoper in November of 1934. To the totalitarian regime that branded it *entartete Musik,* the opera appeared as a highbrow reincarnation of the 1920s' debauchery, which they had swiftly shut down, blaming it on the Jewish perversion of the German spirit.[8] When the two finished acts of *Lulu* premiered in Zurich in 1937, the reviewer for *Die Musik*—then the official music journal of the Nazis—thrashed the opera precisely on account of its degenerate sexuality: "a music of prostitutes and pimps . . . a deliberate tearing at the nerves, a brutal whipping of the air, a tortured piling up of anguish, fear and horror."[9]

A brutal whipping had indeed been in the air during the 1920s. As the metropolis of the Weimar Republic, Berlin was not just the site of a general sexual frenzy. More specifically, it was where the modern iconography of perversion was consolidated as a cultural trope and became part of a lucrative if clandestine industry. A wide array of the visual codes of fetishism and sadomasochism had now been established and were being disseminated both in live performances and print matter. Indeed, the focus on SM is among the chief distinguishing traits of erotic imagery from this time and place. In the words of Mel Gordon: "The pornography that circulated in Weimar Berlin was marked by its unusual emphasis on body worship, extreme fetishism, scatology, dark roleplay and ritualized gender struggle. There was the soft stuff too but the most sought-after girlie mags and sex novels were usually imports or translated editions from Paris or Rome. Local imitations of the same . . . succumbed, even in their erotic cartoons and short stories, to menacing visions and S&M fantasies."[10] Although the kinky inclinations of Weimar Berlin have certainly been mythologized in the popular imaginary—recently in the 2017 crime series *Babylon Berlin*—the establishment of the visual codes of SM is a historical fact.

Compared to the earlier examples dealt with in this book, the distance between the original context and the present-day iconography of perversion is thus drastically reduced. Especially in *Lulu*, they touch both spatially and temporally. No opera before it had portrayed adultery, prostitution, homosexual love, and erotic power struggles with such openness, and it has become intertwined with the notion of the 1920s as an erotically free-spirited epoch. The iconic styles of the time—like that of Louise Brooks's Lulu in *Pandora's Box* or Marlene Dietrich in *Der Blaue Engel*— have often informed modern-day stagings of the opera.[11] Indeed, the seedy atmosphere of Weimar Berlin was right next door to the opera: the real-life equivalents of the variety show in which Lulu dances—as well as hundreds of whorehouses, strip clubs, and gay bars—had their center in Friedrichstadt, literally around the block from the venue where the composer envisioned the premiere of his new work.[12] While Berg was composing his murder scene using a cabaret melody (composed by Wedekind himself), Jack the Ripper appeared as a comic character in the nude-shows of Berlin (fig. 5.1).[13] In Weimar Berlin sadomasochistic sexuality and fetishism turned, for the first time, into a widespread metropolitan underground culture. Once the wave of director's opera hit Berg's operas— starting with the premiere of Friedrich Cerha's three-act version of *Lulu* in 1979, directed by Chéreau and conducted by Boulez—the images of BDSM that cropped up on stage thus appeared, more markedly than in any other opera, as a return of the repressed. In other words, the preposterous history that has hitherto been an effect of the iconography of perversion loses a lot of its preposterousness in *Lulu*.

This chapter is divided into four parts. The first discusses a 2010 staging of *Wozzeck* by Dmitri Tcherniakov, which casts Wozzeck as a male prostitute paid to participate in the kinky scenarios of the men who impersonate the "Captain" and the "Doctor." Here, the BDSM imagery becomes a thin varnish of playacting covering up an inhumane system. In a society that has cast him as subhuman, Wozzeck can only rid himself of his role as

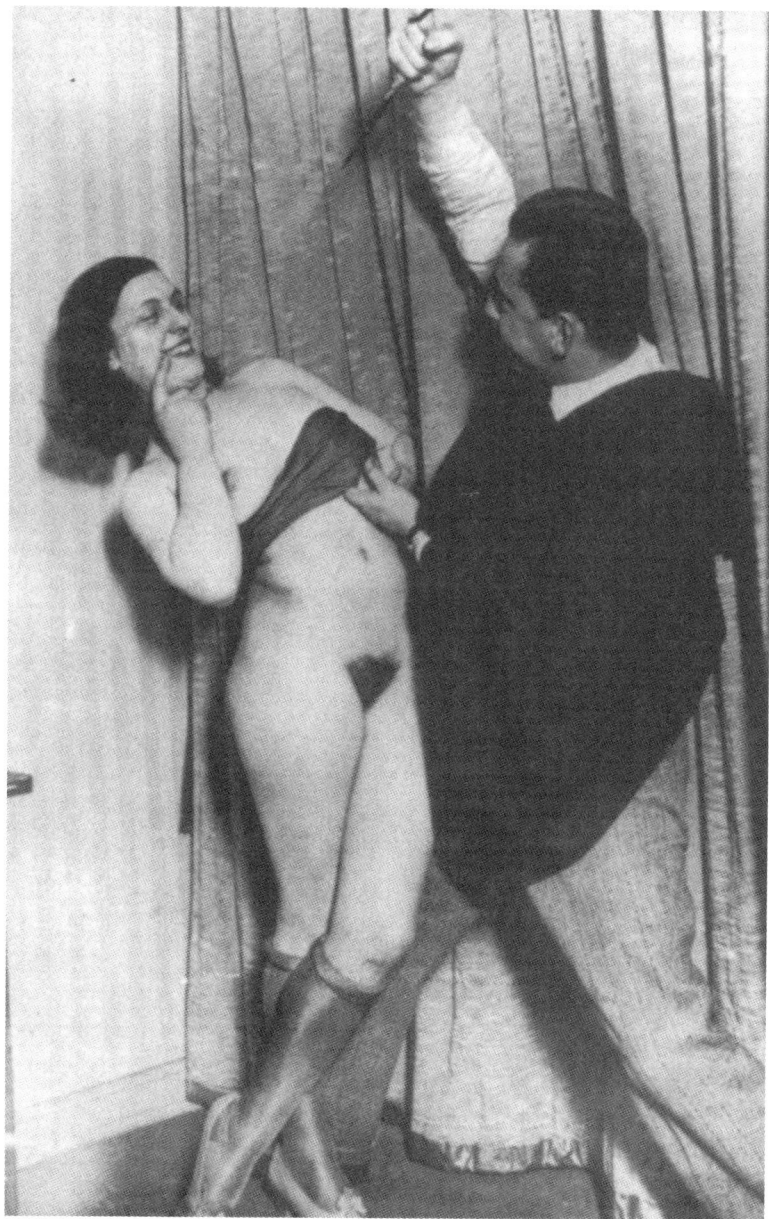

Figure 5.1. Cabaret show from 1920s Berlin, featuring Jack the Ripper. Reproduced in Mel Gordon, *Voluptuous Panic: The Erotic World of Weimar Berlin* (Los Angeles: Feral House, 2006).

a victim by becoming the perpetrator, channeling the violence to which he has been subjected onto the even more powerless Marie. The middle parts involve a number of productions of *Lulu:* most attention is devoted to the two-act version directed by Sven-Eric Bechtolf (Zurich, 2002), where the transformation of Lulu into an inanimate object is particularly salient.[14] In the second part, focus lies on bondage and human-animal role-play in all of these productions and how it is employed to visualize the erotic power struggle between the characters. The third part centers on the idea that *Lulu,* Bechtolf's production in particular, also foregrounds another type of depersonalization: the reduction of a person into an object of aesthetic and erotic appreciation. If, in the previous chapter, we saw conductor and opera-producer characters attempting to subjugate singer characters, Alwa—Alban Berg's onstage alter ego—and Lulu represent a parallel kind of gendered struggle: that between the composer and the material that he struggles (and fails) to control. The fourth part of the chapter, finally, shifts the perspective to focus instead on one unique performer: Canadian soprano and conductor Barbara Hannigan, who has sung *Lulu* not only in productions directed by Krzysztof Warlikowski and Christoph Marthaler but also in concert performances of the *Lulu Suite,* while simultaneously leading the orchestra. In these performances—as well as in those of the *Mysteries* suite from György Ligeti's 1977 opera *The Grand Macabre,* which she actually sings and conducts dressed up as a dominatrix—Hannigan turns the idea of the power dynamic between the singer and conductor on its head by embodying both roles at once. Her take on *Lulu* and *Mysteries* shows how the visual codes of SM can be used to playfully transcend the power structures from which they were derived.

YES, "CAPTAIN"

The real horror of the dehumanization machine in *Wozzeck* is how incontrovertible it seems, particularly in the eyes of its protagonists. Wozzeck and Marie are utterly powerless to change anything in their predicament. It may seem paradoxical, therefore, when Dmitri Tcherniakov's 2010 staging for the Bolshoi—remarkably the first Russian production since 1927—gives his relation to his superiors the appearance of role-play, as if his subservience were an identity to be donned at will. The production starts out by turning the very first scene of the opera into erotic playacting. When we first see Wozzeck and the Captain (sung on the DVD by Georg Nigl and Maxim Paster, respectively), they are dressed in contemporary, civilian clothes and neither of them appears to be in the military. Instead, they dress up as an officer and a private for the purpose of enacting a scene of humiliation. The sub- and supertitles reinforce the point by consistently putting "Captain" in quotation marks. The officer's condescending lecture on morals and Wozzeck's laconically repeated reply—"Jawohl, Herr Hauptmann" (Yes, Captain)—become lines in a military-themed power exchange for the pleasure of the "Captain": before drawing the curtains on the little room where it is to take place, he hands Wozzeck an envelope of cash and goes outside to change. Wozzeck knows the drill. As soon as he has been paid, he starts changing into the uniform that the Captain gives him. He gets the props for the scene out from behind an armchair: a ball-and-chain (which he fixes to his foot) and two wooden footstools.

Wozzeck's role is that of the inanimate object. The role-play begins with him having to sit on one of the footstools while holding up the other as a table on which the Captain can place his cup of coffee. With a kick, his superior removes the one under him, forcing him to remain in an impossibly uncomfortable position (fig. 5.2). The scene becomes an instance of the BDSM practice of human-furniture play, which requires the submissive party to remain motionless for extended periods. In this context the depersonalization scenario becomes a confirmation of Wozzeck's lack of human worth. He is performing a role to which he is actually condemned by society, and to pretend that he is only pretending redoubles the humiliation. He does not last very long, though, and when he falls and spills the coffee the "Captain" has him crawl around on the floor and clean up the mess. He is subsequently kicked around, insulted ("Oh, Er ist dumm, ganz abscheulich dumm!" [Oh, you are dumb, quite revoltingly dumb!]) and forced to polish his superior's leather boots with a toothbrush. While reproaching him for his illegitimate child ("Ohne den Segen der Kirche!" [Without the blessing of the church!]), the Captain shoves a riding crop between his legs and pulls his trousers down before throwing him on the floor with his own belt around his neck.

Figure 5.2. "Yes, Captain." Wozzeck (Georg Nigl) serving as human furniture for the "Captain" (Maxim Paster). *Wozzeck* (dir. Dmitri Tcherniakov, Bolshoi Theatre, 2010).

The effect of this scene depends on the fact that we are first shown that which is outside the border of the role-play: the "reality" of the characters. This reality is neither the crumbling bourgeoisie of Berg's time nor Büchner's prerevolutionary 1830s but a slice of our own present. The curtain initially rises on a cross section of an apartment building, with twelve claustrophobically small rooms, and for several minutes we watch people go about their business in identically furnished rooms among flat-screen TVs and glossy magazines. People cohabitate, but nobody talks. Tcherniakov's version of preposterous history superimposes a bleak vision of late-capitalist alienation on the nineteenth-century class system that Büchner was one of the first to portray, foregrounding the distance as well as the vicinity between them. In this staging, then, the neoliberal promise of freedom through expenditure hides a circumscription of the subject every bit as forceful as that of the *Vormärz* period. Importantly, this opening vision is entirely silent. The opera's music begins at the very moment Paster reenters the room dressed up as the "Captain." In other words, Berg's characteristic opening chord, with the snare-drum roll and string glissandi, becomes a signal announcing the role-play. The onset of the music marks the move into the ritual of eroticized humiliation. The moment of transition between the characters' diegetic reality and their erotic role-playing is thus deliberately focused on stage. Much as in the stagings addressed in previous chapters, however, the border between them is there to be problematized, permeated, and eventually violated. Wozzeck and the "Captain" do not play on equal terms: the sex worker is coerced by his poverty. Eventually, he has had enough, pulls his trousers up, and talks back. At this moment Tcherniakov makes excellent use of Berg's musical drama: we see the "Captain" getting increasingly excited and abusive as the music grows into the scene's climax—Wozzeck's forceful "Wir arme Leut" (We wretched people)—which comes to mark the turning point where he breaks character, throws the belt on the floor, and voices his refusal. In Tcherniakov's interpretation the observation that moral behavior is not available to the poor thus becomes a deconstruction of the limits of the role-play we have just seen: his role as a paid submissive in the "Captain's" fantasy may appear to be a scripted theatrical performance, but it is entirely predicated on his socially inferior position and financial dependence.

If the role-play begins with the "Captain's" entrance, it is less obvious where it ends: insofar as the start of the music signaled the start of erotic ritual in which Wozzeck is abused, the mere fact that it keeps going suggests that he remains trapped in a theater of sexual humiliation. The fourth scene sees another version of a depersonalizing BDSM scenario: in his living room the "Doctor," dressed in scrubs, straps Wozzeck onto a hospital bed, casting him in the role of a helpless guinea pig for his scientific experiments. His position is always one of powerlessness, whether he is catering to the kinks of the "Captain" and the "Doctor" or bullied by the Drum major, who beats him up and seduces Marie in order to define his own manhood ("Was bin ich für ein Mann!" [What a man I am!]). Berg's opera presents us with a textbook phallic hierarchy, where the male subject is defined by the paternal power that always belongs to someone else. In the end his lack leads him to turn his anxiety against the female body in the form of sexual violence. Powerless vis-à-vis the men that surround him, Wozzeck channels his anguish into abuse of the one he can overpower: Marie.

Tcherniakov's staging visualizes this causality by presenting Wozzeck's killing of Marie in the third act as a mirror image of his opening exchange with the "Captain": it has the appearance of a BDSM scene played out in their dining room, yet it ends in death. Musically, the obsessive idea of murder is signified by the ever-present pitch of B, around which the music of the scene is composed. Just as this single note is continuously present, shifting between the different registers, ever more clearly audible, the lethal violence is hovering in the air from the start of the scene but made manifest only at the very end. In Tcherniakov's production Marie (Mardi Byers) is standing on a chair in her underwear, a black-lace blindfold covering her eyes, while Wozzeck slowly, solemnly parades around the table with a riding crop. Like the "Captain" before him, he occasionally brandishes it in the air. If his superior had him dress up to be disciplined, Wozzeck now demands the same of his fiancée: he hands her the same blue dress that she wore when she cheated on him with the Drum major (fig. 5.3). Finally, he applies lipstick on her face, painting a grotesquely oversized mouth. The attribute of feminine seductiveness is parodied, clashing with Marie's increasing angst. Like the dress, it is there to remind her of the guilt of her adultery, recalling the "Captain's" moralizing lecture on children born out of wedlock. Unlike Wozzeck, however, Marie finds no way of stopping the punishment; just as she raises her arms and desperately tries to untie the blindfold, he thrusts a knife into her abdomen. This is one of the more gruesome versions of the actuality effect: he places her body on a chair by the table, where she becomes a literal equivalent of the inanimate object that Wozzeck was forced to playact in the first scene.

Are the blindfold and the riding crop parts of an erotic ritual they have enacted consensually in the past but which has now taken a different turn? Or has he persuaded her to perform it for the first time, with the intent of staging her death as revenge for his own powerlessness? From the audience's position we cannot tell. What we see and hear is only that real terror borrows the external appearance of consensual power exchange, with the effect of becoming even more disturbing. Tcherniakov lets domestic violence slip into the attire of the safe, sane, and consensual: when the lace blindfold, the riding crop, and the ruby lipstick appear against the

Figure 5.3. "Are you afraid, Marie?" Wozzeck (Georg Nigl) terrorizing Marie (Mardi Byers) during a BDSM scene in their living room. *Wozzeck* (dir. Dmitri Tcherniakov, Bolshoi Theatre, 2010).

background of a dining-room table with a flat-screen TV, they do so precisely as commodities of mass-produced mainstream kink. In the social environment where this staging puts them, they seem like merchandise bought to add erotic flavor to a dull love life. As such, they exhibit a certain naivety or innocence, too: while the iconography of BDSM supposedly signals edgy eroticism and excitement, it also signals playacting. It comes with the promise that the violence is *not* for real. The actuality effect (here on its second level) that breaks this promise makes Tcherniakov's version of the scene almost unbearable to watch: it is as if a false varnish of consent were applied to the interplay between Wozzeck and Marie, beneath which the gradually intensifying dread of Berg's music grows until it finally explodes in the act of murder and the *idée fixe* of the note B resounds nakedly through the two grim crescendi that conclude the scene.

On the DVD recording the close-ups of Marie—tense, confused, trembling with fear, and unable to see what Wozzeck is doing—accentuate the horror of the scene and reveal the detailed work that has gone into it. Soprano Mardi Byers remembers dealing with rehearsals in a very detached manner and strictly governed by the director: "there was no room for 'can we try this? can we try this?'"[15] Whereas she remembers Bieito, with whom she has also worked, as very open to ideas from the singers, she describes Tcherniakov as fixated on the details of his own vision: "He would act the whole thing for me," Byers says. "I just remember having to watch every detail of what he was doing, from every shake of the hand to every shake of the knee. Because that's what he wanted, that's what he saw. In many ways it actually broke down the emotional part for me, that it was technical. It was so timed out that I had no time to think." That emotional detachment is necessary not only to maintain control over voice production but also to create the strongest possible impact on the audience: "The better you are at letting it go through you, letting it play your body as a total instrument in that moment, the better it's going to be for the audience. If I put Mardi into that, it's not going to work." At the same time, Byers acknowledges that scenes like these have a particular impact on their performers: "For me, it always comes afterwards," she says; "the next day, it all goes through you, and you just feel exhausted, and you can't get out of bed." Such exertion notwithstanding, the actuality effect here crosses the internal boundaries of the diegesis but does not venture outside it to afflict the real people on stage (that is, it does not go on to what I have called the third level). Byers is clear about not having felt any borders being transgressed and considers Tcherniakov "brilliant in what he does and what he creates." Clearly, she and the other singers are simply professionals doing their job, and very well at that. Yet when the actuality effect breaks through the fiction-within-the-fiction into the reality-within-the-fiction, it inevitably gestures further, into reality. It stages a parallel between the director demanding a compliant performance from his singers and the character demanding a compliant performance from his victim. In the onstage fiction it is Wozzeck who directs the scene, instructing Marie about where to stand, what to wear, how to move.

The fact that Marie's corpse stays on stage throughout the rest of the opera marks her ultimate loss of personhood. No longer a singing subject, she has been entirely reduced to a visible object: a prop stowed in a box of a room next to the TV, like a life-size mannequin or stuffed animal. She has been forced to pretend that she was only pretending: having already been cast as subhuman, she performs the role of an object, which requires no performance at all. Around her dead body, still seated at the dinner table with blindfold on and lipstick smudged, the appearance of business-as-usual is maintained. Wozzeck drowns only metaphorically, in the anonymity of the apartment block where all the neighbors go about their lives. In the final scene he sits at the table and has a vivid conversation with his dead woman, while their child keeps playing his race-car video game—"Hopp, hopp! Hopp, hopp!"—next to his mother's corpse ("he has screen time," as Byers puts it). In the end a society that regards some of its members as subhuman allows them no other role, and whether they are dead objects or merely pretending to be does not seem to matter to anyone. In the Bolshoi *Wozzeck*'s indictment of contemporary society, the commodified style of BDSM receives a heavy blow: here, the visual codes of consensual kink serve only to mock the very idea of consent and reinforce the powerlessness of the oppressed.

LUST ON A LEASH

The opening scene of *Lulu* promises a theater of domination and submission, as arousing as it is thrilling:

Hereinspaziert in die Menagerie,	Step into the menagerie,
Ihr stolzen Herren, Ihr lebenslust'gen Frauen,	You proud gentlemen, you lively ladies,
Mit heißer Wollust und mit kaltem Grauen	To watch with hot lust and cold dread
Die unbeseelte Kreatur zu schauen,	As the soulless animal is tamed
Gebändigt durch das menschliche Genie.	By the human genius.

Whip in hand, the Animal Tamer then announces the dramatis personae as so many wild beasts, while the characters' leitmotifs accompany their appearances: the tiger (Dr. Schön), the bear (The Athlete), the ape (The Marquis), the crocodile (Countess Geschwitz), and finally the snake herself (Lulu). The hierarchies are clear: under the control of the superior human spirit, the animal impulse must be leashed and tamed (*Gebändigt* derives from the same root as bands, bondage, and binding).

This scene is, among other things, an arch-allegory of modernist aesthetics. As Theodor W. Adorno, Berg's pupil, put it: "While the animal trainer promises his audience that they shall see a soulless creature 'tamed by human genius', the music, poised on the outermost dialectical edge, carries out this taming, Lulu's training in cultivated singing, and at the same time undermines it by making her most artificial sound an allegory of . . . unbridled passion."[16] The "cultivated" coloratura singing—Adorno's word is "Ziergesang," meaning ornamental singing but also punning on "Tiergesang," animal singing—is commanded by human genius, ultimately the composer himself. As a modernist masterpiece, *Lulu* appeared toward the end of the long development transferring agency from the singer to the composer, from the performance to the work. In Berg's view the score of an opera was to control not only the slightest musical detail but also the movements of the bodies on stage: "The music must produce everything that the play needs for its transposition to the reality of the stage, and this requires from the composer that he carry out all the most important tasks of an ideal director."[17] As George Perle has argued, the score for *Lulu* consistently ties the characters' gestures, actions, exits, and entrances to musical cues and leitmotifs.[18] This same will to authorial control marks the symmetric large-scale arc of Lulu's rise and fall, with the palindromic piece of film music as the pivotal middle point and her three dead husbands doubling as her three clients in the final act. Perle writes: "The structural symmetries within which the characters are bound in the play, and which give them an almost puppetlike helplessness that mocks their supposedly willed behavior, are clarified and strengthened in the operatic version."[19] The beams, arrows, stems, and lines of Berg's notation, on this view, form an intricate system of bondage that allows the genius to govern his creations down to their tiniest gestures, turning them into puppets on musical strings.

Meanwhile, inside the story, the characters vie with each other for power. The protagonist's sexual agency and her lovers' struggle to control it is the driving force of the drama. She goes by numerous names ("Lulu," "Nelly," "Eva," "Mignon," "Countess Adelaide"), but none of them really seem to stick. The nicknaming is one attempt at governing her anarchic being. Another one is marriage. The Medical Specialist and the Painter believe that they can control her by playing the role of her husband. Doctor

Schön, who knows better, tries instead to marry her off to others, in order to break off their affair and protect his own respectability. The men around her seek to mold her into their own fantasies: the Painter by representing her visually; Alwa by giving her a role in his musical theater; the Prince by eloping with her to Africa; the Athlete by drilling her into a famous acrobat; the Marquis by forcing her to work in a bordello; her customers by purchasing her body; and, finally, Jack the Ripper by stabbing her to death. What unites their behavior is the will to restrict, control, and shape Lulu to fit their sexual wishes.

In contemporary productions this impulse is habitually rigged out in the iconography of perversion. Consider, for instance, the insistent presence of bondage imagery in the relation between Lulu and the Painter. In Bechtolf's Zurich *Lulu*, Laura Aikin poses for her portrait wrapped in newspapers, while her ankles are being tied to the stool on which she is sitting. In Olivier Py's production from Barcelona, Patricia Petibon's Lulu, naked and leaning over a desk, is tied with a rope while he takes her from behind (while a gorilla pleasures himself on a ladder beside them). In the Brussels *Lulu* directed by Krzysztof Warlikowski, Barbara Hannigan's Lulu, in a skimpy red negligee matching the bordello-style drapes behind her, has both arms and both legs fastened with leather straps to a narrow bed, while he alternately tickles and slaps her with a black ostrich plume. Beyond invoking a generic atmosphere of debauchery, these symbolic restrictions of Lulu's body through bondage visually manifest the desire to tame her. Not that she is constrained in any real sense, even in the stage fiction: none of these three Lulus are physically coerced in these scenes, and they are soon untied. But the fantasy of controlling her, which is shared by all her husbands and lovers, is symbolically played out in the form of an erotic game.

Even more than the bondage, however, these productions evoke the trope of the beast and its master as a template for dominant and submissive behavior. We have already witnessed such imagery when Kundry's seduction scene saw her holding a giant snake, symbolizing the insidious sensuality of Wagner's music, or when Lehnhoff's *Tosca* ascribed to Scarpia a fascination with furs and cats. In *Lulu*, however, the insistent thematization of human-animal relations puts this imagery much closer to the heart of the piece. The central power struggle between Lulu and Schön in particular has attracted allusions to human-animal role-play. While the bond-age scenes place Lulu in the submissive position, her later struggle with Doctor Schön puts her on top. When she is still married to the Painter, Schön confidently advises him to rein her in: "Lass Sie Autorität fühlen; sie verlangt nicht mehr, als unbedingt Gehorsam leisten zu dürfen" (Let her feel your authority; she demands no more than to be unconditionally obedient). He will soon learn the difficulty of this task firsthand. At the end of act 1, after she has allegedly fainted during a dance number in the theater, he realizes he cannot free himself from her. In the humiliating scene that leads to their getting married, she forces him to write a letter in which he breaks off the engagement with his fiancée. Word for word, Lulu—playing the role of one of Masoch's dominant heroines—dictates what he must write: "Seit drei Jahren versuche ich, mich loszureißen; ich habe nicht die Kraft dazu. Ich schreibe Ihnen an der Seite der Frau, die mich beherrscht." (For three years now I have tried to break free; I don't have the strength. I write this at the side of the woman who commands me.) The scene marks Lulu's ascendancy to power, which reaches its extreme point as she kills Schön in the second act and which is inverted in the third when the same singer returns in the guise of Jack the Ripper to murder her.

Schön's submission to his mistress's instructions has been staged as a human-animal interaction—to be specific, so-called pony play—with remarkable frequency and varying degrees of subtlety. In fact, the imagery was in place already at the premiere of the three-act version at the Paris Opera in 1979: while Franz Masura's Schön was writing the letter, he crawled around on all fours in black tie, with Teresa Stratas riding on his back. The same move was then repeated in Götz Friedrich's 1981 staging at the Royal Opera House in London, with Günter Reich and Karan Armstrong as horse and rider.[20] In more recent productions of *Lulu*, it seems to have become almost mandatory. Vera Nemirova's staging at the 2010 Salzburg Festival, to begin with, uses it in a developed form.[21] When Lulu returns backstage after her fainting fit, it is clear that her dance number has been a circus act of sorts: the performers accompanying her include an animal tamer with a riding crop and a strange centaur-like crea-ture whose human torso and horse's legs suggest a porous border between animal and human. Patricia Petibon's Lulu, meanwhile, is wearing a circus-horse hat with a white plume. At first, she plays the horse to Michael Volle's Schön, who brandishes a riding crop and smacks it on the ground where Lulu lies. When the scales tip, he drops the crop, and Lulu picks it up. She grabs his hair with her fist, pushes him down on his knees ("Oh, oh, du tust mir weh!" [Oh, oh, you're hurting me!]) and mounts him while he finishes the letter (fig. 5.4). In the same year, Petibon also sings the Barcelona *Lulu* directed by Py, again grabbing Schön's hair, pushing him to the ground, and riding his back (fig. 5.5).[22] Another instance is William Kentridge's production, which premiered in Amsterdam in 2015 and subsequently was taken to New York and London: on the DVD from the Met production this scene sees Marlis Petersen's Lulu mounting Johan Reuter's Schön (fig. 5.6).[23] In Bechtolf's Zurich version the riding does not happen until the second act, when Schön has already been broken in: Aiken's Lulu, in high heels and nylon stockings, rides her husband while chiding him for his sulky mood and spanking his behind with a rose. Here too, however, it serves to mark erotic agency: the pony play coincides with her insistence that he did not marry her—*she* married *him* (fig. 5.7).

This suite of pony-play scenes constitutes a director's-opera tradition in miniature, repeated with great fidelity despite lacking any connection to Berg's stage directions. The imagery itself, far from being a contemporary invention, was well established when Berg wrote the opera. Sexual science had already started paying attention to it around the fin de siècle: in *Psychopathia Sexualis,* for instance, Krafft-Ebing tells of cases of men who enjoy playing the horse to a riding mistress.[24] In Berlin, Magnus Hirschfeld—who ran the Institute for Sexual Science between 1919 and 1933—found even more extensive material. He listed five types of humiliation commonly desired by his male subjects of study, one of which he termed "zoomimischer Metatropismus" (that is, the inversion of a "natural" male-female relationship through the imitation of animals): "In the well-equipped torture chambers of professional mistresses, we find saddles and reins that are made not for horses, but for people, big muzzles strapped on men who walk on all fours and bark."[25] Correspondingly, the smut culture of Weimar Berlin—in which, as Mel Gordon argues, sadomasochistic scenarios were particularly en vogue—often portrayed human-animal dominance (figs. 5.8, 5.9). These images basically

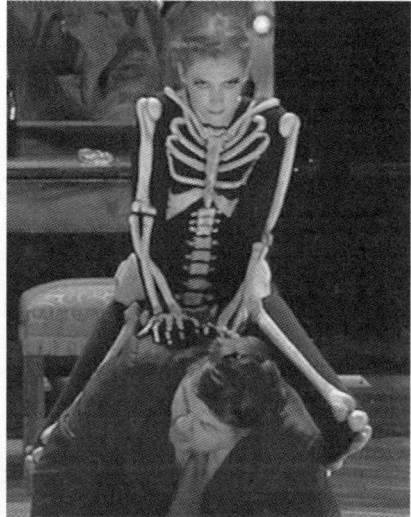

Figures 5.4–7. Dressage domination: Lulu (Patricia Petibon, Marlis Petersen, and Laura Aikin) riding Doctor Schön (Michael Volle, Ashley Holland, Johan Reuter, and Alfred Muff) in recent productions of *Lulu.*

Figures 5.8–9. Step into the menagerie: Pony-play images from Weimar Berlin. Reproduced in Mel Gordon, *Voluptuous Panic: The Erotic World of Weimar Berlin* (Los Angeles: Feral House, 2006).

present an erotic power struggle through the same trope that contemporary directors use for Lulu and Schön, which circulated as pornography in the immediate vicinity of the opera's (planned) premiere venue. *Lulu* thus marks a moment where the later history of opera converges with the iconography of perversion in its early stages, and the pony-play stagings capture it with remarkable consistency.

A CORPUS IN FRAGMENTS

No less insistent than the human-animal role-play is the attempt to turn Lulu into a very particular kind of inanimate object: a work of art. If the newspaper editor Schön and the medical specialist Goll represent the respectable professions of the bourgeois, the Painter and Alwa are artists and no less keen on trying to make Lulu fit their personal desires. Each of them tries to capture her in their own medium: the painter by way of a portrait, the composer by making her a dancer for his cabaret numbers and, later, the topic of an opera. In the productions addressed here, notably, neither the visual nor the audible artworks are content to remain mere representations of Lulu; instead, they are insistently confused with or substituted for her person. This blending of artwork and woman recalls the myth of Pygmalion, the Cypriot sculptor who fashioned an ivory statue so beautiful that he fell in love with it (and married her after Aphrodite had made her come alive). In the stagings discussed here, the artist characters seem to suffer from a Pygmalion complex, obsessed either with fashioning an artwork on the model of Lulu or fashioning Lulu herself according to their aesthetic-erotic taste. Furthermore, this predilection is held up as a mirror to Berg himself and his struggle to complete his second opera.

To begin in the visual end, the Painter is unsurprisingly recast by Bechtolf, Py, and Warlikowski alike as that of a photographer with a vested interest in Lulu's body, and to various degrees, his portrait of her approaches pornographic objectification. In Py's staging the set resembles a European red-light district, where prostitutes and strippers are lit by neon signs with out-of-place messages from highbrow culture ("Mein Herz ist schwer," "schwarze Sonne," "Liebestod" [My heart is heavy, black sun, lovedeath]). The portrait scene in the first act becomes a photo session, which ends when the Painter strips Lulu of her ballerina dress (Petibon is wearing a nude suit) and ties her up. In Warlikowski's Brussels production the portrait is represented by an onstage video screen, showing (moving) images of Hannigan's Lulu posing by herself or with wild animals. Although there is no nudity here, the visual codes of the video portrait are overtly pornographic: Lulu wears minimal lingerie, a blonde wig, heavy makeup, and a diamond leather collar, and we see her licking her lips in slow-motion, sensuously tonguing a bear claw, standing on all fours, lying on her back with legs spread, and so forth. The camera's use of close-ups—on her wide eyes, on her feet—aligns itself with stereotypically fetishist camerawork, as diagnosed by Laura Mulvey. The screen, as it were, assists the gaze of the spectator in dividing Lulu's body into a set of dispersed objects. This visual dismemberment is perhaps most notable in the image of her twitching legs sticking out of the mouth of a giant crocodile: one snap of the jaws, as it were, would push the segmentation from the symbolic into gory reality. In this portrait Lulu is neither dominant mistress nor tamed beast but the prey of a predator.

The threat of dismemberment is given a far more central role in Sven-Eric Bechtolf's mise-en-scène from 2002, to which I will now turn my attention in more detail. The production not only took place in the same house as the 1937 premiere; it also made use of the same version of the score: the two acts finished by Berg, followed by the Variations and Adagio from the *Lulu Suite*. Some twenty years after Cerha's completion, *Lulu* became the focus of a growing interest in the unfinished and fragmentary, and Bechtolf's production was among the first manifestations.[26] Bechtolf's interpretation places emphasis on Lulu as a victim of child abuse, perpetrated by Doctor Schön: a young girl appears frequently on stage, as Lulu's former self. By developing this biographical backstory, merely hinted at in the libretto, Bechtolf seeks to make Lulu more of a person than an idea: "It is clear to see that there is a certain bias for Lulu, and a certain interest in pulling her out of the realm of the eternally feminine and allowing her to become human."[27] Even so, Lulu's humanity is challenged in various ways, not least by the artists who work on her, be they fictional characters or the actual architects of the production.

While less overtly pornographic than Py's Barcelona version, the Zurich production is not necessarily less committed to visual objectification. Like Warlikowski in Brussels, Bechtolf invites the camera to participate in the segmentation of Lulu's body. All the interludes are accompanied by black-and-white film sequences, spattered with scratches and dust dots to evoke the silent-film era from which the opera dates. We see close-up shots from the scenes that have just been played out: the head and breasts of the mannequin, Lulu's feet (tied up), Lulu's armpits (caressed by the razorblade), Lulu's thighs (stroked by the scissors). The blades, juxtaposed with the isolated body parts through rapid cuts, explicitly connect the fetishist gaze to fantasies of dissection and dismemberment. Lulu's portrait is represented by four transparent boxes, each containing a section of a mannequin: head, armless torso, hips, and legs are stacked up to form a statue, nude except for the same glittering flapper-style skull cap

Figure 5.10. "My husband will be here soon." Lulu (Laura Aikin), the Painter (Steve Davislim), and her portrait in the shape of a fragmented mannequin. *Lulu* (dir. Sven-Eric Bechtolf, Opernhaus Zürich, 2002).

worn by Lulu (fig. 5.10). From the first scene, a confusion between Lulu the person and her image—a set of dead objects—is emphasized: the Painter (a cross-dresser in this production, wearing a corset and silk stockings under the black suit) appears to be working on the former rather than the latter. He and Schön adjust Lulu's position, tie her feet and even shave her armpits, and as Schön remarks to the Painter, "Das Haar ist schlecht. Sie sind nicht genügend bei der Sache" (The hair is bad. You are not sufficiently engaged in your work), he runs his hand across Lulu's head, not that of the "portrait." The Painter applies thick red brushstrokes on her torso, suggesting the murder to come, and just after cutting out the breasts of a nude photo, he caresses her legs with a big pair of scissors. After her return from prison in the second act, Lulu has had her head shaved to resemble that of the mannequin. Her body, in other words, is molded in the portrait's image rather than the other way around—and because that image is nothing but a loose assemblage of aestheticized or eroticized objects, this molding comes with an insistent threat of mutilation.

Musical representation plays an even more prominent role in *Lulu* than the visual kind, one that is no less geared toward the erotic. Alwa, who is just as infatuated with Lulu as his father, Doctor Schön, was conceived as a musical self-portrait; not only did Berg refashion Wedekind's playwright character into a composer, but he also clearly suggested that he is the composer of the very opera we are hearing: in the final scene of the first act Berg quotes the snare-drum roll and string glissandi from the opening bars of *Wozzeck,* just before letting Alwa ponder the possibilities and problems of writing an opera about Lulu. By the end of act 2, work appears to be well on the way, because the Athlete lambastes him for the perverse nature of the piece: "Sie haben eine Schauderoper geschrieben, in der die Waden meiner Braut die beiden Hauptfiguren sind, und das kein Hoftheater zur Aufführung bringt. Sie Nachtjacke Sie! Sie Schnodderlumpen!!" (You have written a horror opera, where the calves of my bride play the lead roles and which no theater will ever put on. You lunatic, you! You snot rag!!) The implication, of course, is that Alwa is half Alban. If the former is in some way responsible for composing the opera he is in, his case is also one of pygmalionism: he himself has created the object of his own desire.

Alwa is not the only character in *Lulu* to claim responsibility for the opera, nor is he the first. When the Animal Tamer introduces the opera with the promise of lust and dread, he does so to Alwa's music, the principal theme from the Rondo of the second act. In Perle's words: "Thus the Animal Tamer, inviting the audience to see the beasts in his menagerie, is identified with the composer, Alwa."[28] The musical link—subtle but quite audible for those acquainted with the opera—confirms that the opera we are about to see is, in some sense, his work. In Bechtolf's staging, however, the association between the composer and the characters does not stop with Alwa and the Animal Tamer. In fact, Lulu's male admirers are all curiously alike. The Medical Specialist, the Painter, the Athlete, Schön, the Student, and Alwa all wear the same costume and the same hair: a black silk suit and dark, glossy, well-combed hair. The coiffure is readily identifiable as Alban Berg's own, as seen on every extant photo of him as an adult. Lulu, it would appear, is surrounded by an army of enamored composers who vainly attempt to dominate her. On her own part she

Figure 5.11. "You knew why you took me as your wife, just as well as I knew why I took you as my husband." Lulu (Laura Aikin) singing her centerpiece aria, "Lied der Lulu." *Lulu* (dir. Sven-Eric Bechtolf, Opernhaus Zürich, 2002).

changes outfits as frequently as she changes lovers, but at her crucial moment of self-expression ("Das Lied der Lulu"), her evening gown is graced by a giant, glittering treble clef (fig. 5.11). As she asks Alwa-Alban's opinion of this dress, he replies: "Deine Schneiderin kennt dich offenbar besser als ich—mir erlauben darf, dich zu kennen" (Your seamstress obviously knows you better than I—may allow myself to know you). In this staging his witticism reveals not only jealousy of the carnal (or at least corporeal) knowledge suggested by the close-fitting dress but also the fact that the soprano clef is a sign of her bodily self. Another droll image of the same notion occurs when the Athlete brags about his muscles: Aikin's Lulu seems to approve of his biceps, but shooting up to a high D on the phrase "Wenn Sie nur nicht so lange Ohren hätten" (If only you didn't have such long ears), she grabs his ear and twists it until he squirms in pain. The coloratura is her instrument of domination: identifying his ears as a weak spot, her top notes hit them with unfailing precision, puncturing his inflated masculinity (fig. 5.12).

Figure 5.12. "If only your ears were not so long." Lulu (Laura Aikin) twisting the ear of the acrobat (Rolf Haunstein) while hitting her high note. *Lulu* (dir. Sven-Eric Bechtolf, Opernhaus Zürich, 2002).

The first music Alwa writes for Lulu serves an explicitly erotic purpose: when his father puts her to work as a cabaret dancer, he does so to display her as a sexual object. Her first two husbands are dead, and the task of Alwa's dance music is to find her a third. Alwa's inner Animal Tamer thus reappears as Snake Charmer: his music makes the serpent move seductively. When he, in spite of this, objects to her being abducted, she reminds him: "Sie haben ja doch die Musik dazu komponiert. Es gehen schon einige da unten ganz ernstlich mit sich zu Rate. Ich fühle das, ohne dass ich hinsehe." (But you wrote the music for it. There are already people down there thinking seriously about it. I can feel it without looking.) The stunned Alwa asks, "Wie können Sie denn das fühlen?" (How can you feel that?), and she describes how "Es läuft einem so ein eisiger Schauer am Körper herauf—und wieder hinunter" (It runs like an icy shiver up one's body—and back down again). Berg set this line as an extended chromatic ascent where the soprano part covers all pitches from E4 to C♯6, climaxing with a coloratura trill on the word *herauf* before plunging two full octaves on the words *und wieder hinunter* (example 5.1).[29]

Example 5.1. Alban Berg, *Lulu*, act 1, bars 1068–1076.

These last three words are not in Wedekind's original text, so presumably Berg added the descent when working on the libretto to make possible the conspicuous word-painting and thereby define Lulu's frisson as musical.[30] If she can feel the desire of the audience without looking, it is because she listens. What she hears and feels is Alwa's music, which casts her in the role of the desired seductress. The music *is* her body: it can no more be separated from her limbs than could a shiver of pleasure. In Bechtolf's staging, Aikin's Lulu kneels before Alwa while singing this phrase, running her hands from his crotch to his chest as she ascends and then down again. An autoerotic circuit is created: if her bodily sensation is musically scripted by Berg, her caresses send it back to his onstage alter ego, who gratefully displays his most rapt o-face as she does so. Meanwhile, the audience of Lulu's cabaret number, whose desire is described as the source of her tingling sensation, mirrors the actual audience of the opera, just as Berg is mirrored by Alwa.

The most striking image of Alwa's idea of Lulu as music emerges at the end of the second act. Here, he returns to Lulu's dress and its suggestive way of presenting her body: "Durch dieses Kleid empfinde ich Deinen Wuchs wie Musik" (Through this dress, I feel your shape like music). In the body he desires the composer sees only the material that his genius was born to desire and control. The hymn that follows moves successively upward from her feet until the goal is reached and the hymn climaxes:

> Durch dieses Kleid empfinde ich Deinen Wuchs wie Musik. Diese Knöchel: ein Grazioso; dieses reizende Anschwellen: ein Cantabile; diese Knie: ein Misterioso; und das gewaltige Andante der Wollust. Wie friedlich sich die beiden schlanken Rivalen in dem Bewusstsein aneinanderschmiegen, dass keiner dem andern an Schönheit gleichkommt, bis die launische Gebieterin erwacht, und die beiden Nebenbuhler wie zwei Pole auseinanderweichen. Ich werde Dein Lob singen, dass Dir die Sinne vergehen.

> Through this dress, I feel your body as music. These ankles: a Grazioso; this alluring swell: a Cantabile; these knees: a Misterioso; and the powerful Andante of pleasure. How peacefully the slender rivals slip against each other, knowing that neither can match the other's beauty, until the fickle mistress awakes and the two contenders slide apart like two poles. I will sing your praises until your senses fade.

Figure 5.13. "I feel your body as music." Alwa (Peter Straka) finds himself mesmerized by Lulu's portrait, while ignoring her person. *Lulu* (dir. Sven-Eric Bechtolf, Opernhaus Zürich, 2002).

It takes no more than a modicum of taste to cringe at Alwa's erotic poetry.[31] As farcical as it is, however, it partakes in the sinister aspects of the opera. It deliberately parodies the tradition of lyrical dismemberment that we have seen in *Don Giovanni* and elsewhere. Here, too, the rhetorical fragmentation of the female body foreshadows its literal mutilation. The Zurich production reinforces the point by letting Lulu's disassembled portrait take her place: while he is singing the hymn, Alwa is entirely focused on the four boxes with the mannequin's body parts. In the transition that leads up to the hymn, Berg's score instructs him to look at her portrait, while the four chords associated with the picture are heard.[32] In Bechtolf's production this glance is amplified into an obsessive gaze. During the whole scene, Alwa is unable to tear himself away from the dismembered mannequin: he carries the boxes off one by one and places them on the floor, where he kneels to praise them, ignoring Lulu's attempts to pull him away and persuade him to elope with her (fig. 5.13). The plastic limbs eclipse Lulu the living woman: Alwa is mesmerized by her precisely to the extent that she is transformed into a collection of inanimate objects.

Immediately behind this imaginary dismemberment lurks the actual violence soon to be directed at Lulu's body. Bechtolf is keen on reminding his audience of this fact: throughout, her flesh is repeatedly grazed by scissors, razors, and knives. Since the Zurich production uses the two-act version of the score, the scene with Alwa's poetic dismemberment of Lulu is immediately literalized as physical violence. This scene marks the end of the opera proper, and all that remains is the death of Lulu at the hands of Jack the Ripper. A direct link is thus forged between the hymn that metaphorically fragments Lulu's body and the violence that does so literally, to the accompaniment of the Adagio from the *Lulu Suite*. The passage between these two scenes is the moment of the actuality effect, when the eroticized power and violence that have hitherto been presented as role-play and rhetoric break out into reality. The transition between these scenes, to the Variations movement, is a film sequence where the blades go from grazing the surface to slashing flesh: to the naive tune of Wedekind's cabaret song, uncannily distorted by Berg's polytonal and dodecaphonic variations, we see the razor cutting through a lipstick and pieces of raw meat wrapped in newspaper. Just as in Tcherniakov's *Wozzeck*, the violence is visualized by the application of makeup: a man's hands are seen painting the mouth of a woman in close-up, until suddenly blood gushes from between her lips. As the image of the cut-up body is forced onto the body of the real woman, symbolic segmentation is, once again, made physically manifest as brutality. The final stage image, where the murder of Lulu and her prepubescent double takes place, is dominated by the four boxes containing the female body parts. After throwing Lulu's dead body into an enormous pile of newspapers—like another piece of meat—Jack picks up the head and haunches of the mannequin and carries them off in a bag, while the breasts and feet remain on stage (fig. 5.14).

The visual language in Bechtolf's staging clearly taps into the misogynistic undercurrents of the opera, dwelling on the simultaneous admiration and mutilation of the female body. Insofar as Bechtolf's production sets out to make Lulu human, it does so only to subject her to dehumanization: we see her prepubescent alter ego murdered, the implication being that the adult Lulu has been dead all along. She is consistently equated with her mannequin double and reduced to so many shapely pieces of plastic. This visual fragmentation, moreover, is interlaced with the musi-

Figure 5.14. The final scene of the Zurich *Lulu:* Jack (Alfred Muff) picking up the mannequin's haunches before he leaves. *Lulu* (dir. Sven-Eric Bechtolf, Opernhaus Zürich, 2002).

cal fragmentation: to the composer and his clones, she represents the musical material that is there to be tamed by human genius. The power struggle between the lover-as-composer and Lulu-as-embodied-music is also a struggle between two conceptions of opera: on the one hand as an object—the score in which the modernist composer controls every detail— and on the other as the living performance in which the soprano's voice usurps the authorial position. When Bechtolf shows us Schön as one of Berg's doubles, sneaking around the stage trying to guard his Lulu from the influence of other pretenders, what we see is a vision of the power struggle between operatic agencies. Instead of occupying an elevated position from which he may discipline the onstage bodies—pulling the strings of his puppet performers—the composer has been drawn into his own menagerie, where he needs to fight for his survival while the audience watches and listens with hot lust and cold dread. Like Berg himself, however, the composer clones all die before the third act is finished. When Lulu, cast as the living embodiment of music, rides, spanks, and disciplines her lovers, the vocal performer is in power. At the climax of the second act, this playful dominance turns into real violence, as she kills her husband while wearing the soprano-clef evening gown. When he comes back to murder her, conversely, the male collective of composer lookalikes takes its revenge on the unsurpassable dominance of the high soprano voice, which dies with its famous last scream (emitted in this performance by Lulu herself as Jack slits the throat of her child revenant). The body of music, incorporated by Lulu and doubled by the girl and the mannequin, is cut to pieces. While the two pieces from the *Lulu Suite* stand in for the fragmented corpus of the third act, the murdered child and two pieces of Lulu-the-mannequin's dismembered body remain in their boxes on stage as the curtain falls.

HOW HUMAN IS HANNIGAN?

"I'm a creative animal," says Lulu interpreter Barbara Hannigan. "I don't feel like a female human being when I'm in the creative space. I feel more like a changeable animal. I can flip from being a bird to a wolf to a horse, whatever. It just feels natural for me, to have that animal quality instead of the human quality."[33] Fittingly seated astride a horse while doing the interview, Hannigan evokes the human-animal border for a purpose different from what we have seen so far. The conversation seems casual and the musings offhand, but even so, it is worth asking what "that animal quality" means. It certainly evokes empowerment rather than subservience and perhaps the idea of natural enjoyment rather than self-aware intellect (at least while the music is happening). Above all, however, the emphasis is on the creative metamorphosis and the refusal to be locked into a particular genus or species. Creating music, her comment suggests, is a sort of role-play in itself: it makes one *feel* the freedom of the shapeshifter.

If Hannigan evokes the nonhuman here, critics more typically speak of her as superhuman—a label she has earned by her interest in music that challenges the limits of the vocally possible, which she executes with flawless technique and vivid musicianship, often while simultaneously conducting the performance. Even so, she is shocked by labels like "fearless," "extra-terrestrial," or "superhuman": "I am terribly human, and I am filled with fear."[34] The point is not the self-evident fact of Hannigan being human but that this humanness is connected to the musician's métier: "It's kind of nice to read those things," she acknowledges, "but on the other hand I find it frustrating, because I work very hard, and I prepare very hard, and I think that is the core of what I do. It's the disciplined work."[35] Labeling the performance superhuman tends to dissimulate the rigorous labor that makes possible the move from human fear to the shapeshifter's sense of freedom. Ultimately, what lies behind the seeming paradox of the terribly human and the exhilaratingly animal is the same dialectics pinpointed by Adorno apropos of *Lulu:* at its utmost extreme, virtuoso training can transmute into an expression of boundless enjoyment. The domesticized *Ziergesang* enacts a feral *Tiergesang.*

In the remainder of this chapter I will approach some of Hannigan's performances, and her own comments on them, from this perspective. What is human about opera has nothing to do with lofty metaphysics but with its physical basis in the singing body, its freedoms and constraints, its pleasures and pains. It is from that platform that Hannigan's musicianship allows her to role-play different subject positions in relation to the human. In so doing, she simultaneously evokes and dislodges some of the most insistent tropes of operatic performance and their assumptions about power, agency, and gender—and by now it should come as no surprise that notions of dominance and submission are entangled in those tropes or that the iconography of perversion figures in their onstage representation.

First, we will hear what Hannigan has to say about Lulu. In how far is she a helpless, objectified victim caught in a misogynist story? Hannigan is resolute in her view: "It's about an extraordinary woman, who is, in my opinion, the architect of her own destiny. Even, in my opinion, of her own death."[36] In a talk given at the Southbank Centre the year after the premiere of Warlikowski's production, she emphatically rejects the image of Lulu as a manipulative man-eater who is degraded and finally murdered: "She is one of the most honest people I have ever met, on or off stage. I love her, because she is true to herself, she forces others to see her for who she is." On this view Lulu becomes an image of the free human subject, unswerving in her self-assertion and self-control. What Hannigan voices is the polar opposite of the process of depersonalization that has been the focus of this chapter so far. "What does it feel like to sing Lulu?" Hannigan asks herself: "It feels like my whole body is shaking with resonance. It feels like I become the sound of humanity. It is exhilarating and it is extremely satisfying in a physical way." The *jouissance* of performance is what opens the door to the trope of voice as an index of the liberated and universal subject (and perhaps especially so when the performed role shares some basic identities with the performer—in this case, say, Western, white, female). Then again, the move from the individually to the universally human resembles the move to horse, bird, or wolf. Here, too, the phrase is "feels like": the universality is no more literal than the animality. Like the nonhuman, the panhuman is a role to which Hannigan's musicianship gives her access.

The idea of Lulu's humanity permeates Hannigan's discourse to the extent that she speaks of the character as a person of flesh and blood, for whom she declares an unconditional loyalty. The terms she chooses, however, suggest that the relationship is complicated:

> As you know, Stockholm syndrome is when a captive begins to identify in a positive way with her captor. In my case, I felt like Lulu took me hostage from the moment I signed the contract in 2008. She invaded me, and she took over my mind and my heart and my soul, and I eventually fell in love with her. She lay beside me in bed at night, she woke me up, she was in my dreams, and she became the spring in my step. She became my reason for moving, for looking after myself, and I ended up wanting to defend her to the ends of the earth.

Although these metaphors are doubtlessly tongue-in-cheek, they clearly resonate with the sinister undertones of the opera itself. The position to which Hannigan rhetorically subscribes is also one of unambiguous submission. Having signed the contract, she is essentially at the mercy of a mistress who has taken possession of her not just mentally—mind, heart, soul—but also physically.

Perhaps this is related to the fact that Hannigan first sang Lulu in Warlikowski's production. The Brussels production strongly highlights this bodily control by the prominence it gives to dancing (the choreography is by French dancer and movement director Claude Bardouil). Here, Lulu's dancing in Alwa's show is developed into an ambition to become a classical ballet dancer. In addition to the aforementioned flirtation with pornographic imagery, the ballet theme often dominates the bodies and attire on stage. If the coloratura virtuosity places extreme demands on vocal discipline, this notion is mirrored here by the ballet, which represents a similar extreme in terms of corporeal motion. Hannigan, always excelling in the former, now got a taste of the latter: "So I'm forty-one and I was going on point for the first time. It hurt like hell, and I loved it. I couldn't wait to lace up every morning. And after performances, sometimes we even had a doctor in my dressing room to administer the next prescription for my infected feet. It was fantastic. I could hardly walk." Pushing the body to its limits can be as painful as it is pleasurable. Hannigan's choice of words here is not just suggestive of submission but explicitly tinged with masochism: bodily constraints and physical pain are met with unbridled love and enthusiasm. Perhaps this can be understood as part of her solidarity with her character: in the Brussels production Lulu's willingness to subject herself to pain does not end with tight lacing and hurting feet. She is, as Hannigan says, presented as the architect of her own destiny and death. When she picks up Jack the Ripper as her third customer, it is thus "a conscious choice—and at the end, instead of him murdering her, she takes his hand and, smiling, she drives his knife into her body." If she, as Hannigan puts it, is the architect of her own death, that death may not seem entirely unlike that of the masochistic Scarpia from the previous chapter. Yet the gendered power positions differ enough to give us pause: while his desire to be stabbed comes from a position of absolute power and control, hers comes from absolute desperation and dependence. Indeed, the Stockholm syndrome may be the only apt term for a character making the "conscious choice" of being murdered.

Intentionally or not, the vocabulary Hannigan uses evokes an eros of dominance and submission: a love that surrenders to complete control, an enthusiasm for sensations of pain and bodily restrictions, an extreme physical satisfaction. In one sense these observations have less to do with Hannigan than with the way in which operatic performance repeatedly attracts the imagery of SM in various ways. This attraction occurs for a reason: it simultaneously resonates both with the violence and eroticism carried by the plot and with the bodily discipline and sensuality of operatic singing. Beyond supplying another example of this point, however, Hannigan's unique versatility makes her an instructive example in another way. In her musicianship she inhabits an unusually wide range of positions with respect to the power, agency, and gender at issue here. In the passages quoted above, Hannigan loyally ascribes dominance and agency to the character of Lulu, positing herself as submissive (which, again, is not the same as passive). But what about the other agents involved in opera? "I spend most of my life singing music written by men," says Hannigan. "I am a muse to many composers, most of them male. They work out their demons on me, or so we hope. Alban Berg certainly did so on Lulu. I feel like, when I am singing those characters, I am not just that character, I am also the composer. I am their voice." Whether we think of this image as the composer's mind invading the singer's body or as the singer usurping the authorial position is less important here than the mere fact of their symbiotic coexistence: Hannigan suggests that vocal performance effects a merging of gendered subject positions, where female character and male composer blend into the same body.

She says something similar about her work as a conductor: "I chose . . . one of the few careers where I have absolutely no male competition. I am a soprano. And now . . . I am expanding into the field of conducting, which is completely dominated by men. It's a strange combination. Fortunately, in making music, as far as I'm concerned, I can be both male and female. There is no gender to sound." If there is indeed no gender to sound, which is debatable, there is all the more of it in the music world. Despite the rise of female conductors to stardom in recent years—Marin Alsop, Susanna Mälkki, Simone Young, and others—the dominance noted by Hannigan is still undeniable and still reflected by misogynist dismissals of female conductors.[37] Inevitably, therefore, Hannigan's simultaneous work as a soprano and a conductor attracts the notion of inhabiting distinct gender positions—"I can be both male and female"—and makes it necessary to claim that sound lacks gender (or at least that it ought to). Hannigan's comments suggest that her performances cannot be understood as *independent* from the tenacious gender roles of the music world but rather as working dialectically *with* and *against* them. Nowhere is this strategy clearer than in the performances where Hannigan simultaneously sings and conducts. These concerts, I would argue, need to be understood as a kind of music theater—not primarily because they involve operatic music but because they make the conductor and the soprano visible *as* roles, symbolically charged with their respective configurations of power and agency, yet exchangeable and combinable. If the Brussels *Parsifal* amounted to a rehearsal of a stereotypically gendered power dynamic—whether construed as endorsing or criticizing it—the conducting soprano completely changes the rules of the game.

I first attended such a performance at the Lucerne Festival during the summer of 2015, when the theme of the festival was "PrimaDonna," with a concomitant focus on female soloists, conductors, and composers. Here, Hannigan performed the *Lulu Suite* while leading the Mahler Chamber Orchestra. Singing the centerpiece of the suite—the "Lied der Lulu"—she turned her back to the orchestra yet continued to give cues and tempo. The move was not only theatrical but a kind of minimal staging of the actuality effect in reverse: facing the audience and starting to sing, the conductor became an opera character, half-crossing the boundary into the fiction. This song is Lulu's most clearly stated self-justification. It is the moment when she objects to the husband who wants her to die, when she voices her own human value and asserts her authenticity. When Hannigan simultaneously inhabited the roles of the character and the conductor, the incontrovertible impression was that Lulu also partook in the agency and authority of the conductor. If not just the voice but also the orchestral sound resounded as an extension of Hannigan's body, that was also the body of Lulu, in unerring control of herself and all those surrounding her. At that moment in the concert hall the reading of Lulu as an object, a victim, or a surface for the projected fantasy of others seemed irredeemably false. There was simply no way this role, embodied by Hannigan in this way, was experientially commensurable with such a reduction of Lulu. Instead, all musical agency in the room was concentrated in her person, which dominated every other entity involved in the production and reception of the piece: the audience, the orchestra, and even the composer seemed to yield to the redoubled physical and sensual authority inherent in the rare conflation of vocalist and conductor.

A description of the performance in such terms does indeed constitute a projection of a fantasy onto Lulu, Hannigan, and the concert situation itself. My own experience of the concert certainly drew on received tropes of singing as subjectivity, conducting as control, and my previous experiences of the productions discussed in this book. Also, the multilayered

Figure 5.15. "Pssst! Much discretion—close observation." Gepopo (Barbara Hannigan) singing and conducting the Mahler Chamber Orchestra in György Ligeti's *Mysteries of the Macabre.*

superimposition of roles (singer, conductor, character), or the physical sensuality of live music, does not necessarily have to be presented as a dynamic of dominance and submission. But the fact is that Hannigan herself has done just that—and not just verbally in interviews (as above) but also visually in performance. In her celebrated renditions of György Ligeti's *The Mysteries of the Macabre*—the first piece that she began simultaneously singing and conducting—she goes on stage in a black trench coat, playing the opera character whose pieces Ligeti extracted from *Le Grand Macabre* to form the *Mysteries:* Gepopo, the paranoid chief of the secret police, who only speaks in code. At the words "Pst! Pst! Much discretion!" she rids herself of the coat, revealing a black fetish-style ensemble: corset-style top, fishnet stockings and black high-heel boots. In full dominatrix attire Hannigan's Gepopo instructs—dominates—the musicians in the ensemble with laser-like precision while singing the mind-bogglingly difficult vocal part (fig. 5.15).

Like Hannigan's evocation of the Stockholm syndrome and the pleasure of pain, the Ligeti performance is above all meant to be playful, amusing: "I trust the audience that they know that it's, you know, that it's a joke, right? . . . It's a parody. So even when I'm playing somebody sexy, you know, they know that I'm making fun of it. I'm making fun of this whole outfit, I'm making fun of myself, I'm making fun of classical music."[38] The droll impression, however, does not preclude serious questions. Which aspects, specifically, are being parodied here? Perhaps, for instance, it is the erotically fascinating fascism observed by Susan Sontag. Hannigan's Gepopo—whose name is of course modeled on Gestapo—can be understood as a spoof on the kinkiness stereotypically associated with leather-boot Nazi officers in popular culture. Beyond this, however, the performance also mocks the gendered power position of the conductor. Dressed up like this, Hannigan illustrates that the commands and gestures of leading an orchestra are explicitly involved in the enactment of an eroticized power exchange. Evoking the iconography of perversion, she furnishes the authority of the conductor, the disciplined sensuality of operatic singing, and the bodily control of musicmaking with a visual metaphor on stage. The performance is designed to impress through virtuosity, and as the label of the superhuman suggests, it succeeds. Hannigan stages herself as musician in absolute control, while the dominatrix attire hints at the eroticization of that control.

Even more than her performance of the *Lulu Suite*, that of the *Mysteries* flaunts the fact that a concert performance is no less staged than one at the opera house. But it is less a staging of a specific operatic scene than an operatic staging of classical musicmaking itself. The ensemble plays musicians while also playing subordinates, just as Hannigan plays a conductor while also playing a paranoid dominatrix. Compared to the examples approached in the preceding chapter, where the operatic characters were "playing" singers, conductors, and producers, the same imaginary border is crossed from the opposite direction: it is now the actual conductor-and-singer who is "playing" an operatic character. There, the labor of music-making was inserted into the operatic fiction. Here, an element of operatic fiction appears on the concert stage, which usually displays only the labor of musicmaking. The crossing of a boundary is just as marked as the actuality effect in my other examples, but it moves from the actual to the acted rather than the other way around. First, a concert without theatrical or fictional elements is established, as Hannigan performs Mozart, Rossini, and Fauré in an evening gown. She is a concert performer, and the musicians are musicians. It is only for the last number that she dons the latex attire, thus letting a theater of perversion encroach on the concert situation. Unlike most examples I have been discussing in this book, there is no element of abuse or violence but the foregrounding of and playing-around with the volatile border between the fictional character (the dominatrix chief of police) and the real-life musician (the soprano singing and the conductor conducting) remains, as does the portrayal of music-making as an asymmetric power dynamic.

If one takes the visual cue of this "staging" and pursues the analogy between operatic performance and SM play, Hannigan's passage between various operatic "roles" would appear as the equivalent of the idealized idea of free negotiation of identity and polymorphous pleasure. In BDSM lingo Hannigan's versatility would be precisely that of an operatic "switch": taking on the tasks of the singer, conductor, and director of the performance—even, in some sense, becoming the composer—she inhabits a multitude of different roles, which are typically not only separated but also distributed along axes of gender, power, and agency. From this perspective the performance does not so much exist independently of these roles (in which case the parody would not have hit its mark) as it unhinges and juggles them with dizzying skill. By treating them as exchangeable and combinable roles rather than as given identities, she effectively subverts the gendered norms that still linger in the world of classical music. In this sense Hannigan is indeed a musical shapeshifter.

In the program book for the 2016 Lucerne festival—where Hannigan performed the *Lulu Suite*—the organizers state: "For not until women who conduct, play music, or compose are no longer seen as the exception but become a normal daily experience will objective judgements of artistic achievements be possible."[39] Seeing and hearing Hannigan sing and conduct is unlikely to ever become unexceptional. But precisely by way of their extreme character (and the semiviral attention they attract), performances like her *Lulu Suite* or her dominatrix *Mysteries of the Macabre* will, in a concrete way, make the mere fact of a female conductor seem more normal. These performances underline that what is unique about Barbara Hannigan is not that she is a woman leading an orchestra but that she pushes the physical boundaries of what can be done with music. And she does so not through any superhuman gifts but through an unswerving disciplining of the human body—both her own and her orchestra's—which simultaneously delivers intense pleasure and expands the notion of what the human body can do and be. If her renditions of the *Mysteries* are thus, in a sense, genuinely subversive, it must also be said that if this aspect had been the main point of the performance, the subversion would have failed. Its effectiveness depends entirely on the fact that the pleasure of music is the driving force of the performance or, to paraphrase Hannigan, the fact that singing opera—and, by extension, hearing it—can make the body shake with resonance and deliver the extreme physical satisfaction of perceiving oneself, for a moment, as the sound of humanity.

Epilogue

In a word, we believe there are living powers in what is
called poetry, and that the picture of a crime presented in
the right stage conditions is something infinitely more
dangerous to the mind than if the same crime were
committed in life. We want to make theatre a believable
reality inflicting this kind of tangible laceration, contained
in all true feeling, on the heart and senses.

Antonin Artaud, "Theatre and Cruelty"

The cruelty of deviant opera is of a different species than the one famously
envisioned by Antonin Artaud. Beyond the obvious fact that he was promoting an imagined form of performance rather than critically examining
an existing one, Artaud was careful to point out that he took little interest in
the representation of a literal cruelty. Cruelty, Artaud suggested, is "not synonymous with bloodshed, martyred flesh or crucified enemies"; it is "not a
matter of vicious cruelty, cruelty proliferating with perverted desires."[1] Even
though a staging of one of Marquis de Sade's works was among the envisioned projects, he employed the term in a much broader sense than it has
in everyday usage, referring to a quality that he considered inherent in life.
Consciousness itself, he argued, "gives practising any act in life a blood-red
tinge, its cruel overtones, since it is understood that being alive always
means the death of someone else."[2] From this perspective cruelty is a "hun-
gering after life, cosmic strictness, relentless necessity, in the Gnostic
sense of a living vortex engulfing darkness, in the sense of the inescapably
necessary pain without which life could not continue."[3] Deviant opera,

however, has less to do with Artaud's surrealist metaphysics than with physical representations of concrete power, violence, and eroticism. If there is a significant point of contact to be found, it lies elsewhere—namely, in the insistence on the potential reality of performance: deviant opera, like the theater of cruelty, seeks a "theatre that wakes us up, heart and nerves," whose value lies in "the agonizing magic relationship to reality and danger."[4]

The overarching claim of this book has been that the opera productions it discusses, understood together, make the suggestion that opera is akin to SM. To summarize the foundations of this supposed affinity, I pointed in the first chapter to a number of overlaps or analogies between the two practices: their hyperbolic, self-consciously theatrical quality, their obsession with gendered power asymmetries and eroticism, their intense corporeality permeated by plots and symbols, their inherent promise of pleasure and concomitant risk of unpleasure, and the resulting need for both verbal and nonverbal communication and critical negotiation. The mise-en-scènes discussed in this book (and others like them) bring these aspects to the fore. But as the succeeding chapters have devoted closer interpretative attention to a number of operatic works, productions, and performances, a more specific analogy has gradually taken shape: when opera is staged as SM, it shows a proclivity for overstepping certain boundaries *within* its theatrical space, which evokes an overstepping of the boundaries *surrounding* that theatrical space as well. This is what I have tried to pin down by calling it "the actuality effect." It is borne out by the repeated tendency of the addressed stagings to deploy SM imagery in a move from the figurative evocation of suffering to its literal manifestation on stage (on the first level), from the fiction-within-the-fiction to the diegetic reality (on the second level), and from enacted diegesis to the involvement of the real selves of the performers (on the third level). These productions, therefore, present opera as analogous to SM not only to emphasize its intertwinement of power, violence, gender, and desire but also to hint at the possibility that those dark undercurrents are in some sense *for real*, that they could overflow the boundaries of theatrical space. From this perspective deviant stagings are preoccupied with a longing for authenticity on behalf of opera; their focus of attention is precisely theater's relation to reality and danger.

It is instructive in this respect to compare deviant opera with performance art that works with suffering as a means of expression. Since the
1970s there has been a steady presence of artists subjecting their bodies
to actual pain: Marina Abramović, Chris Burden, Carlos Martiel, Adriana
Disman, and many others have hurt themselves in the name of their art.[5]
Abramović summarizes the rationale of this art—or at least her own—in
an interview from 2010: "To be a performance artist, you have to hate
theatre. Theatre is fake, there is a black box, you pay for a ticket, and you
sit in the dark and see somebody playing somebody else's life. The knife is
not real, the blood is not real, and the emotions are not real. Performance
is just the opposite: the knife is real, the blood is real, and the emotions are
real."[6] A concept of performance that rejects all role-play as fake is inimical
not only to theater but to both opera and BDSM as a safe, sane, and consensual practice. Real knives never come near Carmen or Scarpia, and stories like that of Jon Vickers or Maria Callas drawing blood from their colleagues fortunately remain exceptions. Real emotion is the mortal enemy
of a controlled production of vocal tone and timbre. Yet opera's insistent
staging of the actuality effect bespeaks a longing for the real that is related
to that expressed by Abramović. With reference to his Komische Oper
Entführung, Calixto Bieito said: "For me, the stage is no set, something
made presentable, but an installation of reality. For instance, if I want
jeans on stage, I don't fetch something that looks like jeans. It is about life
and death."[7] If we bracket the difference between real denim and real
blades, this rationale has a particular resonance in contemporary culture.

Painting with the broadest possible brush, one might say that modernity has seen art edge from representation of cruelty to simulation of
cruelty and, more recently, to arrive at the threshold of a presentation of
cruelty. From Ancient Greece onward, the representation of violence in
premodern art was almost always governed by strict taboos and styliza-
tions, whereas in the real world executions and torture regularly served as
public entertainment. As Enlightenment values took hold, modernity
largely expelled the display of real cruelty from the public sphere, and a
taboo was put on state-sanctioned torture in general (at least officially). At
the same time, the taboos governing the aesthetic representation of cruelty gradually loosened, and art became open to a simulation of cruelty.
Once gallows and guillotines had disappeared from the town squares, vio-

lence eventually reappeared with ever-greater realism on theater stages as well as in movie theaters and video games. Today, one of art's many responses to a culture increasingly defined by a superabundance of images detached from reality—a narrative that has now been repeated and varied for the last four decades—is a spreading hunger for authenticity, which faces particularly difficult topics in suffering and sexuality.[8]

In his seminal account of postdramatic theater—that is, the post-1960s theater that seeks in various ways to escape its role as servant to a dramatic narrative—Hans-Thies Lehmann points to what he calls the "irruption of the real": postdramatic theater, he asserts, "is the first to turn the level of the real explicitly into a 'co-player,'" and the "self-mutilations of performance artists" are a problematic part of this tendency from a moral point of view.[9] In Lehmann's view "the main point is not the assertion of the real as such (as is the case in the . . . sensationalist products of the porn industry), but the unsettling that occurs through the *indecidability* [of] whether one is dealing with reality or fiction." The aesthetics of postdramatic theater works "by 'treading the borderline,' by permanently switching . . . between 'real' contiguity (connection with reality) and 'staged' construct. It is in this sense that postdramatic theatre means: theatre of the real."[10] The actuality effect obsesses over the same borderline. It represents a deliberate overstepping of it—but in most cases only represents it. When Rinaldo's fantasy of a dominant schoolmistress takes physical shape on stage, when Zerlina's hyperbolic language is materialized into either playful bondage or violent abuse, or when Wozzeck starts off a BDSM scene that ends in murder, the actuality effect is played out within the confines of the represented fiction. At the same time, the crossing over from one diegetic layer to the next necessarily evokes the fantasy of the crossing over from fiction into reality. That fantasy, even if it is not realized, is inherent in the actuality effect.

What makes the actuality effect, understood in these terms, particular to opera is its ambivalent relation to the operatic voice. That voice is the ultimate source and expression of operatic ecstasy, as well as the bodily sign of suffering—a stylized scream of both pain and pleasure. On the one hand, it is a guarantor of artificiality: no matter what level of realism is displayed visually, opera's particular mode of singing reveals it at every moment as ritualized contrivance. This is true not least because if a singer lets him- or herself be overcome by actual emotion, vocal technique immediately and unmistakably falters: without the mastery of vocal artifice the actuality effect would remain ineffective. If and when the real irrupts into opera, therefore, it does so against an ever-present foil of the unreal. On the other hand, the singing voice can itself be heard as an irruption of the real. "The experience of the real, of the fact that no fictive illusions are created," writes Lehmann, "is often accompanied by disappointment about the reduction, the apparent 'poverty.'"[11] In opera, however, that reality has the advantage of including the materiality of voice: if the fictive illusions were to be completely stripped away, what remained would be breathing bodies emitting song. Something similar happens if the fiction is in some sense coextensive with reality, as it is in several instances of the actuality effect: when an opera singer playacts an opera singer in *Tosca*, or when the veil of fiction is momentarily removed, as when Anna Larsson's Kundry names herself "Anna" in the Brussels *Parsifal*, or when an orchestra is simultaneously conducted by Barbara Hannigan and by her dominatrix Gepopo, the result becomes a double exposure of, or oscillation between, representation and presentation. This ambiguity, as I have stressed, forms another facet of operatic performance that is highlighted by the analogy with BDSM: in any kind of consensual power exchange the coexistence of the self and the role is essential. To reinforce this point, I will conclude with a brief discussion of two underground performances taking place in intimate venues, far from the large opera houses. Each in its own way turns the personal investment of the singer into a central aspect of performance.

Returning to where I started, I would like to point to the configuration of the playacted and the personal in Sammie Gorham's kinky adaptation of Wolf-Ferrari, which I mentioned in the preface. In *Il segreto di Susanna* the protagonist's husband whiffs tobacco on returning home and suspects his wife of infidelity. The secret that he eventually discovers is that she is a smoker herself. In Gorham's present-day version, *Susanna's Secret: A BDSM Opera* (2018), the secret is instead that she is an SM aficionado: she plays the dominatrix to Sante (a mute role, who is walked around on a leash, strapped to a Saint Andrew's Cross, and whipped), but wishes deep down to be dominated by her husband (fig. E.1). Once the secret is revealed, she hands her purportedly vanilla husband a flogger, his eyes light up, and everyone is happy. In other words, the adaptation's concern

Figure E.1. "Please don't forget your safe word this time." Susanna (Sammie Gorham) giving Sante (Jordan Marchese) a tender flogging. *Susanna's Secret: A BDSM Opera* (dir. Sammie Gorham, Seattle Modern Opera Company, 2018).

with authenticity takes the shape of a coming-out process: Susanna dares to discover her true self and is liberated by it. But beyond the story level, Gorham's production itself was paralleled by a personal story mirroring that of the opera. The limited-edition program pamphlet included an essay, "Sammie's Secret: A Life in Opera + BDSM." Reflecting on her personal experiences, she recounts when and how she learned about her own taste for pain and bondage (like her version of Susanna, she identifies as a switch with a preference for submission). The idea of doing the performance, Gorham told me when I interviewed her, came around the time when she had started dating her current partner, who also ended up playing the silent part of Sante—that is, the pot-smoking friend whom

Susanna flogs in the opera. The role-play, of course, focuses less on the dark and edgy aspects of BDSM than on the drolly experimental, but this does not belie the personal connection. Gorham, for instance, identifies herself as a "Bratty Submissive," that is, a sub who will "tease and poke and prod until their Dom/Domme reacts with a punishment (in some cases, *fun*-ishment)."[12] The impetus and framing of *Susanna's Secret* thus appears to hinge on the analogy between the self-explorations of Susanna and Sammie, publicly staging a personal relationship to sexuality that is as playful as it is intimate.

In 2016, Swedish baritone and performance artist Joa Helgesson discovered his predilection for body suspension—that is, the insertion of metal hooks into the tissue of the hypodermis, which are then used to raise the body into the air. He shares the interest with his partner, microbiologist and performance artist Anna Zakrisson of Doctor Anna's Imaginarium, with whom he also performs. Helgesson and Zakrisson are part of the body suspension scene, which is not the same as the BDSM community, although they overlap: "I have never met anyone who has [body suspension] as a BDSM fetish," he observes, "but many people who do this also do BDSM things, like bondage, shibari, and so on. I think it has to do with a different way of relating to pain. . . . I think there is a curiosity and fearlessness that bring those worlds together."[13] At the 2017 International Body Suspension Symposium, Helgesson incorporated his hobby in his profession as a singer for the first time. His own adaptation of scenes from Claudio Monteverdi's *Orfeo* (1607) for keyboard and viola was performed at the Malzfabrik in Berlin (literally a malt factory, now repurposed into a creative cultural space). While Beto Rea and Eugenia Monti from the Santa Sangre Body Rituals played Orfeo and Eurydice, Helgesson sang Hades but also both of their vocal parts—Eurydice's in the original key, with a harsh, piercing falsetto far above his own baritone range, while the viola part contorted into atonal glissandi. All three actors had hooks attached to their back, with a construction of ropes and pulleys connecting Hades's hooks to those of Orfeo and Eurydice (fig. E.2). As the lovers ascended from the underworld, Helgesson slowly pulled them up into the air until, at the moment of Orfeo's turnaround, Eurydice was released and slowly dropped back into Hades's arms, her lover helplessly hovering below the ceiling. For Helgesson, who professes a longtime inter-

Figure E.2. Hooked on Hades: Eurydice (Eugenia Monti) being welcomed back into the underworld by Hades (Joa Helgesson). *Orfeo* (dir. Joa Helgesson, Malzfabrik, 2017). © Anja Hüttner, 2017. Reproduced by kind permission.

est in dark and melancholy art, pursuing the combination of opera and body suspension is a matter of exploring the authenticity of performed pain: "We often talk about singing from one's pain, or how to represent inner pain on stage. But does it really make sense to represent pain in the way it is conventionally done? Can we ever be completely honest in our expressions?"[14]

The focus on authenticity is further underlined by the fact that both Helgesson and Gorham trace their present interests back to childhood experiences. Gorham, once tied up in a make-believe dungeon while playing Aladdin, comments: "I knew this was something I liked that wasn't normal."[15] Helgesson, meanwhile, says, "I have always been fascinated by pain. I remember in primary school, I used to challenge friends to bang my head against the wall and jump on my hands. . . . At one point I fell from a tree and, sure, it hurt like hell—I don't think I enjoyed it—but still, I somehow longed for something like that to happen. The possibility of something momentous happening."[16] The implication is that the exploration of pain is something that has deep roots within the individual that can be made to resonate in operatic performance. This cherishing of the idea of emotional authenticity is often crucial to the self-understanding of BDSM practitioners. As Staci Newmahr puts it: "SM participants seek authenticity in emotional, physical, and psychological *experience,* rather than in their presentation to others."[17] The same can be said for the spectacle of opera: the sense of emotional authenticity remains intact to the devotee despite the awareness of make-believe, artifice, and hyperbole that marks the performance. While a production might embrace or reject it, this quest for emotional authenticity through the paradoxical detour of role-play is a crucial facet of the affinity between BDSM and opera. The actuality effect can be understood as an expression of that quest, which may involve real pain as well as real pleasure.

In these two performances, moreover, it is possible to talk about the irruption of the real in Lehmann's sense. Here, that "real" is not simply the bodily presence of a singer becoming visible at the expense of the represented character. It takes the form of a personal investment of the performers' relationship to the experience of physical pain—light and explicitly erotic in the case of Gorham's *Susanna's Secret,* more severe and sensual without being sexual in Helgesson's *Orfeo.* In both cases, that real pain takes place within a circle of consent (and, in the body-suspension performance, within meticulous procedures of knowledge, safety, and hygiene). The initiative here necessarily comes from the performers themselves: onstage flogging—to say nothing of suspending the performers from hooks in their bodies—would have been unthinkable had it been the idea of an experimentally minded director coaxing a reluctant singer into agreeing.

These two performances mark an end point of deviant opera, as the most actual of its third-level actuality effects. Here, the singers deliberately stage their own personal relation to sexuality and suffering, respectively, as openly as is possible within the boundaries of aesthetic practice. At the same time, that end point is gestured at in every single one of the productions I have written about in this book: each time the actuality effect bursts through a boundary within the theatrical fiction, its vibrations echo across the wider boundaries of the operatic space, reaching the people who are performing, watching, and listening, and reminding them that the border between the enacted and the actual can be fragile and volatile. The circuits of power and pleasure that crisscross that border are what drive opera and SM individually, as well as their combination on stage. Therefore, the notion of an affinity between them also highlights their relation to their own outer limits: the safe, sane, and consensual ultimately becomes an image of the aesthetic autonomy of art and its uncertain status in contemporary culture. The drama enacted for pleasure within those confines is haunted at every moment by the sinister realities outside them. As performative practices, both opera and BDSM are intensely aware of their precarious borders and ceaselessly return to the fantasy of their breakdown.

Notes

1. *Safe Word* is the second of three one-act operas on sexual themes that premiered together under the title *Three Way*. The score, from which I am quoting the Domme's line (at page 100), is available for perusal on the composer's website, www.robertpaterson.com, and published as Robert Paterson, *Three Way: A Trio of One-Act Operas: Piano/Vocal Score* (New York: Bill Holab Music, 2017).

2. I use these two acronyms more or less synonymously, although BDSM is a more recent coinage—it began to spread in the early 1990s—and thus connotes the contemporary subculture more specifically than does SM, which has been around for several more decades, sometimes in the versions S&M or S/M. For an introductory discussion of the complexities of BDSM terminology see Margot Weiss, *Techniques of Pleasure: BDSM and the Circuits of Sexuality* (Durham, NC: Duke University Press, 2011), vii–x.

3. Sammie Gorham, Skype interview by the author, 27 March 2019.

4. Paterson, *Three Way*, 100.

1. The volume is part of the pornographic series "Library Illustrative of Social Progress," published by John Camden Hotten. Hotten claimed that the series

206   NOTES TO PAGES 2-5

was based on a collection of texts dating back to the 1770s, which was found in the library of the historian Henry Thomas Buckle. This source, however, is questioned in Henry Spencer Ashbee, *Bibliography of Prohibited Books*, vol. 1 (1877; New York: Jack Brussel, 1962), 239–41.

2. *Lady Bumtickler's Revels*, 25.

3. *Lady Bumtickler's Revels*, 84–85

4. *Lady Bumtickler's Revels*, 87–88.

5. The productions alluded to here are the following (the years are those of the premiere): Wolfgang Amadeus Mozart's *Die Entführung aus dem Serail* (dir. Calixto Bieito, Komische Oper Berlin, 2004) and *Così fan tutte* (dir. Robert Borgmann, Deutsche Oper, 2016); Gaetano Donizetti's *Lucia di Lammermoor* (dir. Katie Mitchell, Royal Opera House, 2016); Giuseppe Verdi's *Macbeth* (dir. Liliana Cavani, Teatro Regio di Parma, 2006) and *Rigoletto* (dir. David McVicar, Royal Opera House, 2001); Richard Wagner's *Die Walküre* (dir. La Fura dels Baus/Carlus Padrissa, Palau de les Arts Reina Sofia, 2007); Camille Saint-Saëns's *Samson et Dalila* (dir. Omri Nitzan and Amir Nizar Zuabi, Vlaamse Opera, 2009); Jules Massenet's *Manon* (dir. Coline Serreau, Opéra Bastille, 2012); Giacomo Puccini's *Manon Lescaut* (dir. Mariusz Treliński, La Monnaie, 2013) and *Tosca* (dir. Pierre Audi, Opéra Bastille, 2014); Richard Strauss's *Salome* (dir. Sofia Jupither, Kungliga Operan Stockholm, 2013) and *Ariadne auf Naxos* (dir. William Friedkin, Los Angeles Opera, 2004); Ermanno Wolf-Ferrari's *Il segreto di Susanna* (dir. Sammie Gorham, Seattle Modern Opera Company, 2018); György Ligeti's *Le grand macabre* (dir. La Fura dels Baus/Àlex Ollé and Valentina Carrasco, La Monnaie, 2009); Thomas Adès's *Powder Her Face* (dir. Orpha Phelan, Det Kongelige Teater, 2016); George Benjamin's *Written on Skin* (dir. Katie Mitchell, Festival International d'Art Lyrique d'Aix-en-Provence, 2012); Peter Eötvös's *Le Balcon* (dir. Damien Bigourdan, L'Opéra de Lille, 2015); and Christoffer Elgh's *Valerie's Voice* (dir. Helena Röhr, Aliasteatern, 2019).

6. For a discussion of the term *perversion*—the traditional, pathologizing usage and the attempts to recuperate it for critical purposes, as well as references to further reading—see Will Stockton, "The Liberal World of Perversion," *GLQ: A Journal of Lesbian and Gay Studies* 17, no. 2–3 (2011): 389–403. See also Molly Anne Rothenberg, Dennis A. Foster, and Slavoj Žižek, eds., *Perversion and the Social Relation* (Durham, NC: Duke University Press, 2003), which describes "an increasing valorization of the perverse for its analytic possibilities as well as for its revolutionary potential" (2). See also Andrea Beckmann, *The Social Construction of Sexuality and Perversion: Deconstructing Sadomasochism* (Basingstoke: Palgrave Macmillan, 2009), 84–85.

7. The Latin roots of these words emphasize the act of moving away *(de-)* from a road *(via)* and of thoroughly *(per-)* turning around *(vertere)*.

8. For discussions of the terminology see Gundula Kreuzer and Clemens Risi, "*Regietheater* in Transition: An Introduction to Barbara Beyer's 'Interviews with

Contemporary Opera Directors,'" *Opera Quarterly* 27, no. 2–3 (2011): 303–6; and Ulrich Müller, *"Regietheater*/Director's Theater," in *The Oxford Handbook of Opera,* ed. Helen M. Greenwald (Oxford: Oxford University Press, 2014), 582–606.

9. For a passionate defense of such intentionalism see Robert Donington, *Opera and Its Symbols: The Unity of Words, Music and Staging* (New Haven, CT: Yale University Press, 1992).

10. Clemens Risi, *Oper in Performance: Analysen zur Aufführungsdimension von Operninszenierungen* (Berlin: Theater der Zeit, 2017), 12. Unless otherwise indicated, all translations are my own.

11. Carolyn Abbate and Roger Parker, *A History of Opera* (New York: Norton, 2012), 33.

12. A few examples from the press will illustrate this habit of formulation, which can be amply confirmed by a quick search in online discussion forums devoted to opera: Heather MacDonald, "The Abduction of Opera: Can the Met Stand Firm against the Trashy Productions of Trendy Nihilists?" *City Journal* (Summer 2007); David Mellor, "Carry on Nurse: Strauss's Magical *Ariadne auf Naxos* Is Revenge for the War," *Daily Mail,* 25 May 2013; Rian Evans, "Manon Lescaut—Review," *The Guardian,* 10 February 2014; Michael Church, "The Force of Destiny, Coliseum, Theatre Review: Calixto Bieito's Perverse Production Is Saved by Brilliant Singing," *Independent,* 10 November 2015; Rupert Christiansen, *"Lucia di Lammermoor,* Royal Opera House, Verdict: 'Too Leaden Even for the Hecklers,'" *The Telegraph,* 8 April 2016.

13. On *Fifty Shades* see Ruth A. Deller, Sarah Harman, and Bethan Jones, "Introduction to the Special Issue: Reading the *Fifty Shades* 'Phenomenon,'" *Sexualities* 16, no. 8 (2013): 859–63. On women in BDSM see Ani Ritchie and Meg Barker, "Feminist SM: A Contradiction in Terms or a Way of Challenging Traditional Gendered Dynamics through Sexual Practice?" *Lesbian and Gay Psychology Review* 6, no. 3 (2005): 227–39; as well as Beckmann, *The Social Construction;* and Weiss, *Techniques of Pleasure.*

14. Hannah Furness, "Royal Opera House to Join the #Metoo Era as It Challenges Misogyny on Stage by Asking: 'Does Opera Hate Women?'" *Daily Telegraph,* 25 December 2018.

15. Catherine Clément, *Opera, or the Undoing of Women,* trans. Betsy Wing (London: Tauris, 1997).

16. Mary Ann Smart, introduction to *Siren Songs: Representations of Gender and Sexuality in Opera,* ed. Mary Ann Smart (Princeton, NJ: Princeton University Press, 2000), 4.

17. Susan McClary, *Feminine Endings: Music, Gender, and Sexuality* (1991; Minneapolis: University of Minnesota Press, 2002); Lawrence Kramer, *After the Lovedeath: Sexual Violence and the Making of Culture* (Berkeley: University of California Press, 1997).

18. Paul Robinson, "It's Not over until the Soprano Dies," *New York Times*, 1 January 1989. Carolyn Abbate, "Opera; or, The Envoicing of Women," in *Musicology and Difference: Gender and Sexuality in Music Scholarship*, ed. Ruth A. Solie (Berkeley: University of California Press, 1992), 225–58.

19. Nina Eidsheim, *Sensing Sound: Singing and Listening as Vibrational Practice* (Durham, NC: Duke University Press, 2015); Jelena Novak, *Postopera: Reinventing the Voice-Body* (Farnham: Ashgate, 2015).

20. See, e.g., Suzanne Aspden, "'A Great Private Party': The Participatory Theatrics of Country-House Operagoing," *Opera Quarterly* 35, no. 1–2 (2019): 96–117; Ryan Minor, "Opera and/as Theatricality: Notes from across the Aisle," *Opera Quarterly* 35, no. 1–2 (2019): 143–46; and Heather Wiebe, "Opera and Relational Aesthetics," *Opera Quarterly* 35, no. 1–2 (2019): 139–42.

21. Wiebe, "Opera and Relational Aesthetics," 139.

22. A recent example is "Opera at the Multiplex," ed. Christopher Morris and Joseph Attard, a special issue of *Opera Quarterly* 34, no. 4 (2018). The same journal has published numerous articles on the topic, notable ones including David J. Levin, "The Mise-en-scène of Mediation: Wagner's *Götterdämmerung* (Stuttgart Opera, Peter Konwitschny, 2000–2005)," *Opera Quarterly* 27, no. 2–3 (2011): 219–34; Richard Will, "Zooming In, Gazing Back: *Don Giovanni* on Television," *Opera Quarterly* 27, no. 1 (2011): 32–65; Emanuele Senici, "Porn Style? Space and Time in Live Opera Videos," *Opera Quarterly* 26, no. 1 (2010): 63–80; and Christopher Morris, "Digital Diva: Opera on Video," *Opera Quarterly* 26, no. 1 (2010): 96–119.

23. Gundula Kreuzer, *Curtain, Gong, Steam: Wagnerian Technologies of Nineteenth-Century Opera* (Oakland: University of California Press, 2018); Lydia Goehr, "The Domestic Diva: Toward an Operatic History of the Telephone," in *Technology and the Diva: Sopranos, Opera, and Media from Romanticism to the Digital Age*, ed. Karen Henson (Cambridge: Cambridge University Press, 2016), 104–23.

24. Nicholas Mathew and Mary Ann Smart, "Elephants in the Music Room: The Future of Quirk Historicism," *Representations* 132 (2015): 72.

25. Arman Schwartz, "Opera and Objecthood: Sedimentation, Spectatorship, and *Einstein on the Beach*," *Opera Quarterly* 35, no. 1–2 (2019): 42. Schwartz is referring to the following studies of these technologies: Francesca Vella, "(De) railing Mobility: Opera, Stasis, and Locomotion on Late-Nineteenth-Century Italian Tracks," *Opera Quarterly* 34, no. 1 (2018): 3–28; Kreuzer, *Curtain, Gong, Steam;* Senici, "Porn Style?"; and Morris, "Digital Diva."

26. Tom Sutcliffe, *Believing in Opera* (Princeton, NJ: Princeton University Press, 1997); David J. Levin, *Unsettling Opera: Staging Mozart, Verdi, Wagner, and Zemlinsky* (Chicago: University of Chicago Press, 2007).

27. In addition to Kreuzer and Risi, "*Regietheater* in Transition," see their "A Note from the Guest Editors," *Opera Quarterly* 27, no. 2–3 (2011): 149–52;

Mary Ann Smart, "Resisting Rossini, or Marlon Brando Plays Figaro," *Opera Quarterly* 27, no. 2–3 (2011): 153–78; and Joy H. Calico's chapter "Brecht's Legacy for Opera: Estrangement and the Canon," in *Brecht at the Opera* (Berkeley: University of California Press, 2008), 140–63. Valuable books on the topic include Alison Latham and Roger Parker, eds., *Verdi in Performance* (New York: Oxford University Press, 2001); Jürgen Schläder, ed., *OperMachtTheaterBilder: Neue Wirklichkeiten des Regietheaters* (Berlin: Henschel, 2006); Ortrud Gutjahr, ed., *Regietheater! Wie sich über Inszenierungen streiten lässt* (Würzburg: Königshausen & Neumann, 2008); and Robert Sollich, Clemens Risi, Sebastian Reus, and Stephan Jöris, eds., *Angst vor der Zerstörung: Der Meister Künste zwischen Archiv und Erneuerung* (Berlin: Theater der Zeit, 2008).

28. Sutcliffe, *Believing in Opera*, 14.

29. Sutcliffe, 30.

30. Levin, *Unsettling Opera*, 46; Kreuzer and Risi, "*Regietheater* in Transition," 304.

31. Mary Ann Smart, "An Operatic Alphabet," paper presented at the Seventy-Seventh Annual Meeting of the American Musicological Society in San Francisco, 10–13 November 2011.

32. Smart, "An Operatic Alphabet," n.p.

33. See "Rihanna Feat. Britney Spears—S&M Remix—Live—Billboard Music Awards 2011," YouTube.com, www.youtube.com/watch?v=IaTMIDAvu LUVSpFTRQ.

34. Paul Bentley, "'Mummy Porn': *Fifty Shades of Grey* Outstrips Harry Potter to Become Fastest Selling Paperback of All Time," *Daily Mail*, 18 June 2012.

35. See G. Falk and Thomas S. Weinberg, "Sadomasochism and Popular Western Culture," in *S and M: Studies in Sadomasochism*, ed. Thomas S. Weinberg and G. W. L. Kamel (Buffalo, NY: Prometheus, 1983), 37–144; Margot Weiss, "Mainstreaming Kink: The Politics of BDSM Representation in U.S. Popular Media," in *Sadomasochism: Powerful Pleasures*, ed. Peggy J. Kleinplatz and Charles Moser (Binghamton, NY: Harrington Park Press, 2006), 103–32; Catherine Scott, *Thinking Kink: The Collision of BDSM, Feminism and Popular Culture* (Jefferson, NC: McFarland, 2015).

36. Susan Sontag, "Fascinating Fascism," in *Under the Sign of Saturn* (New York: Picador, 2002), 105. The essay was originally published in the *New York Review of Books* 22, no. 1 (6 February 1975).

37. E. L. James, *Fifty Shades of Grey* (London: Arrow, 2012), 98.

38. Weiss, "Mainstreaming Kink."

39. Robert V. Bienvenu, "The Development of Sadomasochism as a Cultural Style in the Twentieth-Century United States" (PhD diss., Indiana University, 1998); see also Weiss, *Techniques of Pleasure*, viii.

40. Mel Gordon, *Voluptuous Panic: The Erotic World of Weimar Berlin* (Los Angeles: Feral House, 2006).

41. Thomas S. Weinberg, "Sadomasochism and the Social Sciences: A Review of the Sociological and Social Psychological Literature," in *Sadomasochism: Powerful Pleasures*, ed. Peggy J. Kleinplatz and Charles Moser (Binghamton, NY: Harrington Park, 2006), 36.

42. Susan Wright, "Discrimination of SM-Identified Individuals," in *Sadomasochism: Powerful Pleasures*, ed. Peggy J. Kleinplatz and Charles Moser (Binghamton, NY: Harrington Park, 2006), 217–32.

43. Charles Moser and Peggy J. Kleinplatz, "Introduction: The State of Our Knowledge on SM," in *Sadomasochism: Powerful Pleasures*, ed. Peggy J. Kleinplatz and Charles Moser (Binghamton, NY: Harrington Park, 2006), 5.

44. david stein, "'Safe Sane Consensual': The Making of a Shibboleth," *Boybear*. web.archive.org/web/20110911035825/http://www.boybear.us/ssc.pdf.

45. Academic authors are no exception. For instance, Catherine Scott refuses to mention the title *Fifty Shades of Grey*, continuously referring to it as "that book," in an attempt "to placate those (including myself) who were already sick of hearing the books discussed at the time, and are even sicker of them two years later." Scott, *Thinking Kink*, 1.

46. Weiss, *Techniques of Pleasure*, 11.

47. Weiss, 101–42. Matthew Weait notes that BDSM vocabulary of consent, freedom, and choice links it to liberalism: SM "exists at the limit point of liberalism itself." Matthew Weait, "Sadomasochism and the Law," in *Safe, Sane and Consensual: Contemporary Perspectives on Sadomasochism*, ed. Darren Langdridge and Meg Barker (New York: Palgrave Macmillan, 2007), 79.

48. See, e.g., Weiss, *Techniques of Pleasure*, 5, 34–60; and Anonymous, "SM International," in *Sadomasochism: Powerful Pleasures*, ed. Peggy J. Kleinplatz and Charles Moser (Binghamton, NY: Harrington Park, 2006), 265. For a discussion of the demographics of operagoing see Georgia Cowart, "Audiences," in *The Oxford Handbook of Opera*, ed. Helen M. Greenwald (Oxford: Oxford University Press, 2014), 666–84.

49. For comprehensive accounts of this development and its prehistory in the early twentieth century see Sutcliffe, *Believing in Opera;* Levin, *Unsettling Opera*, 1–35; Evan Baker, *From the Score to the Stage: An Illustrated History of Continental Opera Production and Staging* (Chicago: University of Chicago Press, 2013), 253–368; and Müller, *"Regietheater/*Director's Theatre."

50. A fair amount of scholarly work exists on the centenary *Ring*. See, e.g., Jean-Jacques Nattiez, *Tétralogies: Wagner, Boulez, Chéreau* (Paris: Bourgois, 1983); Michael Ewans, "The Bayreuth Centenary *Ring* by Patrice Chéreau and Pierre Boulez," *Miscellanea Musicologica* 14 (1985): 167–74; Patrick Carnegy, *Wagner and the Art of the Theatre* (New Haven, CT: Yale University Press, 2006), 354–64; and Sutcliffe, *Believing in Opera*, 99–124.

51. Kreuzer has interrogated the historiography ascribing this role to Chéreau's *Ring*, arguing that it is overly focused on Germany and thus blind to

creative stage work during the 1930s and 1940s. See Gundula Kreuzer, "Voices from Beyond: *Don Carlos* and the Modern Stage," *Cambridge Opera Journal* 18, no. 2 (2006): 151–79.

52. On the work of Sellars see Sutcliffe, *Believing in Opera,* 195–226; and Levin, *Unsettling Opera,* 69–98.

53. Experiments that tamper with the musical stratum of opera are rarer. For instance, Christoph Marthaler's Paris staging of *Le nozze di Figaro* substituted various strange keyboard sounds for the harpsichord in the recitatives, and his Hamburg *Lulu* (2017) used a new chamber-music arrangement of the unfinished third act and concluded with a complete performance of Berg's Violin Concerto. See Axel Englund, "An Incomplete Life: *Lulu* and the Performance of Unfinishedness," *Opera Quarterly* 35, no. 1–2 (2019): 20–39. For an in-depth discussion of operatic music as continuously revisable, see Roger Parker, *Remaking the Song: Operatic Visions and Revisions from Handel to Berio* (Berkeley: University of California Press, 2006).

54. Wholesale attempts at historically informed performance are very rare, for both practical and aesthetic reasons. See Mary Hunter, "Historically Informed Performance," in *The Oxford Handbook of Opera,* ed. Helen M. Greenwald (Oxford: Oxford University Press, 2014), 606–26.

CHAPTER 1

1. Mathieu-François Pidansat de Mairobert, quoted and translated in Thomas Wynn, "Prostitutes and Erotic Performances in Eighteenth-Century Paris," in *Prostitution and Eighteenth-Century Culture: Sex, Commerce and Morality,* ed. Ann Lewis and Markman Ellis (London: Routledge, 2012), 92. See also Georgia Cowart, "Of Women, Sex, and Folly: Opera under the Old Regime," *Cambridge Opera Journal* 6, no. 3 (1994): 205–20; and Cowart, "Audiences," 669.

2. Margaret Reynolds, "Ruggiero's Deceptions, Cherubino's Distractions," in *En Travesti: Women, Gender, Subversion, Opera,* ed. Corinne E. Blackmer and Patricia Juliana Smith (New York: Columbia University Press, 1995), 133.

3. See Thomas McGeary, "'Warbling Eunuchs': Opera, Gender, and Sexuality on the London Stage, 1705–1742," *Restoration and Eighteenth-Century Theatre Research* 7, no. 1 (1992): 11–15.

4. Søren Kierkegaard, *Either/Or: Part 1,* ed. and trans. Howard V. Hong and Edna H. Hong (1843; Princeton, NJ: Princeton University Press, 1987), 48.

5. Wayne Koestenbaum, *The Queen's Throat: Opera, Homosexuality, and the Mystery of Desire* (1993; 2nd ed., New York: Da Capo, 2001).

6. Laurence Dreyfus, *Wagner and the Erotic Impulse* (Cambridge, MA: Harvard University Press, 2010).

7. Eduard Hanslick, *Concerte, Componisten und Virtuosen der letzten fünf-zehn Jahre. 1870-1885* (Berlin: Allgemeiner Verein für Deutsche Literatur, 1886), 77–78; Richard Batka and Willibald Nagel, *Allgemeine Geschichte der Musik: Dritter Band* (Stuttgart: Carl Grüninger, 1909), 68; Dreyfus, *Wagner and the Erotic Impulse*, 34, 39.

8. Charles Baudelaire, *Correspondance: Tome 1, 1832-1860*, ed. Claude Pichois and Jean Ziegler (Paris: Bibliothèque de la Pléiade, 1973), 673. Translation in *Selected Letters of Charles Baudelaire: The Conquest of Solitude*, trans. and ed. Rosemary Lloyd (Chicago: University of Chicago Press, 1986), 146. See also Dreyfus, *Wagner and the Erotic Impulse*, 17–23.

9. Robert G. L. Waite, *The Psychopathic God: Adolf Hitler* (New York: Basic Books, 1977), 99; Glenn B. Infield, *Hitler's Secret Life: The Mystery of the Eagle's Nest* (New York: Stein and Day, 1979), 88–89. In the words of another observer, Hitler "feasts his sado-masochism on Wagner." Elwin Humphreys Powell, *The Design of Discord: Studies of Anomie* (New Brunswick, NJ: Transaction, 1988), 180.

10. Angela Carter, *The Bloody Chamber* (1979; New York: Penguin, 2015), 6.

11. Carter, *The Bloody Chamber*, 43.

12. Carolyn Abbate, "Music—Drastic or Gnostic?" *Critical Inquiry* 30, no. 3 (2004): 505–36.

13. Michelle Duncan, "The Operatic Scandal of the Singing Body: Voice, Presence, Performativity," *Cambridge Opera Journal* 16, no. 3 (2004): 283–306.

14. Risi, *Oper in Performance*, 84–111.

15. See Martha Feldman and Judith T. Zeitlin, eds., *The Voice as Something More: Essays toward Materiality* (Chicago: University of Chicago Press, 2019); Eidsheim, *Sensing Sound*; Karmen MacKendrick, *The Matter of Voice: Sensual Soundings* (New York: Fordham University Press, 2016); Adriana Cavarero, *For More Than One Voice: Toward a Philosophy of Vocal Expression*, trans. Paul A. Kottman (2003; Stanford: Stanford University Press, 2005).

16. Modern versions of this skepticism stretch from Susan Sontag's famous polemic against interpretation in *Against Interpretation and Other Essays* (New York: Noonday Press, 1966) to Hans Ulrich Gumbrecht's critique of the humanities' hermeneutic bedrock in *The Production of Presence: What Meaning Cannot Convey* (Stanford: Stanford University Press, 2004) and beyond. In opera studies its most famous iteration is Abbate, "Music—Drastic or Gnostic?" This article has had a significant impact on music scholarship, but it has also been criticized on various accounts—for its rigidly dichotomous understanding of eventness and meaning as mutually exclusive, for its taking for granted what "real" opera is, and for its caricatured image of hermeneutics as inherently totalizing. See, e.g., Levin, *Unsettling Opera*, 8–10; Duncan, "The Operatic Scandal," 286–89; and Lawrence Kramer, *Interpreting Music* (Berkeley: University of California Press, 2010), 87. The antihermeneutic note still resonates, for instance, in Risi's more

recent work on director's opera, which posits as its theoretical foundation the move "Beyond Interpretation." Risi, *Oper in Performance,* 30–57.

17. Roland Barthes, *S/Z,* trans. R. Howard (1970; New York: Farrar, Straus and Giroux, 1975), 110.

18. Michel Poizat, *The Angel's Cry: Beyond the Pleasure Principle in Opera,* trans. Arthur Denner (1986; Ithaca, NY: Cornell University Press, 1992), 105.

19. Samuel D. Abel, *Opera in the Flesh: Sexuality in Operatic Performance* (Boulder, CO: Westview, 1997), 82. See also Mitchell Morris, "Reading as an Opera Queen," in *Musicology and Difference: Gender and Sexuality in Music Scholarship,* ed. Ruth A. Solie (Berkeley: University of California Press, 1992), 184–200. For a critical view on this mode of writing see David J. Levin, "Is There a Text in This Libido? *Diva* and the Rhetoric of Contemporary Opera Criticism," in *Between Opera and Cinema,* ed. Jeongwon Joe and Rose Theresa (New York: Routledge, 2002), 121–32.

20. Risi, *Oper in Performance,* 153.

21. Suzanne Cusick, "On a Lesbian Relation with Music: A Serious Effort Not to Think Straight," in *Queering the Pitch: The New Gay and Lesbian Musicology,* ed. Philip Brett, Elizabeth Wood, and Gary C. Thomas (New York: Routledge, 1994), 67–84; Terry Castle, "In Praise of Brigitte Fassbaender: Reflections on Diva Worship," in *En Travesti: Women, Gender, Subversion, Opera,* ed. Corinne E. Blackmer and Patricia Juliana Smith (New York: Columbia University Press, 1995), 20–58; Laura Wahlfors, "Resonances and Dissonances: Listening to Waltraud Meier's Envoicing of Isolde," in *On Voice,* ed. Walter Bernhart and Lawrence Kramer (Amsterdam: Rodopi, 2014), 57–76.

22. Abbate, "Envoicing of Women," 254.

23. Laura Mulvey, "Visual Pleasure and Narrative Cinema" (1975), in *Film Theory and Criticism: Introductory Readings,* ed. Leo Braudy and Marshall Cohen (New York: Oxford University Press, 1999), 833–44.

24. For a critique of Mulvey see Noël Carroll, "The Image of Women in Film: A Defense of a Paradigm," *Journal of Aesthetics and Art Criticism* 48, no. 4 (1990): 349–60. See also the discussion on the gaze in Roberta Sassatelli, "Interview with Laura Mulvey: Gender, Gaze, and Technology in Film Culture," in *Theory, Culture & Society* 28, no. 5 (2011): 123–43.

25. Linda Hutcheon and Michael Hutcheon, *Bodily Charm: Living Opera* (Lincoln: University of Nebraska Press, 2000), 106–12.

26. Clemens Risi, "Opera in Performance: 'Regietheater' and the Performative Turn," *Opera Quarterly* 35, no. 1–2 (2019): 17; Eidsheim, *Sensing Sound,* 3 et passim; Martha Feldman, "Voice Gap Crack Break," in *The Voice as Something More: Essays toward Materiality,* ed. Martha Feldman and Judith T. Zeitlin (Chicago: University of Chicago Press, 2019), 196.

27. In one of her Kittleresque moments Abbate argues that "musical performance challenges notions of autonomy by staging the performer's servitude, even

automatism, and upends assumptions about human subjectivity by invoking mechanism: human bodies wired to notational prescriptions." Abbate, "Music—Drastic or Gnostic," 508. James Q. Davies, "'I Am an Essentialist': Against the Voice Itself," in *The Voice as Something More: Essays toward Materiality,* ed. Martha Feldman and Judith T. Zeitlin (Chicago: University of Chicago Press, 2019), 144.

28. A sustained argument for this view is made in Hartmut Böhme, *Fetishism and Culture: A Different Theory of Modernity,* trans. Anna Galt (Berlin: De Gruyter, 2014), 4–13 et passim.

29. For a lucid history of fetishism in the sexual sense see Böhme, *Fetishism and Culture,* 296–322.

30. See, e.g., Marcia J. Citron, *Opera on Screen* (New Haven, CT: Yale University Press, 2000); Marcia J. Citron, *When Opera Meets Film* (Cambridge: Cambridge University Press, 2010); and João Pedro Cachopo, "Opera's Screen Metamorphosis: The Survival of a Genre or a Matter of Translation?" *Opera Quarterly* 30, no. 14 (2014): 315–29; as well as the aforementioned Morris and Attard, "Opera at the Multiplex"; Levin, "The Mise-en-scène of Mediation"; Will, "Zooming In, Gazing Back"; Morris, "Digital Diva"; and Senici, "Porn Style?"

31. Mulvey, "Visual Pleasure and Narrative Cinema."

32. Böhme, *Fetishism and Culture,* 33.

33. For different kinds of eulogies see Theodor W. Adorno, "Opera and the Long-Playing Record" (1969), trans. Thomas Y. Levin, *October* 55 (1990): 62–66; and Koestenbaum, *The Queen's Throat,* 46–83.

34. Susan Sontag states, e.g., that "sadomasochistic sexuality is more theatrical than any other" in "Fascinating Fascism," 103; and Lacan says that the "ascetic who flagellates himself does it for a third party," in Jacques Lacan, *The Seminar of Jacques Lacan: Book XI: The Four Fundamental Concepts of Psychoanalysis,* ed. Jacques-Alain Miller, trans. Alan Sheridan (New York: Norton, 1981), 183. See also Race Bannon, "SM as Erotic Theater," in *SM Classics,* ed. Susan Wright (New York: Masquerade, 1999), 19–26.

35. Niklaus Largier, *In Praise of the Whip: A Cultural History of Arousal,* trans. Graham Harman (2001; New York: Zone, 2007), 13.

36. See Weiss, *Techniques of Pleasure,* 220.

37. See Charles Moser, "S/M (Sadomasochistic) Interactions in Semi-public Settings," *Journal of Homosexuality* 36, no. 2 (1998): 19–29.

38. The idea of nongenital pleasure, for instance, was important to Michel Foucault's notion of SM: "These practices [of SM] are insisting that we can produce pleasure with very odd things, very strange parts of our bodies, in very unusual situations, and so on." Michel Foucault, *Ethics: Subjectivity and Truth,* vol. 1 of *The Essential Works of Foucault, 1954–1984,* ed. Paul Rabinow and trans. Robert Hurley et al. (New York: New Press, 1997), 165. See also Moser, "S/M (Sadomasochistic) Interactions," 26–27; Beckmann, *The Social Construction,*

87–89; and Robin Bauer, *Queer BDSM Intimacies: Critical Consent and Pushing Boundaries* (Basingstoke: Palgrave Macmillan, 2014), 58–60.

39. David J. Levin, introduction to *Opera through Other Eyes*, ed. David J. Levin (Stanford: Stanford University Press, 1994), 13.

40. Richard von Krafft-Ebing, *Psychopathia Sexualis: Revised and Enlarged Twelfth Edition* (1903; London: William Heinemann, 1939), 84–85.

41. Laura Hinton, *The Perverse Gaze of Sympathy: Sadomasochistic Sentiments from "Clarissa" to "Rescue 911"* (Albany: State University of New York Press, 1999), 7.

42. Judith Butler, *Bodies That Matter* (1993; London: Routledge, 2011), 122.

43. Butler, however, is careful to query the notion of hyperbolic citation: "Does the denaturalization of the norm succeed in subverting the norm, or is this a denaturalization in the service of a perpetual reidealization, one that can only oppress, even as, or precisely when, it is embodied most effectively?" Butler, *Bodies That Matter*, 129. Butler does not mention SM as an example of such denaturalization, but in a very early text she is strongly critical, above all, of the discourse of authenticity that tends to accompany SM practices. See Judy Butler, "Lesbian S&M: The Politics of Dis-illusion," in *Against Sadomasochism: A Radical Feminist Analysis*, ed. Robin Ruth Linden et al. (Palo Alto: Frog in the Well, 1982).

44. Staci Newmahr, *Playing on the Edge: Sadomasochism, Risk, and Intimacy* (Bloomington: Indiana University Press, 2011), 108. See also Weiss, *Techniques of Pleasure*, 190–92.

45. See Robin Ruth Linden et al., *Against Sadomasochism: A Radical Feminist Analysis* (Palo Alto: Frog in the Well, 1982). Later criticism can be found in Sandra Lee Bartky, "Feminine Masochism and the Politics of Personal Transformation," in *Femininity and Domination: Studies in the Phenomenology of Oppression* (New York: Routledge, 1990), 45–62. Without rejecting BDSM as such, Weiss also questions the notion of BDSM as a safely bracketed space. Weiss, *Techniques of Pleasure*.

46. See Samois Collective, *Coming to Power: Writings and Graphics on Lesbian S/M* (Palo Alto: Up Press, 1981), which prompted the anthology by Linden et al as a response. For a more recent apologia see Beckmann, *The Social Construction*.

47. Foucault, whose enthusiasm vis-à-vis the pleasure culture of the San Francisco leather scene in the early 1980s is a standard reference for BDSM theorists, was very much aware of this challenge. Asked by an interviewer whether we can be sure "that these new pleasures won't be exploited in the way advertising uses the stimulation of pleasure as a means of social control," Foucault responded: "We can never be sure. In fact, we can always be sure *it will* happen, and that everything that has been created or acquired, any ground that has been gained will, at a certain moment be used in such a way." Michel Foucault, *Foucault Live:*

Collected Interviews, 1961–1984, ed. Sylvère Lotringer, trans. Lysa Hochroth and John Johnson (New York: Semiotext(e), 1996), 85.

48. Clément, *Opera*, 75–76.

49. Ellie M. Hisama, "A Feminist Staging of Britten's *The Rape of Lucretia*," *Journal of the American Musicological Society* 71, no. 1 (2018): 237–43.

50. Tim Ashley, "*Guillaume Tell* Review—Sex, Violence and Protracted Booing," *The Guardian*, 30 June 2015; Rupert Christiansen, "*Guillaume Tell*, Royal Opera House, Review—'Lame and Pretentious,'" *The Telegraph*, 30 June 2015; Alexandra Coghlan, "The Gang Rape Was the Least Offensive Thing about Royal Opera's New *William Tell*," *The Spectator*, 4 July 2015.

51. Claire Seymour, "*Guillaume Tell*, Covent Garden," *Opera Today*, 30 June 2015, www.operatoday.com/content/2015/06/guillaume_tell_.php; Clare Colvin, "Review: Rossini's *Guillaume Tell* at the Royal Opera House," *Daily Express*, 5 July 2016.

52. Anonymous, "*William Tell:* Nudity and Rape Scene Greeted with Boos at Royal Opera House," *The Guardian*, 30 June 2015.

53. Anonymous, "*William Tell:* Nudity and Rape Scene."

54. For prominent accounts see Levin, *Unsettling Opera*, vii–xiv; Risi, *Oper in Performance;* and Risi, "Opera in Performance."

55. Antje Kaiser, ed., *Die Entführung aus dem Serail.* Program book (Berlin: Komische Oper, 2018), 4, 7, 8.

56. Micaela Baranello, "Staging Opera Ballet," *Journal of the American Musicological Society* 71, no. 1 (2018): 226.

57. In interviews with female practitioners of BDSM, ethnographer of sexuality Corie Hammers has studied how rape play enables some survivors of sexual trauma to reenact their experience and thus disrupt the bodily disintegration by a bodily recuperation: it means, as one interviewee puts it, "taking back the control of my own body." Corie Hammers, "Corporeality, Sadomasochism and Sexual Trauma," *Body & Society* 20, no. 2 (2014): 80.

58. Clemens Risi, "Opera in Performance—In Search of New Analytical Approaches," *Opera Quarterly* 27, no. 2–3 (2012): 291.

59. Risi, 292.

60. Abel, *Opera in the Flesh*, 99, 102.

61. Weiss, *Techniques of Pleasure*, 84.

62. Gary Switch, "Origin of RACK: RACK vs. SSC," www.leathernroses.com/generalbdsm/garyswitchrack.htm. See also Weiss, *Techniques of Pleasure*, 84; and Newmahr, *Playing on the Edge*, 147.

63. Hammers, "Corporeality," 80. See also Newmahr, *Playing on the Edge*, 75–80.

64. Theodore Bennett, "Unorthodox Rules: The Instructive Potential of BDSM Consent for Law," *Journal of Positive Sexuality* 4, no. 1 (2018): 4–11.

Queer theorist Robin Bauer also defines BDSM as a "communicative sexuality," in Bauer, *Queer BDSM Intimacies,* 85–88. On the "4Cs" see D. J. Williams et al., "From 'SSC' and 'RACK' to the '4Cs': Introducing a new Framework for Negotiating BDSM Participation," *Electronic Journal of Human Sexuality* 17 (2014): www.ejhs.org/volume17/BDSM.html.

65. For a sustained examination of Brecht's relation to the opera, including his influence on *Regietheater,* see Calico, *Brecht at the Opera,* 140–63 et passim. See also Laurenz Lütteken, "Wider den Zeitgeist der Beliebigkeit: Ein Plädoyer für die Freiheit des Textes und die Grenzen der Interpretation," *Wagnerspectrum* 2 (2005): 23; Stephen Hinton, *Weill's Musical Theater: Stages of Reform* (Berkeley: University of California Press, 2012), 147–48; and Tim Carter, "What Is Opera?" in *The Oxford Handbook of Opera,* ed. Helen M. Greenwald (Oxford: Oxford University Press, 2014), 23.

66. See, e.g., Bertolt Brecht, "*Verfremdung* Effects in Chinese Acting," in *Brecht on Theatre: The Development of an Aesthetic,* 3rd ed., ed. Marc Silberman, Steve Giles, and Tom Kuhn, (London: Bloomsbury, 2014), 151–58.

67. In Brecht's words: "I can imagine that one day they will only be able to feel their old pleasure when the alienation effect is offered." Quoted in Hubert Witt, ed., *Brecht as They Knew Him,* trans. John Peet (Berlin: Seven Seas, 1974), 228.

68. Peter Brooker, "Key Words in Brecht's Theory and Practice of Theatre," in *The Cambridge Companion to Brecht,* 2nd ed., ed. Peter Thomson and Glendyr Sacks (Cambridge: Cambridge University Press, 2006), 218. More polemically put, the tendency of staging against-the-grain "has become more normative, tedious and . . . arbitrary than the assumed convention against which such theatre always claimed to offer resistance ever was or wanted to be." Lütteken, "Wider den Zeitgeist der Beliebigkeit," 23.

69. Calico, *Brecht at the Opera,* 143–45.

70. Risi, "Opera in Performance—In Search of New Analytical Approaches," 292.

71. Jens Larsen, preperformance talk in connection with the very final performance of the production at the Komische Oper, 28 April 2018.

72. Volker Blech, "Wie aus einer Ersatzsängerin ein Opernstar wird," interview with Maria Bengtsson, *Berliner Morgenpost,* 31 March 2013.

73. Larsen, preperformance talk, 28 April 2018.

CHAPTER 2

1. See, e.g., Helen Hills, "The Baroque: The Grit in the Oyster of Art History," in *Rethinking the Baroque,* ed. Helen Hills (Farnham, Surrey: Ashgate, 2011), 13.

2. Hills, 13.

3. Suzanne Aspden, "'An Infinity of Factions': Opera in Eighteenth-Century Britain and the Undoing of Society," *Cambridge Opera Journal* 9, no. 1 (1997): 1–19. Joseph Kerman paraphrases Benedetto Marcello as calling opera a "societal disease," also noting that he was an exception among Italian critics: in the early eighteenth century the moral dubiousness of opera was less acutely felt in Italy, where one was used to it, than abroad. Joseph Kerman, *Opera as Drama* (1956; Berkeley: University of California Press, 2005), 39.

4. Kerman, *Opera as Drama*, 40–41.

5. For a comprehensive examination of hyperbole and the baroque see Christopher D. Johnson, *Hyperboles: The Rhetoric of Excess in Baroque Literature and Thought* (Cambridge, MA: Harvard University Department of Comparative Literature, 2010).

6. This usage was first introduced in Gérard Genette, *Narrative Discourse: An Essay in Method*, trans. Jane E. Lewin (1972; Ithaca, NY: Cornell University Press, 1980), 234–35. Since then, the concept has become widespread in narratological theory, and Genette himself elaborated on it in *Métalepse* (Paris: Seuil, 2004).

7. The revival of Handel's works has also been instrumental in the development of director's opera, the two occurring more or less simultaneously. It is perhaps symptomatic that the three opening chapters in Schläder's *OperMachtTheaterBilder*—by Barbara Zuber, Corinna Herr, and Christopher Balme—are all dedicated to innovative productions of Handel.

8. Abbate and Parker, *A History of Opera*, 90.

9. I am quoting here Nathan Link's review of the DVD in *Opera Quarterly* 24, no. 3–4 (2008): 314. Link, in turn, quotes Andrew Clark, "*Giulio Cesare in Egitto*, Glyndebourne," *Financial Times*, 5 July 2005; and Robert Thicknesse, "*Giulio Cesare*: Robert Thicknesse at Glyndebourne," *The Times* (London), 5 July 2005.

10. Winton Dean, *Handel's Operas, 1726–1741* (Woodbridge: Boydell Press, 2006), 489.

11. Gilles Deleuze, *The Fold: Leibniz and the Baroque*, trans. Tom Conley (1988; London: Continuum, 2006). See, e.g., Omar Calabrese, *Neo-baroque: A Sign of the Times*, trans. Charles Lambert (Princeton, NJ: Princeton University Press, 1992); and Angela Ndalianis, *Neo-baroque Aesthetics and Contemporary Entertainment* (Cambridge, MA: MIT Press, 2004).

12. See, e.g., Kelly A. Wacker, ed., *Baroque Tendencies in Contemporary Art* (Newcastle: Cambridge Scholars, 2007).

13. Mieke Bal, *Quoting Caravaggio: Contemporary Art, Preposterous History* (Chicago: University of Chicago Press, 1999).

14. Bal, *Quoting Caravaggio*, 15.

15. Mieke Bal, "Baroque Matters," in *Rethinking the Baroque*, ed. Helen Hills (Farnham, Surrey: Ashgate, 2011), 188.

16. Bal, 188.

17. Winton Dean and John Merrill Knapp, *Handel's Operas, 1704–1726* (Woodbridge: Boydell Press, 2014), 172.

18. Dean and Knapp, *Handel's Operas, 1704–1726*, 173.

19. See, e.g., Reynolds, "Ruggiero's Deceptions, Cherubino's Distractions"; Abbate and Parker, *A History of Opera*, 76; and Wendy Heller, "Reforming Achilles: Gender, 'Opera Seria' and the Rhetoric of the Enlightened Hero," *Early Music* 26, no. 4 (1998): 562–81.

20. Martha Feldman, *The Castrato: Reflections on Natures and Kinds* (Oakland: University of California Press, 2015), xvii.

21. The popular *Rinaldo* was revived in 1712, 1713, 1714–15, 1717, and 1731. Dean and Knapp, *Handel's Operas, 1704–1726*, 183.

22. Wendy Heller, "The Beloved's Image: Handel's *Admeto* and the Statue of Alcestis," *Journal of the American Musicological Society* 58, no. 3 (2005): 559–637.

23. Corinne E. Blackmer and Patricia Juliana Smith, introduction to *En Travesti: Women, Gender, Subversion, Opera*, ed. Corinne E. Blackmer and Patricia Juliana Smith (New York: Columbia University Press, 1995), 9.

24. See Michel Foucault, *The Will to Knowledge: The History of Sexuality, Volume 1*, trans. Robert Hurley (1976; London: Penguin, 1998), 51–74.

25. Martha Feldman, "Denaturing the Castrato," *Opera Quarterly* 24, no. 3–4 (2008): 178.

26. McClary develops this argument in relation to Bizet's *Carmen*. See McClary, *Feminine Endings*, 56–67.

27. Dean, *Handel's Operas, 1726–1741*, 487, 489. On the countertenor revival see Peter Giles, *The History and Technique of the Counter-Tenor* (London: Scholar Press, 1994); and Corinna Herr, Arnold Jacobshagen, and Kai Wessel, eds., *Der Countertenor: Die männliche Falsettstimme vom Mittelalter zur Gegenwart* (Mainz: Schott, 2012).

28. Dean and Knapp, *Handel's Operas, 1704–1726*, 183.

29. See, e.g., Aspden, "An Infinity of Factions"; and McGeary, "'Warbling Eunuchs.'"

30. Quoted in McGeary, "'Warbling Eunuchs,'" 5–6.

31. See McGeary, 11–15. McGeary stresses the fact that the sex change would not have appeared as the change from one pole of a binary system into another but, in accordance with the notion of female genitalia being essentially an inverted/underdeveloped version of the male, as a descending of the Chain of Being, from the masculine to the feminine.

32. Hugh Canning, "Hard to Handel," *Sunday Times* (London), 10 July 2011.

33. Reynolds, "Ruggiero's Deceptions, Cherubino's Distractions," 136.

34. The exception is Almirena's strident first aria, "Combatti da forte," which, as critics often note, is quite out of character. Dean and Knapp, *Handel's Operas,*

1704–1726, 178. Carsen's production, however, excises it, letting Almirena make her first appearance with "Augelletti."

35. The interview is part of the "Director's Notes" feature on the Opus Arte DVD of *Rinaldo* (2012).

36. For an accessible introduction to this aspect of Lacan see Slavoj Žižek, *How to Read Lacan* (London: Granta, 2006), 34.

37. Gilles Deleuze, *Coldness and Cruelty* (1967), in Gilles Deleuze and Leopold von Sacher-Masoch, *Masochism: Coldness and Cruelty; Venus in Furs*, trans. Jean McNeil and Aude Willm (New York: Zone, 1991), 33. Richard Krafft-Ebing, *Psychopathia Sexualis: Mit besonderer Berücksichtigung der conträren Sexualempfindung*, 9th ed. (Stuttgart: Ferdinand Fink, 1894), 131.

38. Böhme, *Fetishism and Culture*.

39. Deleuze, *The Fold*, 141.

40. Deleuze, 141.

41. Barbara Zuber, "Bildzauber—Zauberbilder: Die Ästhetik des Wunderbaren in Jossi Wielers und Christof Loys Inszenierungen von Händels *Alcina*," in *OperMachtTheaterBilder: Neue Wirklichkeiten des Regietheaters*, ed. Jürgen Schläder (Berlin: Henschel, 2006), 25.

42. Although details of "Ein Kind wird geschlagen" (1919), Freud's earliest attempt at accounting for masochistic inclinations, differ from those represented in Rinaldo on several accounts (the Freudian child would be considerably younger than a boarding-school pupil at the moment of "original" beating, for instance), the basic causal relation between corporeal punishment and later sexual fantasies is the same.

43. British law banned corporal punishment in all schools (i.e., private as well as state schools) only in 1998. In the late 1970s, for instance, the Purley High School for Boys in London ended up at the center of a heated debate because of its record-high employment of caning. Smoking—for which "Rinaldo" is being unjustly punished at Glyndebourne—was in fact one of the typical minor offenses that led to this particular method of disciplining. For an archive of articles on corporal punishment in the UK, see the website of the World Corporal Punishment Research at www.corpun.com.

CHAPTER 3

1. The phrase is Margaret Reynolds's, in "Ruggiero's Deceptions," 141.

2. For a comprehensive collection of essays on its legacy see Lydia Goehr and Daniel Herwitz, eds., *The Don Giovanni Moment: Essays on the Legacy of an Opera* (New York: Columbia University Press, 2008).

3. See, e.g., Jeremy Tambling, "Losey's 'fenomeni morbosi': Don Giovanni," in *Opera, Ideology and Film* (Manchester: Manchester University Press, 1987),

159–75; Will, "Zooming In, Gazing Back"; and Axel Englund, "Thrilling Opera: Conflicts of the Mind and the Media in Kasper Holten's *Juan*," in *Music, Narrative and the Moving Image: Varieties of Plurimedial Interrelations*, ed. Walter Bernhart and David Francis Urrows (Leiden: Rodopi/Brill, 2019), 185–98.

4. This quotation is from the website of the Halifax Summer Opera Festival 2018, which presented a *Giovanni* directed by Jason Davis and Nina Scott-Stoddart. See http://halifaxsummeroperafestival.com/?page_id=117324. Other companies evoking the Me Too movement in connection to their *Don Giovanni* productions include Opera Hong Kong, Opera Queensland, OperaBend, The Core Ensemble, Opera on Location, Theater Lübeck, Northwestern, Baltimore Concert Opera, Teatro Filarmonico Verona, Wermland Opera, Skånska Operan, Petite Opera, Purchase College Opera, Houston Grand Opera, and Edmonton Opera.

5. Richard Will, "*Don Giovanni* and the Resilience of Rape Culture," *Journal of the American Musicological Society* 71, no. 1 (2018): 218–20.

6. Will, 218.

7. Will, 221.

8. Will, 222.

9. In addition to Will's work see, for instance, Wye Jamison Allanbrook, *Rhythmic Gesture in Mozart: "Le nozze di Figaro" & "Don Giovanni"* (Chicago: University of Chicago Press, 1983), 227–29; Ralph P. Locke, "What Are These Women Doing in Opera?" in *En Travesti: Women, Gender, Subversion, Opera*, ed. Corinne E. Blackmer and Patricia Juliana Smith (New York: Columbia University Press, 1995), 67–69; Clément, *Opera*, 33–34; and Felicity Baker, "The Figures of Hell in the *Don Giovanni* Libretto," in *Words about Mozart: Essays in Honour of Stanley Sadie*, ed. Dorothea Link and Judith Nagley (Woodbridge: Boydell Press, 2005), 97–98.

10. Will, "*Don Giovanni*," 222.

11. See, e.g., Kristi Brown-Montesano's contribution from December 2017 to the AMS blog *Musicology Now:* "Holding Don Giovanni Accountable," www.musicologynow.org/2017/12/holding-don-giovanni-accountable.html.

12. Theodor W. Adorno, "Huldigung an Zerlina" (1953), in *Gesammelte Schriften, Bd. 17: Musikalische Schriften IV: Moments musicaux, Impromptus*, ed. Rolf Tiedemann (Frankfurt: Suhrkamp, 1982), 34–35. Translation quoted from Berthold Hoeckner, "Homage to Adorno's 'Homage to Zerlina,'" *Musical Quarterly* 87, no. 3 (2004): 511.

13. Hoeckner, "Homage," 513.

14. Charles Ford, *Music, Sexuality and the Enlightenment in Mozart's "Figaro," "Don Giovanni" and "Così fan tutte"* (Farnham, Surrey: Ashgate, 2012), 182–85.

15. See, e.g., Allanbrook, *Rhythmic Gesture in Mozart*, 262; and Kristi Brown-Montesano, *Understanding the Women of Mozart's Operas* (Berkeley: University of California Press, 2007), 69.

16. See, e.g., Wye Jamison Allanbrook, Mary Hunter, and Gretchen A. Whee-lock, "Staging Mozart's Women," in *Siren Songs: Representations of Gender and Sexuality in Opera*, ed. Mary Ann Smart (Princeton, NJ: Princeton University Press, 2000), 64; and Brown-Montesano, *Understanding the Women*, 70.

17. Allanbrook advocates a staging that lets Zerlina keep a distanced self-awareness vis-à-vis the game she is playing and points to how utterly incompat-ible Sellars's painful imagery and static close-ups are with Zerlina's wit and the ambiguous layering of the rhythmic gesture in Mozart's score. Allanbrook, Hunter, and Wheelock, "Staging Mozart's Women," 62–66.

18. Marisa Martins, email interview by author, 8 September 2019.

19. The quotations are taken from Charlotte Higgins, "ENO Retests Market with Bieito's Dirty Don," *The Guardian*, 29 September 2004.

20. Unlike Bieito's *Entführung* it has received fairly little scholarly attention, the chief exception being Sarah Wright's treatment of it in the context of differ-ent cultural manifestations of the Don Juan myth. See Sarah Wright, *Tales of Seduction: The Figure of Don Juan in Spanish Culture* (New York: Tauris, 2007), 157–86.

21. Wright, *Tales of Seduction*, 163, 181.

22. Wright, 159.

23. Quoted in Brown-Montesano, *Understanding the Women*, 62. Brown-Montesano develops this observation by showing how this class-based flattery recurs insistently in various renderings of the Don Juan myth.

24. Brown-Montesano, *Understanding the Women*, 67–68.

25. See Alessandra Campana, "To Look Again (at *Don Giovanni*)," in *The Cambridge Companion to Eighteenth-Century Opera*, ed. Anthony R. DelDonna and Pierpaolo Polzonetti (Cambridge: Cambridge University Press, 2009), 149. While Anna's aria aligns itself with what Susan McClary, in her analysis of *L'Orfeo*, designates a rhetoric of lament, Zerlina's is patently an instance of the other orphic rhetoric: that of seduction. See McClary, *Feminine Endings*, 46.

26. Brown-Montesano, *Understanding the Women*, 70.

27. In Allanbrook's words the rhythms of the gavotte "mime an arch parody of submission" ("Staging Mozart's Women," 63). The subservient character of her appeal is also announced musically by the descending motive with which she opens her aria. Throughout the first stanza her phrases retain this trajectory of self-abasement; whether through stepwise movement or broken triads they are always downward bound. At the recapitulation after the contrasting second stanza, in which her vocal line endeavors for a moment to claim the ascending leading note, the effect is all the more striking yet far from unambiguous in terms of initiative and power. Here, the flute, bassoon, and obbligato cello sink through an extended phrase, and the voice and strings enter in a docile imitation of this gesture as the music returns to the tonic key: it is as if the soprano voice had itself set up a structure with which it can now comply, playing the obedient

servant to an authority that was in fact established by its own opening phrase. At this moment, then, a multilayered dynamic of agency and acquiescence is created by musical means, while the whole ensemble, as it were, bows down in utter meekness at Masetto's feet.

28. For an incisive account of this tradition in poetry, film, and psychoanalytic theory see Eliane DalMolin, *Cutting the Body: Representing Woman in Baudelaire's Poetry, Truffaut's Cinema, and Freud's Psychoanalysis* (Ann Arbor: University of Michigan Press, 2000).

29. As Eliane DalMolin has suggested, the cutting of a woman's hair can serve as a "reversed castration scenario," which potentially "leaves her in an ambivalent sexual position." DalMolin, *Cutting the Body*, 82.

30. Anthony Rudel, *Imagining Don Giovanni* (New York: Atlantic Monthly Press, 2001), 151.

31. Marquis de Sade, *The 120 Days of Sodom, or the School of Libertinage*, trans. Will McMorran and Thomas Wynn (London: Random House, 2016), 384.

32. Ford, *Music, Sexuality and the Enlightenment*, 55; see also 205–7.

33. Deleuze, *Coldness and Cruelty*, 25–26.

34. Deleuze, 27.

35. Deleuze, 28.

36. Deleuze, 28–29.

37. Deleuze, 29.

38. As Lacan suggested as early as 1963, Sade is thus paradoxically close to his contemporary Immanuel Kant, and *Philosophy in the Bedroom* "gives the truth" of *Critique of Practical Reason*. Jacques Lacan, "Kant with Sade," trans. James B. Swenson Jr., *October* 51 (1989): 55. Žižek returns to this idea in *Opera's Second Death*, arguing that the libertine's commitment to destruction becomes a categorical imperative of sorts, the seamy underside of Enlightenment ethics. He brings it to bear, however, not on *Don Giovanni* but on *Tristan*. See Slavoj Žižek and Mladen Dolar, *Opera's Second Death* (New York: Routledge, 2002), 141.

39. Slavoj Žižek, *For They Know Not What They Do: Enjoyment as a Political Factor* (London: Verso, 1991), 114.

40. Žižek and Dolar, *Opera's Second Death*, 46.

41. The mirroring of these scenes has also been noted by Anna-Elena Pääkkölä, who analyzes the SM aspects of Guth's production in her dissertation, "Sound Kinks: Sadomasochistic Erotica in Audiovisual Music Performances" (PhD diss., University of Turku, 2016), 184–85.

42. Pääkkölä takes a different approach to Guth's Zerlina, arguing that she is to be understood as a Sadean character yet one that undermines any essentializing claims that might attach to her role: "In this production, Zerlina is not girly, cute or innocent, but rather reveals the three stances as queer performatives." "Sound Kinks," 181–82.

43. Andrea Beckmann's sociological account of SM, based on ethnographical interviews and participant observation in London in the early 2000s, identifies a generational gap: while an "old scene" was marked by unchangeable roles (typically with female doms and male subs), the current SM scene, according to Beckmann, is marked by "switching" to a much higher degree; that is, the assignment of dominant and submissive roles is not fixed according to sex or gender but is itself an object of play and negotiation. Beckmann, *The Social Construction,* chap. 3, esp. 116–24.

44. Brown-Montesano, who writes about the importance of the *manine* figure in Giovanni's seductive rhetoric, also notes that Zerlina skewers it in this number. Brown-Montesano, *Understanding the Women,* 79.

45. Pääkkölä, using Lynda Hart's concept of "the queer real," also notes that the Salzburg staging of this number "blurs the lines between represented violence and represented SM." "Sound Kinks," 187–88.

CHAPTER 4

1. Nina Stemme et al., "705 kvinnliga sångare i upprop mot trakasserier och sexism," *Dagens Nyheter,* 13 November 2017 (updated 16 November 2017), www.dn.se/kultur-noje/705-kvinnliga-sangare-i-upprop-mot-trakasserier-och-sexism.

2. Michael Cooper, "David Daniels, Opera Star, Is Arrested on Sexual Assault Charge," *New York Times,* 30 January 2019.

3. Michael Cooper, "James Levine's Final Act at the Met Ends in Disgrace," *New York Times,* 12 March 2018; "Allegations against Plácido Domingo Deemed Credible by L.A. Opera," *New York Times,* 10 March 2020.

4. For the seminal exposition of this argument, dating the start of the change to around 1800, see Lydia Goehr, *The Imaginary Museum of Musical Works: An Essay in the Philosophy of Music* (Oxford: Clarendon, 1992), 224–32. In relation to opera see Karen Henson, *Opera Acts: Singers and Performance in the Late Nineteenth Century* (Cambridge: Cambridge University Press, 2014).

5. See chapter 3 of James Kennaway, *Bad Vibrations: The History of the Idea of Music as a Cause of Disease* (Farnham, Surrey: Ashgate, 2012).

6. Dreyfus, *Wagner and the Erotic Impulse,* 135–50.

7. Dreyfus, 2.

8. Baudelaire, *Selected Letters,* 146. See also Dreyfus, *Wagner and the Erotic Impulse,* 17–23.

9. Dreyfus, *Wagner and the Erotic Impulse,* 37.

10. J. L. Klein, *Geschichte des Dramas. VIII. Das spanische Drama. Erster Band* (Leipzig: T. O. Weigel, 1871), 738. See also Dreyfus, *Wagner and the Erotic Impulse,* 34.

11. Klein, *Geschichte des Dramas,* 738. Nicolas Slonimsky, *Lexicon of Musical Invective: Critical Assaults on Composers since Beethoven's Time* (1953; New York: Norton, 2000), 114. See also Dreyfus, *Wagner and the Erotic Impulse,* 39.

12. Friedrich Nietzsche, *Nietzsche contra Wagner,* in *Kritische Studienausgabe in 15 Bänden,* ed. Giorgio Colli and Mazzino Montinari, vol. 6 (Munich: Deutsche Taschenbuch, 1999), 431.

13. Nietzsche declared his hatred against this sexuality in an 1888 letter to Malwida von Meysenbug, quoted in Jutta Georg and Renate Reschke, eds., *Nietzsche und Wagner: Perspektiven ihrer Auseinandersetzung* (Berlin: de Gruyter, 2016), 60.

14. Anna Larsson, Skype interview by author, 25 July 2019.

15. Friedrich Nietzsche, *The Case of Wagner,* in *The Birth of Tragedy and The Case of Wagner,* trans. Walter Kaufmann (New York: Vintage, 1967), 184.

16. Friedrich Nietzsche, *The Birth of Tragedy,* in *The Birth of Tragedy and The Case of Wagner,* trans. Walter Kaufmann (New York: Vintage, 1967), 25.

17. Master K, *The Beauty of Kinbaku, or Everything You Ever Wanted to Know about Japanese Erotic Bondage When You Suddenly Realized You Didn't Speak Japanese,* 2nd ed. (New York: King Cat Ink, 2014), 9–19 et passim.

18. For an exploration of fin de siècle aestheticism, its connection to sadomasochism as a turning-away from bourgeois normativity, and its expression through the metaphor of flower cultivation, see chapter 3 of Romana Byrne, *Aesthetic Sexuality: A Literary History of Sadomasochism* (London: Bloomsbury, 2013).

19. Larsson, interview.

20. Max Nordau, *Degeneration,* trans. anonymous (New York: D. Appleton, 1895), 181–82.

21. Nietzsche, *The Case of Wagner,* 184.

22. Nietzsche, 180.

23. Quoted in Gunilla Brodrej, "Dirigentväldet är direkt farligt för unga kvinnor," interview with Anna Larsson, *Expressen,* 27 October 2017.

24. Quoted in Brodrej, "Dirigentväldet."

25. Anna Larsson, "Sextrakasserier i operahusen," *Dalarnas Tidningar,* 21 September 2012.

26. See Suzanne Stewart's interpretation of Parsifal's compassion for Amfortas as sexual fantasy and pornography, in *Sublime Surrender: Male Masochism at the Fin-de-siècle* (Ithaca, NY: Cornell University Press, 1988), 108.

27. Poizat, *The Angel's Cry,* 194, 198–99; see also Stewart, *Sublime Surrender,* 107.

28. Richard Wagner, "Über Schauspieler und Sänger," in *Gesammelte Schriften und Dichtungen,* vol. 9, 3rd ed. (Leipzig: C. F. W. Siegel, n.d.), 161.

29. Dreyfus, *Wagner and the Erotic Impulse,* 57.

30. Dreyfus, 57.

31. Wagner, "Über Schauspieler und Sänger," 229.

32. Wagner, 218.

33. Wagner, 218.

34. Wagner, 226.

35. On the idea of perversion as a necessary part of normality, see Rothenberg, Foster, and Žižek, *Perversion and the Social Relation*, 2–4.

36. Alexandra Wilson, *The Puccini Problem: Opera, Nationalism and Modernity* (Cambridge: Cambridge University Press, 2007), 69.

37. Kerman, *Opera as Drama*, 205.

38. Fausto Torrefranca, *Giacomo Puccini e l'opera internazionale* (Torino: Fratelli Bocca, 1912). See also Wilson, *The Puccini Problem*, 125–54.

39. Torrefranca, *Giacomo Puccini*, 54.

40. For a development of this argument see Arman Schwartz, "Rough Music: *Tosca* and *Verismo* Reconsidered," *Nineteenth Century Music* 31, no. 3 (2008): 228–44.

41. Nikolaus Lehnhoff, *Die Oper ist das Reich des Scheins: Inszenierungen von Nikolaus Lehnhoff*, ed. Birgit Pargner (Leipzig: Henschel, 2015), 116.

42. Scarpia, in both Puccini's and Sardou's works, is repeatedly and casually referred to as a sadist. See, e.g., Mosco Carner, *Giacomo Puccini: Tosca* (Cambridge: Cambridge University Press, 1985), 52–53, 83; Eric A. Plaut, *Grand Opera: Mirror of the Western Mind* (Chicago: Ivan R. Dee, 1993), 242–44; Susan Vandiver Nicassio, *Tosca's Rome: The Play and the Opera in Historical Perspective* (Chicago: University of Chicago Press, 1999), 185, 203, 207–10.

43. This is one of the changes Puccini himself introduced in the libretto: the librettists first wrote it as a question, "Tu mì odii?" Carner, *Tosca*, 20.

44. Slavoj Žižek, *Welcome to the Desert of the Real* (London: Verso, 2002), 21–22. Elsewhere, Žižek actually comments in passing on Scarpia's need for Tosca's contempt but does not consider it in terms of masochism; see Žižek and Dolar, *Opera's Second Death*, 109.

45. See, e.g., Žižek, *Welcome to the Desert*, 21; and Deleuze, *Coldness and Cruelty*.

46. Deleuze, *Coldness and Cruelty*, 32.

47. Deleuze, 33.

48. Lehnhoff, *Die Oper*, 116.

49. Leopold von Sacher-Masoch, *Venus in Furs* (1870), in Gilles Deleuze and Leopold von Sacher-Masoch, *Masochism: Coldness and Cruelty; Venus in Furs*, trans. Jean McNeil and Aude Willm (New York: Zone, 1989), 153, 178.

50. Sacher-Masoch, 189, 202.

51. Sacher-Masoch, 197, 214–15, 246–47.

52. Poizat, *The Angel's Cry*, 32–37 et passim.

53. Kramer, *After the Lovedeath*, 150.

54. It is a "song act" in the sense suggested by Lawrence Kramer: a reflective moment staging its own genre, which constitutes a call for interpretation. See

Lawrence Kramer, "Meaning," in *The Oxford Handbook of Opera*, ed. Helen M. Greenwald (Oxford: Oxford University Press, 2014), 356.

55. Poizat, *The Angel's Cry,* 104.

56. Sacher-Masoch, *Venus in Furs,* 220, 254.

57. Sacher-Masoch, 234.

58. Newmahr, *Playing on the Edge,* 144–86; Bauer, *Queer BDSM Intimacies,* 162–63.

59. See Bauer, *Queer BDSM Intimacies,* 145; and Weiss, *Techniques of Pleasure,* 61–62.

60. Quoted in Weiss, *Techniques of Pleasure,* 85.

61. Quoted in Weiss, 92.

62. Weiss, 88.

63. See Tambling, *Opera, Ideology, Film,* 53; or Mary Ann Smart, "The Lost Voice of Rosine Stoltz," in *En Travesti: Women, Gender, Subversion, Opera,* ed. Corinne E. Blackmer and Patricia Juliana Smith (New York: Columbia University Press, 1995), 171.

64. Christa Ludwig, *In My Own Voice: Memoirs,* trans. Regina Domeraski (New York: Limelight, 1999), 77.

65. David Bret, *Maria Callas: The Tigress and the Lamb* (London: Robson, 1997), 217, 237.

66. Bret, 217.

67. Arianna Huffington, *Maria Callas: The Woman behind the Legend* (New York: Cooper Square Press, 2002), 257.

68. Tito Gobbi on interpretation in Carner, *Giacomo Puccini: Tosca,* 81.

69. Carner, *Giacomo Puccini: Tosca,* 89.

70. See their web pages at www.dasniyasommer.de and www.francisdath.info, respectively.

71. Larsson, interview.

CHAPTER 5

1. See, e.g., Martha Feldman, "The Interstitial Voice: An Opening," *Journal of the American Musicological Society* 68, no. 3 (2015): 657–58. See also Nina Eidsheim, *The Race of Sound: Listening, Timbre, and Vocality in African American Music* (Durham, NC: Duke University Press, 2019).

2. Feldman, "The Interstitial Voice," 657–58.

3. For a recent take on posthumanism and opera see Christopher Morris, "Casting Metal: Opera Studies after Humanism," *Opera Quarterly* 35, no. 1–2 (2019): 77–95.

4. Gloria G. Brame, William D. Brame, and Jon Jacobs, *Different Loving: The World of Sexual Dominance and Submission* (New York: Villard, 1996), 151.

The *Ullstein Enzyklopädie der Sexualität* lists a similar yet slightly vaguer category under the heading "Metamorphosismus," where masochistic inclination creates a desire to be transformed into a thing, an animal, or slave in order to be an object of contempt or abuse. See Ernest Borneman, *Ullstein Enzyklopädie der Sexualität* (Frankfurt am Main: Ullstein, 1990), 489.

5. Matei Calinescu, *Five Faces of Modernity: Modernism, Avant-garde, Decadence, Kitsch, Postmodernism* (1977; Durham, NC: Duke University Press, 1987), 125.

6. Sontag, "Fascinating Fascism," 105.

7. In April of 1933 he wrote to Erich Kleiber, who had led the premiere of *Wozzeck* there eight years earlier: "When this new opera is produced in Germany of today there'll be an outburst of the most colossal indignation." Quoted in Douglas Jarman, *Alban Berg: Lulu* (Cambridge: Cambridge University Press, 1991), 7.

8. Gordon, *Voluptuous Panic*, 253–55.

9. Quoted in Jarman, *Alban Berg: Lulu*, 42.

10. Gordon, *Voluptuous Panic*, 171.

11. The productions by Bechtolf and Kentridge, for instance, are full of visual allusions to the 1920s.

12. Gordon, *Voluptuous Panic*, 33, 36–37.

13. Gordon, 59.

14. Alban Berg, *Lulu*, dir. Sven-Eric Bechtolf (TDK, DVD DVWW-OPLULU, 2006).

15. Mardi Byers, interview by author, 14 September 2019.

16. Theodor W. Adorno, *Alban Berg: Master of the Smallest Link*, trans. Juliane Brand and Christopher Hailey (1968; Cambridge: Cambridge University Press, 1991), 131.

17. Berg's words are from an essay on *Wozzeck*, quoted in George Perle, "Some Thoughts on an Ideal Production of *Lulu*," *Journal of Musicology* 7, no. 2 (1989): 244.

18. See Perle, "Some Thoughts."

19. George Perle, *The Operas of Alban Berg*, vol. 2, *Lulu* (Berkeley: University of California Press, 1985), 66.

20. See Douglas Jarman, "Friedrich's *Lulu*," *International Alban Berg Society Newsletter* 10 (1981): 14.

21. Alban Berg, *Lulu*, dir. Vera Nemirova (Unitel Classica, DVD D4779, 2012).

22. Alban Berg, *Lulu*, dir. Olivier Py (Deutsche Grammophon, DVD 00440 073 4637, 2011).

23. Alban Berg, *Lulu*, dir. William Kentridge (Nonesuch, DVD 0075597945379, 2016).

24. Krafft-Ebing, *Psychopathia Sexualis*, 108–11.

25. Magnus Hirschfeld, *Sexualpathologie: Ein Lehrbuch für Ärzte und Studierende. Zweiter Teil* (Bonn: A. Marcus & E. Webers, 1918), 241.

26. See Englund, "An Incomplete Life."

27. See "Lulu—The Lethal Victim," dir. Reiner E. Moritz, a bonus feature on Alban Berg, *Lulu*, dir. Sven-Eric Bechtolf (DVD DVWW-OPLULU. TDK, 2006).

28. Perle, *Operas of Alban Berg*, 2:62.

29. This ornament is more-or-less impossible to execute as it is written; most singers use the ossia, and even Barbara Hannigan, who always excels in making the almost unachievable seem like child's play, streamlines it slightly on the DVD recording from La Monnaie.

30. The cuts to which Berg subjected Wedekind's text equate the music with the "Schauer": in Wedekind's play she simply says that she can feel the audience thinking about marrying her (referring to Schön's plan of placing her in the theater).

31. The embarrassment of the poetry notwithstanding, Berg does not shy away from sustaining the analogy between himself and the composer: as has been noted by Perle and others, the musical movements to which Alwa alludes correspond vaguely to sections of Berg's own *Lyric Suite*. (See Perle, *Operas of Alban Berg*, 2:59; and Jarman, *Alban Berg: Lulu*, 22.) Thus the "Andante der Wollust," which is there in Wedekind's play, is suggestive of the second movement of the suite ("II. Andante amoroso") and the "Misterioso," which Berg substituted for Wedekind's "Capriccio," of the third ("III. Allegro misterioso").

32. Berg, *Lulu, Akt 1-2*, 632 (m. 1094).

33. Barbara Seiler, dir., "Barbara Hannigan: I'm a Creative Animal," *Concert Documentary* (DVD ACC 20327. Accentus Music, 2015).

34. Seiler.

35. Seiler.

36. See Hannigan's talk at Women of the World Festival 2013 at the Southbank Centre, "Opera Singer Barbara Hannigan on Why She Loves 'Lulu,'" www.youtube.com/watch?v=6AhnOFwfBnM. The direct quotes from Hannigan in the following four paragraphs are taken from this talk.

37. See, e.g., Zachary Woolfe, "Missing from Podiums: Women," *New York Times*, 20 December 2013.

38. Seiler, "Barbara Hannigan."

39. Hubert Achermann and Michael Haefliger's introduction to Susanne Stähr, ed., *PrimaDonna*, program book for the Lucerne Festival (Lucerne: Stiftung Lucerne Festival, 2016), 5.

EPILOGUE

1. Antonin Artaud, *The Theatre and Its Double*, trans. Victor Corti (1938; Richmond, Surrey: Alma Classics, 2013), 72, 81.

2. Artaud, 73.

3. Artaud, 73.

4. Artaud, 60, 63.

5. For an incisive account of this type of art see Jennifer Doyle, *Hold It against Me: Difficulty and Emotion in Contemporary Art* (Durham, NC: Duke University Press, 2013).

6. Robert Ayers, "'The Knife Is Real, the Blood Is Real, and the Emotions Are Real.'—Robert Ayers in Conversation with Marina Abramović" (2010), www.askyfilledwithshootingstars.com/wordpress/?p=1197.

7. Interview in Kaiser, *Entführung*, 11.

8. The most influential version of this story is no doubt Fredric Jameson, *Postmodernism, or, the Cultural Logic of Late Capitalism* (Durham, NC: Duke University Press, 1991). Recently, studies of contemporary theater and performance have also argued that the longing for authenticity marks a departure from the postmodern: see Andy Lavender, *Performance in the Twenty-First Century: Theatres of Engagement* (London: Routledge, 2016); and Daniel Schulze, *Authenticity in Contemporary Theatre and Performance: Make it Real* (London: Bloomsbury, 2017).

9. Hans-Thies Lehmann, *Postdramatic Theatre,* trans. Karen Jürs-Munby (1999; London: Routledge, 2006), 100–101.

10. Lehmann, 101, 103.

11. Lehmann, 100–101.

12. Sammie Gorham, Skype interview by author, 27 March 2019. Sammie Gorham, "Sammie's Secret: A Life in Opera + BDSM," essay for the program book for *Susanna's Secret,* performed at Mount Analogue, Seattle, 20 January–14 February 2018.

13. Joa Helgesson, Skype interview by author, 28 March 2019.

14. Quoted in Arvid Jurjaks, "En smärtsam jakt på operans anatomi," *OPUS,* 1 June 2018, https://opusmagasin.se/en-smartsam-jakt-pa-operans-anatomi.

15. Gorham, "Sammie's Secret."

16. Helgesson, interview.

17. Newmahr, *Playing on the Edge,* 72–73. See also Beckmann, *The Social Construction,* 184.

Works Cited

Abbate, Carolyn. "Music—Drastic or Gnostic?" *Critical Inquiry* 30, no. 3 (2004): 505–36.

———. "Opera; or, The Envoicing of Women." In Solie, *Musicology and Difference*, 225–58.

Abbate, Carolyn, and Roger Parker. *A History of Opera*. New York: Norton, 2012.

Abel, Samuel D. *Opera in the Flesh: Sexuality in Operatic Performance*. Boulder, CO: Westview Press, 1997.

Adorno, Theodor W. *Alban Berg: Master of the Smallest Link*. 1968. Translated by Juliane Brand and Christopher Hailey. Cambridge: Cambridge University Press, 1991.

———. "Huldigung an Zerlina." 1953. In *Gesammelte Schriften, Bd. 17: Musikalische Schriften IV: Moments musicaux, Impromptus*. Edited by Rolf Tiedemann, 34–35. Frankfurt: Suhrkamp, 1982.

———. "Opera and the Long-Playing Record." 1969. Translated by Thomas Y. Levin. *October* 55 (1990): 62–66.

Allanbrook, Wye Jamison. *Rhythmic Gesture in Mozart: "Le nozze di Figaro" & "Don Giovanni."* Chicago: University of Chicago Press, 1983.

Allanbrook, Wye Jamison, Mary Hunter, and Gretchen A. Wheelock. "Staging Mozart's Women." In *Siren Songs: Representations of Gender and Sexuality in Opera*, edited by Mary Ann Smart, 47–66. Princeton, NJ: Princeton University Press, 2000.

Anonymous. *Lady Bumtickler's Revels: A Comic Opera, in Two Acts*. London: George Peacock, 1872.

———. "SM International." In Kleinplatz and Moser, *Sadomasochism*, 263–80.

———. "*William Tell:* Nudity and Rape Scene Greeted with Boos at Royal Opera House." *The Guardian*, 30 June 2015.

Artaud, Antonin. *The Theatre and Its Double*. 1938. Translated by Victor Corti. Richmond, Surrey: Alma Classics, 2013.

———. "Theatre and Cruelty." In Artaud, *The Theatre and Its Double*, 60–62.

Ashbee, Henry Spencer. *Bibliography of Prohibited Books*. Vol. 1. 1877. New York: Jack Brussel, 1962.

Ashley, Tim. "*Guillaume Tell* Review—Sex, Violence and Protracted Booing." *The Guardian*, 30 June 2015.

Aspden, Suzanne. "'A Great Private Party': The Participatory Theatrics of Country-House Operagoing." *Opera Quarterly* 35, no. 1–2 (2019): 96–117.

———. "'An Infinity of Factions': Opera in Eighteenth-Century Britain and the Undoing of Society." *Cambridge Opera Journal* 9, no. 1 (1997): 1–19.

Ayers, Robert. "'The Knife Is Real, the Blood Is Real, and the Emotions Are Real': Robert Ayers in Conversation with Marina Abramović." A Sky Filled with Shooting Stars website, 2010. www.askyfilledwithshootingstars.com /wordpress/?p=1197.

Baker, Evan. *From the Score to the Stage: An Illustrated History of Continental Opera Production and Staging*. Chicago: University of Chicago Press, 2013.

Baker, Felicity. "The Figures of Hell in the *Don Giovanni* Libretto." In *Words about Mozart: Essays in Honour of Stanley Sadie*, edited by Dorothea Link and Judith Nagley, 77–106. Woodbridge: Boydell Press, 2005.

Bal, Mieke. "Baroque Matters." In Hills, *Rethinking the Baroque*, 183–202.

———. *Quoting Caravaggio: Contemporary Art, Preposterous History*. Chicago: University of Chicago Press, 1999.

Bannon, Race. "SM as Erotic Theater." In *SM Classics*, edited by Susan Wright, 19–26. New York: Masquerade, 1999.

Baranello, Micaela. "Staging Opera Ballet." *Journal of the American Musicological Society* 71, no. 1 (2018): 223–26.

Barthes, Roland. *S/Z*. 1970. Translated by R. Howard. New York: Farrar, Straus and Giroux, 1975.

Bartky, Sandra Lee. "Feminine Masochism and the Politics of Personal Transformation." In *Femininity and Domination: Studies in the Phenomenology of Oppression*, 45–62. New York: Routledge, 1990.

Batka, Richard, and Willibald Nagel. *Allgemeine Geschichte der Musik: Dritter Band*. Stuttgart: Carl Grüninger, 1909.

Baudelaire, Charles. *Correspondance: Tome 1, 1832-1860*. Edited by Claude Pichois and Jean Ziegler. Paris: Bibliothèque de la Pléiade, 1973.

———. *Selected Letters of Charles Baudelaire: The Conquest of Solitude*. Edited and translated by Rosemary Lloyd. Chicago: University of Chicago Press, 1986.

Bauer, Robin. *Queer BDSM Intimacies: Critical Consent and Pushing Boundaries*. Basingstoke: Palgrave Macmillan, 2014.

Beckmann, Andrea. *The Social Construction of Sexuality and Perversion: Deconstructing Sadomasochism*. Basingstoke: Palgrave Macmillan, 2009.

Bennett, Theodore. "Unorthodox Rules: The Instructive Potential of BDSM Consent for Law." *Journal of Positive Sexuality* 4, no. 1 (2018): 4–11.

Bentley, Paul. "'Mummy Porn': *Fifty Shades of Grey* Outstrips Harry Potter to Become Fastest Selling Paperback of All Time." *Daily Mail*, 18 June 2012.

Bienvenu, Robert V. "The Development of Sadomasochism as a Cultural Style in the Twentieth-Century United States." PhD diss., Indiana University, 1998.

Blackmer, Corinne E., and Patricia Juliana Smith, eds. *En Travesti: Women, Gender, Subversion, Opera*. New York: Columbia University Press, 1995.

———. Introduction to Blackmer and Smith, *En Travesti*, 1–19.

Blech, Volker. "Wie aus einer Ersatzsängerin ein Opernstar wird." Interview with Maria Bengtsson. *Berliner Morgenpost*, 31 March 2013.

Böhme, Hartmut. *Fetishism and Culture: A Different Theory of Modernity*. Translated by Anna Galt. Berlin: De Gruyter, 2014.

Borneman, Ernest. *Ullstein Enzyklopädie der Sexualität*. Frankfurt am Main: Ullstein, 1990.

Brame, Gloria G., William D. Brame, and Jon Jacobs. *Different Loving: The World of Sexual Dominance and Submission*. New York: Villard, 1996.

Brecht, Bertolt. "*Verfremdung* Effects in Chinese Acting." In *Brecht on Theatre: The Development of an Aesthetic*. 3rd ed. Edited by Mark Silberman, Steve Giles, and Tom Kuhn, 151–58. London: Bloomsbury, 2014.

Bret, David. *Maria Callas: The Tigress and the Lamb*. London: Robson, 1997.

Brodrej, Gunilla. "Dirigentväldet är direkt farligt för unga kvinnor." Interview with Anna Larsson. *Expressen*, 27 October 2017.

Brooker, Peter. "Key Words in Brecht's Theory and Practice of Theatre." In *The Cambridge Companion to Brecht*. 2nd ed. Edited by Peter Thomson and Glendyr Sacks, 209–24. Cambridge: Cambridge University Press, 2006.

Brown-Montesano, Kristi. "Holding Don Giovanni Accountable." *Musicology Now*, December 2017. www.musicologynow.org/2017/12/holding-don-giovanni-accountable.html.

———. *Understanding the Women of Mozart's Operas*. Berkeley: University of California Press, 2007.

Butler, Judith. *Bodies That Matter*. 1993. London: Routledge, 2011.

Butler, Judy [Judith]. "Lesbian S&M: The Politics of Dis-illusion." In *Against Sadomasochism: A Radical Feminist Analysis*, edited by Robin Ruth Linden et al., 168–75. Palo Alto: Frog in the Well, 1982.

Byrne, Romana. *Aesthetic Sexuality: A Literary History of Sadomasochism*. London: Bloomsbury, 2013.

Cachopo, João Pedro. "Opera's Screen Metamorphosis: The Survival of a Genre or a Matter of Translation?" *Opera Quarterly* 30, no. 14 (2014): 315–29.

Calabrese, Omar. *Neo-baroque: A Sign of the Times*. Translated by Charles Lambert. Princeton, NJ: Princeton University Press, 1992.

Calico, Joy H. *Brecht at the Opera*. Berkeley: University of California Press, 2008.

Calinescu, Matei. *Five Faces of Modernity: Modernism, Avant-garde, Decadence, Kitsch, Postmodernism*. 1977. Durham, NC: Duke University Press, 1987.

Campana, Alessandra. "To Look Again (at *Don Giovanni*)." In *The Cambridge Companion to Eighteenth-Century Opera*, edited by Anthony R. DelDonna and Pierpaolo Polzonetti, 140–52. Cambridge: Cambridge University Press, 2009.

Canning, Hugh. "Hard to Handel." *Sunday Times* (London), 10 July 2011.

Carnegy, Patrick. *Wagner and the Art of the Theatre*. New Haven, CT: Yale University Press, 2006.

Carner, Mosco. *Giacomo Puccini: Tosca*. Cambridge: Cambridge University Press, 1985.

Carroll, Noël. "The Image of Women in Film: A Defense of a Paradigm." *Journal of Aesthetics and Art Criticism* 48, no. 4 (1990): 349–60.

Carter, Angela. *The Bloody Chamber*. 1979. New York: Penguin, 2015.

Carter, Tim. "What Is Opera?" In Greenwald, *Oxford Handbook of Opera*, 15–32.

Castle, Terry. "In Praise of Brigitte Fassbaender: Reflections on Diva Worship." In Blackmer and Smith, *En Travesti*, 20–58.

Cavarero, Adriana. *For More Than One Voice: Toward a Philosophy of Vocal Expression*. 2003. Translated by Paul A. Kottman. Stanford: Stanford University Press, 2005.

Christiansen, Rupert. "*Guillaume Tell*, Royal Opera House, Review—'Lame and Pretentious.'" *The Telegraph*, 30 June 2015.

———. "*Lucia di Lammermoor*, Royal Opera House, Verdict: 'Too Leaden Even for the Hecklers.'" *The Telegraph*, 8 April 2016.

Church, Michael. "The Force of Destiny, Coliseum, Theatre Review: Calixto Bieito's Perverse Production Is Saved by Brilliant Singing." *Independent*, 10 November 2015.

Citron, Marcia J. *Opera on Screen*. New Haven, CT: Yale University Press, 2000.

———. *When Opera Meets Film*. Cambridge: Cambridge University Press, 2010.

Clark, Andrew. "*Giulio Cesare in Egitto*, Glyndebourne." *Financial Times*, 5 July 2005.

Clément, Catherine. *Opera, or the Undoing of Women*. Translated by Betsy Wing. London: Tauris, 1997. Originally published as *L'opéra, ou, La défait des femmes* (Paris: B. Grasset, 1979).

Coghlan, Alexandra. "The Gang Rape Was the Least Offensive Thing about Royal Opera's New *William Tell*." *The Spectator*, 4 July 2015.

Colvin, Clare. "Review: Rossini's *Guillaume Tell* at the Royal Opera House." *Daily Express*, 5 July 2016.

Cooper, Michael. "Allegations against Plácido Domingo Deemed Credible by L.A. Opera." *New York Times*, 10 March 2020.

———. "David Daniels, Opera Star, Is Arrested on Sexual Assault Charge." *New York Times*, 30 January 2019.

———. "James Levine's Final Act at the Met Ends in Disgrace." *New York Times*, 12 March 2018.

Cowart, Georgia. "Audiences." In Greenwald, *Oxford Handbook of Opera*, 666–84.

———. "Of Women, Sex, and Folly: Opera under the Old Regime." *Cambridge Opera Journal* 6, no. 3 (1994): 205–20.

Cusick, Suzanne. "On a Lesbian Relation with Music: A Serious Effort Not to Think Straight." In *Queering the Pitch: The New Gay and Lesbian Musicology*, edited by Philip Brett, Elizabeth Wood, and Gary C. Thomas, 67–84. New York: Routledge, 1994.

DalMolin, Eliane. *Cutting the Body: Representing Woman in Baudelaire's Poetry, Truffaut's Cinema, and Freud's Psychoanalysis*. Ann Arbor: University of Michigan Press, 2000.

Davies, James Q. "'I Am an Essentialist': Against the Voice Itself." In Feldman and Zeitlin, *The Voice as Something More*, 142–68.

Dean, Winton. *Handel's Operas, 1726–1741*. Woodbridge: Boydell Press, 2006.

Dean, Winton, and John Merrill Knapp. *Handel's Operas, 1704–1726*. Woodbridge: Boydell Press, 2014.

Deleuze, Gilles. *Coldness and Cruelty*. 1967. In Gilles Deleuze and Leopold von Sacher-Masoch, *Masochism: Coldness and Cruelty; Venus in Furs*. Translated by Jean McNeil and Aude Willm, 9–138. New York: Zone, 1991.

———. *The Fold: Leibniz and the Baroque*. 1988. Translated by Tom Conley. London: Continuum, 2006.

Deller, Ruth A., Sarah Harman, and Bethan Jones. "Introduction to the Special Issue: Reading the *Fifty Shades* 'Phenomenon.'" *Sexualities* 16, no. 8 (2013): 859–63.

de Sade, Donatien Alphonse François [Marquis de Sade]. *The 120 Days of Sodom, or the School of Libertinage*. Translated by Will McMorran and Thomas Wynn. London: Random House, 2016.

Donington, Robert. *Opera and Its Symbols: The Unity of Words, Music and Staging*. New Haven, CT: Yale University Press, 1992.

Doyle, Jennifer. *Hold It against Me: Difficulty and Emotion in Contemporary Art.* Durham, NC: Duke University Press, 2013.

Dreyfus, Laurence. *Wagner and the Erotic Impulse.* Cambridge, MA: Harvard University Press, 2010.

Duncan, Michelle. "The Operatic Scandal of the Singing Body: Voice, Presence, Performativity." *Cambridge Opera Journal* 16, no. 3 (2004): 283–306.

Eidsheim, Nina Sun. *The Race of Sound: Listening, Timbre, and Vocality in African American Music.* Durham, NC: Duke University Press, 2019.

———. *Sensing Sound: Singing and Listening as Vibrational Practice.* Durham, NC: Duke University Press, 2015.

Englund, Axel. "An Incomplete Life: *Lulu* and the Performance of Unfinished-ness." *Opera Quarterly* 35, no. 1–2 (2019): 20–39.

———. "Thrilling Opera: Conflicts of the Mind and the Media in Kasper Holten's *Juan.*" In *Music, Narrative and the Moving Image: Varieties of Plurimedial Interrelations,* edited by Walter Bernhart and David Francis Urrows, 185–98. Leiden: Rodopi/Brill, 2019.

Evans, Rian. "Manon Lescaut—Review." *The Guardian,* 10 February 2014.

Ewans, Michael. "The Bayreuth Centenary *Ring* by Patrice Chéreau and Pierre Boulez." *Miscellanea Musicologica* 14 (1985): 167–74.

Falk, G., and Thomas S. Weinberg. "Sadomasochism and Popular Western Culture." In *S and M: Studies in Sadomasochism,* edited by Thomas S. Weinberg and G. W. L. Kamel, 37–144. Buffalo, NY: Prometheus, 1983.

Farrell, C[olin]. Corpun: World Corporal Punishment Research. www.corpun.com.

Feldman, Martha. *The Castrato: Reflections on Natures and Kinds.* Oakland: University of California Press, 2015.

———. "Denaturing the Castrato." *Opera Quarterly* 24, no. 3–4 (2008): 178–99.

———. "The Interstitial Voice: An Opening." *Journal of the American Musicological Society* 68, no. 3 (2015): 653–59.

———. "Voice Gap Crack Break." In Feldman and Zeitlin, *The Voice as Something More,* 188–209.

Feldman, Martha, and Judith T. Zeitlin, eds. *The Voice as Something More: Essays toward Materiality.* Chicago: University of Chicago Press, 2019.

Ford, Charles. *Music, Sexuality and the Enlightenment in Mozart's "Figaro," "Don Giovanni" and "Così fan tutte."* Farnham, Surrey: Ashgate, 2012.

Foucault, Michel. *Ethics: Subjectivity and Truth.* Vol. 1 of *The Essential Works of Foucault, 1954–1984.* Edited by Paul Rabinow and translated by Robert Hurley et al. New York: New Press, 1997.

———. *Foucault Live: Collected Interviews, 1961–1984.* Edited by Sylvère Lotringer and translated by Lysa Hochroth and John Johnson. New York: Semiotext(e), 1996.

———. *The Will to Knowledge: The History of Sexuality, Volume 1.* Translated by Robert Hurley. 1976. London: Penguin, 1998.

Furness, Hannah. "Royal Opera House to Join the #MeToo Era as It Challenges Misogyny on Stage by Asking: 'Does Opera Hate Women?'" *Daily Telegraph*, 25 December 2018.

Genette, Gérard. *Métalepse*. Paris: Seuil, 2004.

———. *Narrative Discourse: An Essay in Method*. 1972. Translated by Jane E. Lewin. Ithaca, NY: Cornell University Press, 1980.

Georg, Jutta, and Renate Reschke, eds. *Nietzsche und Wagner: Perspektiven ihrer Auseinandersetzung*. Berlin: De Gruyter, 2016.

Giles, Peter. *The History and Technique of the Counter-Tenor*. London: Scholar Press, 1994.

Goehr, Lydia. "The Domestic Diva: Toward an Operatic History of the Telephone." In *Technology and the Diva: Sopranos, Opera, and Media from Romanticism to the Digital Age*, edited by Karen Henson, 104–23. Cambridge: Cambridge University Press, 2016.

———. *The Imaginary Museum of Musical Works: An Essay in the Philosophy of Music*. Oxford: Clarendon, 1992.

Goehr, Lydia, and Daniel Herwitz, eds. *The Don Giovanni Moment: Essays on the Legacy of an Opera*. New York: Columbia University Press, 2008.

Gordon, Mel. *Voluptuous Panic: The Erotic World of Weimar Berlin*. Los Angeles: Feral House, 2006.

Gorham, Sammie. "Sammie's Secret: A Life in Opera + BDSM." In Program book. *Susanna's Secret: A BDSM Opera*. Seattle, WA: Mount Analogue and Operamuse, 2018.

Greenwald, Helen M., ed. *The Oxford Handbook of Opera*. Oxford: Oxford University Press, 2014.

Gumbrecht, Hans Ulrich. *The Production of Presence: What Meaning Cannot Convey*. Stanford: Stanford University Press, 2004.

Gutjahr, Ortrud, ed. *Regietheater! Wie sich über Inszenierungen streiten lässt*. Würzburg: Königshausen & Neumann, 2008.

Hammers, Corie. "Corporeality, Sadomasochism and Sexual Trauma." *Body & Society* 20, no. 2 (2014): 68–90.

Hanslick, Eduard. *Concerte, Componisten und Virtuosen der letzten fünfzehn Jahre. 1870–1885*. Berlin: Allgemeiner Verein für Deutsche Literatur, 1886.

Heller, Wendy. "The Beloved's Image: Handel's *Admeto* and the Statue of Alcestis." *Journal of the American Musicological Society* 58, no. 3 (2005): 559–637.

———. "Reforming Achilles: Gender, 'Opera Seria' and the Rhetoric of the Enlightened Hero." *Early Music* 26, no. 4 (1998): 562–81.

Henson, Karen. *Opera Acts: Singers and Performance in the Late Nineteenth Century*. Cambridge: Cambridge University Press, 2014.

Herr, Corinna, Arnold Jacobshagen, and Kai Wessel, eds. *Der Countertenor: Die männliche Falsettstimme vom Mittelalter zur Gegenwart*. Mainz: Schott, 2012.

Higgins, Charlotte. "ENO Retests Market with Bieito's Dirty Don." *The Guardian,* 29 September 2004.

Hills, Helen. "The Baroque: The Grit in the Oyster of Art History." In Hills, *Rethinking the Baroque,* 11–38.

———, ed. *Rethinking the Baroque.* Farnham, Surrey: Ashgate, 2011.

Hinton, Laura. *The Perverse Gaze of Sympathy: Sadomasochistic Sentiments from "Clarissa" to "Rescue 911."* Albany: State University of New York Press, 1999.

Hinton, Stephen. *Weill's Musical Theater: Stages of Reform.* Berkeley: University of California Press, 2012.

Hirschfeld, Magnus. *Sexualpathologie: Ein Lehrbuch für Ärzte und Studierende. Zweiter Teil.* Bonn: A. Marcus & E. Webers, 1918.

Hisama, Ellie M. "A Feminist Staging of Britten's *The Rape of Lucretia.*" *Journal of the American Musicological Society* 71, no. 1 (2018): 237–43.

Hoeckner, Berthold. "Homage to Adorno's 'Homage to Zerlina.'" *Musical Quarterly* 87, no. 3 (2004): 510–22.

Huffington, Arianna. *Maria Callas: The Woman behind the Legend.* New York: Cooper Square Press, 2002.

Humphreys Powell, Elwin. *The Design of Discord: Studies of Anomie.* New Brunswick, NJ: Transaction, 1988.

Hunter, Mary. "Historically Informed Performance." In Greenwald, *Oxford Handbook of Opera,* 606–26.

Hutcheon, Linda, and Michael Hutcheon. *Bodily Charm: Living Opera.* Lincoln: University of Nebraska Press, 2000.

Infield, Glenn B. *Hitler's Secret Life: The Mystery of the Eagle's Nest.* New York: Stein and Day, 1979.

James, E. L. *Fifty Shades of Grey.* London: Arrow, 2012.

Jameson, Fredric. *Postmodernism, or, the Cultural Logic of Late Capitalism.* Durham, NC: Duke University Press, 1991.

Jarman, Douglas. *Alban Berg: Lulu.* Cambridge: Cambridge University Press, 1991.

———. "Friedrich's *Lulu.*" *International Alban Berg Society Newsletter* 10 (1981): 13–14.

Johnson, Christopher D. *Hyperboles: The Rhetoric of Excess in Baroque Literature and Thought.* Cambridge, MA: Harvard University Department of Comparative Literature, 2010.

Jurjaks, Arvid. "En smärtsam jakt på operans anatomi." *OPUS,* 1 June 2018. https://opusmagasin.se/en-smartsam-jakt-pa-operans-anatomi.

Kaiser, Antje, ed. *Die Entführung aus dem Serail.* Program book. Berlin: Komische Oper, 2018.

Kennaway, James. *Bad Vibrations: The History of the Idea of Music as a Cause of Disease.* Farnham, Surrey: Ashgate, 2012.

Kerman, Joseph. *Opera as Drama*. 1956. Berkeley: University of California Press, 2005.

Kierkegaard, Søren. *Either/Or: Part 1*. 1843. Edited and translated by Howard V. Hong and Edna H. Hong. Princeton, NJ: Princeton University Press, 1987.

Klein, J[ulius] L[eopold]. *Geschichte des Dramas. VIII. Das spanische Drama. Erster Band*. Leipzig: T. O. Weigel, 1871.

Kleinplatz, Peggy J., and Charles Moser, eds. *Sadomasochism: Powerful Pleasures*. Binghamton, NY: Harrington Park, 2006.

Koestenbaum, Wayne. *The Queen's Throat: Opera, Homosexuality and the Mystery of Desire*. 1993. 2nd ed. New York: Da Capo, 2001.

Krafft-Ebing, Richard von. *Psychopathia Sexualis: Mit besonderer Berücksichtigung der conträren Sexualempfindung*. 9th ed. Stuttgart: Ferdinand Fink, 1894.

———. *Psychopathia Sexualis: Revised and Enlarged Twelfth Edition*. 1903. Translated by F. J. Rebman. London: William Heinemann, 1939.

Kramer, Lawrence. *After the Lovedeath: Sexual Violence and the Making of Culture*. Berkeley: University of California Press, 1997.

———. *Interpreting Music*. Berkeley: University of California Press, 2011.

———. "Meaning." In Greenwald, *Oxford Handbook of Opera*, 352–70.

Kreuzer, Gundula. *Curtain, Gong, Steam: Wagnerian Technologies of Nineteenth-Century Opera*. Oakland: University of California Press, 2018.

———. "Voices from Beyond: *Don Carlos* and the Modern Stage." *Cambridge Opera Journal* 18, no. 2 (2006): 151–79.

Kreuzer, Gundula, and Clemens Risi. "A Note from the Guest Editors." *Opera Quarterly* 27, no. 2–3 (2011): 149–52.

———. "*Regietheater* in Transition: An Introduction to Barbara Beyer's 'Interviews with Contemporary Opera Directors.'" *Opera Quarterly* 27, no. 2–3 (2011): 303–6.

Lacan, Jacques. "Kant with Sade." Translated by James B. Swenson Jr. *October* 51 (1989): 55–75.

———. *The Seminar of Jacques Lacan: Book XI: The Four Fundamental Concepts of Psychoanalysis*. Edited by Jacques-Alain Miller and translated by Alan Sheridan. New York: Norton, 1981.

Largier, Niklaus. *In Praise of the Whip: A Cultural History of Arousal*. 2001. Translated by Graham Harman. New York: Zone, 2007.

Larsson, Anna. "Sextrakasserier i operahusen." *Dalarnas Tidningar*, 21 September 2012.

Latham, Alison, and Roger Parker, eds. *Verdi in Performance*. New York: Oxford University Press, 2001.

Lavender, Andy. *Performance in the Twenty-First Century: Theatres of Engagement*. London: Routledge, 2016.

Lehmann, Hans-Thies. *Postdramatic Theatre.* 1999. Translated by Karen Jürs-Munby. London: Routledge, 2006.

Lehnhoff, Nikolaus. *Die Oper ist das Reich des Scheins: Inszenierungen von Nikolaus Lehnhoff.* Edited by Birgit Pargner. Leipzig: Henschel, 2015.

Levin, David J. Introduction to *Opera through Other Eyes*, edited by David J. Levin, 1–18. Stanford: Stanford University Press, 1994.

———. "Is There a Text in This Libido? *Diva* and the Rhetoric of Contemporary Opera Criticism." In *Between Opera and Cinema*, edited by Jeongwon Joe and Rose Theresa, 121–32. New York: Routledge, 2002.

———. "The Mise-en-scène of Mediation: Wagner's *Götterdämmerung* (Stuttgart Opera, Peter Konwitschny, 2000–2005)." *Opera Quarterly* 27, no. 2–3 (2011): 219–34.

———. *Unsettling Opera: Staging Mozart, Verdi, Wagner, and Zemlinsky.* Chicago: University of Chicago Press, 2007.

Linden, Robin Ruth, et al., eds. *Against Sadomasochism: A Radical Feminist Analysis.* Palo Alto: Frog in the Well, 1982.

Link, Nathan. "George Frideric Handel: Giulio Cesare." *Opera Quarterly* 24, no. 3–4 (2008): 313–24.

Locke, Ralph P. "What Are These Women Doing in Opera?" In Blackmer and Smith, *En Travesti*, 59–98.

Ludwig, Christa. *In My Own Voice: Memoirs.* Translated by Regina Domeraski. New York: Limelight, 1999.

Lütteken, Laurenz. "Wider den Zeitgeist der Beliebigkeit: Ein Plädoyer für die Freiheit des Textes und die Grenzen der Interpretation." *Wagnerspectrum* 2 (2005): 23–30.

MacDonald, Heather. "The Abduction of Opera: Can the Met Stand Firm against the Trashy Productions of Trendy Nihilists?" *City Journal* (Summer 2007): www.city-journal.org/html/abduction-opera-13034.html.

MacKendrick, Karmen. *The Matter of Voice: Sensual Soundings.* New York: Fordham University Press, 2016.

Master, K. *The Beauty of Kinbaku, or Everything You Ever Wanted to Know about Japanese Erotic Bondage When You Suddenly Realized You Didn't Speak Japanese.* 2nd ed. New York: King Cat Ink, 2014.

Mathew, Nicholas, and Mary Ann Smart. "Elephants in the Music Room: The Future of Quirk Historicism." *Representations* 132 (2015): 61–78.

McClary, Susan. *Feminine Endings: Music, Gender, and Sexuality.* 1991. Minneapolis: University of Minnesota Press, 2002.

McGeary, Thomas. "'Warbling Eunuchs': Opera, Gender, and Sexuality on the London Stage, 1705–1742." *Restoration and Eighteenth-Century Theatre Research* 7, no. 1 (1992): 11–15.

Mellor, David. "Carry on Nurse: Strauss's Magical *Ariadne auf Naxos* Is Revenge for the War." *Daily Mail*, 25 May 2013.

Minor, Ryan. "Opera and/as Theatricality: Notes from across the Aisle." *Opera Quarterly* 35, no. 1–2 (2019): 143–46.

Morris, Christopher. "Casting Metal: Opera Studies after Humanism." *Opera Quarterly* 35, no. 1–2 (2019): 77–95.

———. "Digital Diva: Opera on Video." *Opera Quarterly* 26, no. 1 (2010): 96–119.

Morris, Christopher, and Joseph Attard, eds. "Opera at the Multiplex." Special issue, *Opera Quarterly* 34, no. 4 (2018).

Morris, Mitchell. "Reading as an Opera Queen." In Solie, *Musicology and Difference*, 184–200.

Moser, Charles. "S/M (Sadomasochistic) Interactions in Semi-public Settings." *Journal of Homosexuality* 36, no. 2 (1998): 19–29.

Moser, Charles, and Peggy J. Kleinplatz. "Introduction: The State of Our Knowledge on SM." In Kleinplatz and Moser, *Sadomasochism*, 1–15.

Müller, Ulrich. "*Regietheater*/Director's Theatre." In Greenwald, *Oxford Handbook of Opera*, 582–605.

Mulvey, Laura. "Visual Pleasure and Narrative Cinema." 1975. In *Film Theory and Criticism: Introductory Readings*, edited by Leo Braudy and Marshall Cohen, 833–44. New York: Oxford University Press, 1999.

Nattiez, Jean-Jacques. *Tétralogies: Wagner, Boulez, Chéreau*. Paris: Bourgois, 1983.

Ndalianis, Angela. *Neo-baroque Aesthetics and Contemporary Entertainment*. Cambridge, MA: MIT Press, 2004.

Newmahr, Staci. *Playing on the Edge: Sadomasochism, Risk, and Intimacy*. Bloomington: Indiana University Press, 2011.

Nietzsche, Friedrich. *The Birth of Tragedy and The Case of Wagner*. Translated by Walter Kaufmann. New York: Vintage, 1967.

———. *Nietzsche contra Wagner*. In *Kritische Studienausgabe in 15 Bänden*. Edited by Giorgio Colli and Mazzino Montinari. Vol. 6, 413–45. Munich: Deutsche Taschenbuch, 1999.

Novak, Jelena. *Postopera: Reinventing the Voice-Body*. Farnham, Surrey: Ashgate, 2015.

Nordau, Max. *Degeneration*. 1892. Anonymous translator. New York: D. Appleton, 1895.

Pääkkölä, Anna-Elena, "Sound Kinks: Sadomasochistic Erotica in Audiovisual Music Performances." PhD diss., University of Turku, 2016.

Parker, Roger. *Remaking the Song: Operatic Visions and Revisions from Handel to Berio*. Berkeley: University of California Press, 2006.

Perle, George. *The Operas of Alban Berg*. Vol. 2, *Lulu*. Berkeley: University of California Press, 1985.

———. "Some Thoughts on an Ideal Production of *Lulu*." *Journal of Musicology* 7, no. 2 (1989): 244–53.

Plaut, Eric A. *Grand Opera: Mirror of the Western Mind.* Chicago: Ivan R. Dee, 1993.

Poizat, Michel. *The Angel's Cry: Beyond the Pleasure Principle in Opera.* 1986. Translated by Arthur Denner. Ithaca, NY: Cornell University Press, 1992.

Reynolds, Margaret. "Ruggiero's Deceptions, Cherubino's Distractions." In Blackmer and Smith, *En Travesti,* 132–51.

Risi, Clemens. "Opera in Performance—In Search of New Analytical Approaches." *Opera Quarterly* 27, no. 2–3 (2012): 283–95.

———. "Opera in Performance: 'Regietheater' and the Performative Turn." *Opera Quarterly* 35, no. 1–2 (2019): 7–19.

———. *Oper in Performance: Analysen zur Aufführungsdimension von Operninszenierungen.* Berlin: Theater der Zeit, 2017.

Ritchie, Ani, and Meg Barker. "Feminist SM: A Contradiction in Terms or a Way of Challenging Traditional Gendered Dynamics through Sexual Practice?" *Lesbian and Gay Psychology Review* 6, no. 3 (2005): 227–39.

Robinson, Paul. "It's Not Over until the Soprano Dies." *New York Times,* 1 January 1989.

Rothenberg, Molly Anne, Dennis A. Foster, and Slavoj Žižek, eds. *Perversion and the Social Relation.* Durham, NC: Duke University Press, 2003.

Rudel, Anthony. *Imagining Don Giovanni.* New York: Atlantic Monthly Press, 2001.

Sacher-Masoch, Leopold von. *Venus in Furs.* 1870. In Gilles Deleuze and Leopold von Sacher-Masoch, *Masochism: Coldness and Cruelty; Venus in Furs.* Translated by Jean McNeil and Aude Willm, 141–271. New York: Zone, 1991.

Samois Collective. *Coming to Power: Writings and Graphics on Lesbian S/M.* Palo Alto: Up Press, 1981.

Sassatelli, Roberta. "Interview with Laura Mulvey: Gender, Gaze, and Technology in Film Culture." *Theory, Culture & Society* 28, no. 5 (2011): 123–43.

Schläder, Jürgen, ed. *OperMachtTheaterBilder: Neue Wirklichkeiten des Regietheaters.* Berlin: Henschel, 2006.

Schulze, Daniel. *Authenticity in Contemporary Theatre and Performance: Make it Real.* London: Bloomsbury, 2017.

Schwartz, Arman. "Opera and Objecthood: Sedimentation, Spectatorship, and *Einstein on the Beach.*" *Opera Quarterly* 35, no. 1–2 (2019): 40–62.

———. "Rough Music: *Tosca* and *Verismo* Reconsidered." *Nineteenth Century Music* 31, no. 3 (2008): 228–44.

Scott, Catherine. *Thinking Kink: The Collision of BDSM, Feminism and Popular Culture.* Jefferson, NC: McFarland, 2015.

Senici, Emanuele. "Porn Style? Space and Time in Live Opera Videos." *Opera Quarterly* 26, no. 1 (2010): 63–80.

Seymour, Claire. "*Guillaume Tell*, Covent Garden." *Opera Today*, 30 June 2015. www.operatoday.com/content/2015/06/guillaume_tell_.php.

Slonimsky, Nicolas. *Lexicon of Musical Invective: Critical Assaults on Composers since Beethoven's Time*. 1953. New York: Norton, 2000.

Smart, Mary Ann. Introduction to *Siren Songs: Representations of Gender and Sexuality in Opera*, edited by Mary Ann Smart, 3–16. Princeton, NJ: Princeton University Press, 2000.

———. "The Lost Voice of Rosine Stoltz." In Blackmer and Smith, *En Travesti*, 169–89.

———. "An Operatic Alphabet." Paper presented at the Seventy-Seventh Annual Meeting of the American Musicological Society in San Francisco, 10–13 November 2011.

———. "Resisting Rossini, or Marlon Brando Plays Figaro." *Opera Quarterly* 27, no. 2–3 (2011): 153–78.

Solie, Ruth A., ed. *Musicology and Difference: Gender and Sexuality in Music Scholarship*. Berkeley: University of California Press, 1992.

Sollich, Robert, Clemens Risi, Sebastian Reus, and Stephan Jöris, eds. *Angst vor der Zerstörung: Der Meister Künste zwischen Archiv und Erneuerung*. Berlin: Theater der Zeit, 2008.

Sontag, Susan. *Against Interpretation and Other Essays*. New York: Noonday Press, 1966.

———. "Fascinating Fascism." In *Under the Sign of Saturn*, 73–105. New York: Picador, 2002.

Stähr, Susanne, ed. *PrimaDonna*. Program book. Lucerne: Stiftung Lucerne Festival, 2016.

stein, david. "'Safe Sane Consensual': The Making of a Shibboleth." *Boybear*. web.archive.org/web/20110911035825/http://www.boybear.us/ssc.pdf.

Stemme, Nina, et al. "705 kvinnliga sångare i upprop mot trakasserier och sexism." *Dagens Nyheter*, 13/16 November 2017.

Stewart, Suzanne R. *Sublime Surrender: Male Masochism at the Fin-de-siècle*. Ithaca, NY: Cornell University Press, 1988.

Stockton, Will. "The Liberal World of Perversion." *GLQ: A Journal of Lesbian and Gay Studies* 17, no. 2–3 (2011): 389–403.

Sutcliffe, Tom. *Believing in Opera*. Princeton, NJ: Princeton University Press, 1997.

Switch, Gary. "Origin of RACK; RACK vs. SSC." www.leathernroses.com/generalbdsm/garyswitchrack.htm.

Tambling, Jeremy. *Opera, Ideology and Film*. Manchester: Manchester University Press, 1987.

Thicknesse, Robert. "*Giulio Cesare:* Robert Thicknesse at Glyndebourne." *The Times* (London), 5 July 2005.

Torrefranca, Fausto. *Giacomo Puccini e l'opera internazionale.* Torino: Fratelli Bocca, 1912.

Vandiver Nicassio, Susan. *Tosca's Rome: The Play and the Opera in Historical Perspective.* Chicago: University of Chicago Press, 1999.

Vella, Francesca. "(De)railing Mobility: Opera, Stasis, and Locomotion on Late-Nineteenth-Century Italian Tracks." *Opera Quarterly* 34, no. 1 (2018): 3–28.

Wacker, Kelly A., ed. *Baroque Tendencies in Contemporary Art.* Newcastle: Cambridge Scholars, 2007.

Wagner, Richard. "Über Schauspieler und Sänger." In *Gesammelte Schriften und Dichtungen.* Vol. 9, 157–230. 3rd ed. Leipzig: C. F. W. Siegel, n.d.

Wahlfors, Laura. "Resonances and Dissonances: Listening to Waltraud Meier's Envoicing of Isolde." In *On Voice,* edited by Walter Bernhart and Lawrence Kramer, 57–76. Amsterdam: Rodopi, 2014.

Waite, Robert G. L. *The Psychopathic God: Adolf Hitler.* New York: Basic Books, 1977.

Weait, Matthew. "Sadomasochism and the Law." In *Safe, Sane and Consensual: Contemporary Perspectives on Sadomasochism,* edited by Darren Langdridge and Meg Barker, 63–82. New York: Palgrave Macmillan, 2007.

Weinberg, Thomas S. "Sadomasochism and the Social Sciences: A Review of the Sociological and Social Psychological Literature." In Kleinplatz and Moser, *Sadomasochism,* 17–40.

Weiss, Margot. "Mainstreaming Kink: The Politics of BDSM Representation in U.S. Popular Media." In Kleinplatz and Moser, *Sadomasochism,* 103–32.

———. *Techniques of Pleasure: BDSM and the Circuits of Sexuality.* Durham, NC: Duke University Press, 2011.

Wiebe, Heather. "Opera and Relational Aesthetics." *Opera Quarterly* 35, no. 1–2 (2019): 139–42.

Will, Richard. "*Don Giovanni* and the Resilience of Rape Culture." *Journal of the American Musicological Society* 71, no. 1 (2018): 218–20.

———. "Zooming In, Gazing Back: *Don Giovanni* on Television." *Opera Quarterly* 27, no. 1 (2011): 32–65.

Williams, D. J., et al. "From 'SSC' and 'RACK' to the '4Cs': Introducing a new Framework for Negotiating BDSM Participation." *Electronic Journal of Human Sexuality* 17 (2014): www.ejhs.org/volume17/BDSM.html.

Wilson, Alexandra. *The Puccini Problem: Opera, Nationalism and Modernity.* Cambridge: Cambridge University Press, 2007.

Witt, Hubert, ed. *Brecht as They Knew Him.* Translated by John Peet. Berlin: Seven Seas, 1974.

Woolfe, Zachary. "Missing from Podiums: Women." *New York Times,* 20 December 2013.

Wright, Sarah. *Tales of Seduction: The Figure of Don Juan in Spanish Culture*. New York: Tauris, 2007.

Wright, Susan. "Discrimination of SM-Identified Individuals." In Kleinplatz and Moser, *Sadomasochism*, 217–32.

Wynn, Thomas, "Prostitutes and Erotic Performances in Eighteenth-Century Paris." In *Prostitution and Eighteenth-Century Culture: Sex, Commerce and Morality*, edited by Ann Lewis and Markman Ellis, 87–98. London: Routledge, 2016.

Žižek, Slavoj. *For They Know Not What They Do: Enjoyment as a Political Factor*. London: Verso, 1991.

———. *How to Read Lacan*. London: Granta, 2006.

———. *Welcome to the Desert of the Real*. London: Verso, 2002.

Žižek, Slavoj, and Mladen Dolar. *Opera's Second Death*. New York: Routledge, 2002.

Zuber, Barbara. "Bildzauber—Zauberbilder: Die Ästhetik des Wunderbaren in Jossi Wielers und Christof Loys Inszenierungen von Händels *Alcina*." In Schläder, *OperMachtTheaterBilder*, 9–26.

MUSICAL SCORES

Berg, Alban. *Lulu*. Akt 1–2. UE No. 13640A. Vienna: Universal Edition, 2017.

Paterson, Robert. *Three Way: A Trio of One-Act Operas: Piano/Vocal Score*. New York: Bill Holab Music, 2017.

AUDIOVISUAL SOURCES

Berg, Alban. *Lulu*. Directed by Sven-Eric Bechtolf. DVD DVWW-OPLULU. TDK, 2006.

———. *Lulu*. Directed by William Kentridge. DVD 0075597945379. Nonesuch Records, 2016.

———. *Lulu*. Directed by Vera Nemirova. DVD D4779. Unitel Classica, 2012.

———. *Lulu*. Directed by Olivier Py. DVD 00440 073 4637. Deutsche Grammophon, 2011.

———. *Lulu*. Directed by Krzysztof Warlikowski. DVD BAC109. Bel Air Classiques, 2014.

———. *Wozzeck*. Directed by Dmitri Tcherniakov. DVD BAC068. Bel Air Classiques, 2012.

Handel, George Frideric. *Alcina*. Directed by Jossi Wieler and Sergio Morabito. DVD 102 300. Arthaus Musik, 2013.

———. *Rinaldo*. Directed by Robert Carsen. DVD OA 1081 D. Opus Arte, 2012.

Hannigan, Barbara. "Opera Singer Barbara Hannigan on Why She Loves 'Lulu.'" www.youtube.com/watch?v=6AhnOFwfBnM.

Mozart, Wolfgang Amadeus. *Don Giovanni*. Directed by Calixto Bieito. DVD OA 0921 D. Opus Arte, 2006.

———. *Don Giovanni*. Directed by Claus Guth. DVD 2072548. Unitel Classica, 2010.

Puccini, Giacomo. *Tosca*. Directed by Robert Carsen. DVD 074 3420. Decca, 2011.

———. *Tosca*. Directed by Nikolaus Lehnhoff. DVD 074 3201. Decca, 2007.

"Rihanna Feat. Britney Spears—S&M Remix—Live—Billboard Music Awards 2011." YouTube.com. www.youtube.com/watch?v=IaTMIDAvuLUVSpFTRQ.

Seiler, Barbara, dir. "Barbara Hannigan: I'm a Creative Animal." *Concert Documentary*. DVD ACC 20327. Accentus Musik, 2015.

Wagner, Richard. *Parsifal*. Directed by Romeo Castellucci. DVD BAC097. Bel Air Classiques, 2013.

Index

Abbate, Carolyn, 9, 29–30, 213n27
Abel, Samuel, 43; *Opera in the Flesh* of, 28–29
Abramović, Marina, 196
Aci, Galatea e Polifemo (Handel), 58
actuality effect, 45–50, 118, 120, 149, 151, 194–203; depersonalization as, 155–56; in Barcelona production of *Don Giovanni*, 101, 116–117; in Brussels production of *Parsifal*, 124, 130; in Glyndebourne production of *Rinaldo*, 83; in Hannigan's concert performances, 189, 191; in Moscow production of *Wozzeck*, 163–65; in Salzburg production of *Don Giovanni*, 110, 112, 116–117; in Stuttgart production of *Alcina*, 83; relation to *Verfremdungseffekt*, 46–47; three levels of, 47–48; in *Tosca*, 135, 137, 144, 146; in Zurich production of *Lulu*, 182
Adorno, Theodor W., 87, 107, 167, 185
adultery, 157, 163
aesthetics, 43, 91, 173, 203; campy, 52; modernist, 167; postmodernist, 52
Aikin, Laura, 168, 170, 171*fig.*, 175*fig.*, 177, 177*fig.*, 178*fig.*, 180

Alcina (Handel), 53, 59–61, 72–81, 75*fig.*, 80*fig.*, 83, 93, 110
Alsop, Marin, 188
Amalric, Mathieu, 25
Amsterdam, 170
À Rebours (Huysmans), 126
Ariosto, Ludovico, 53
Armstrong, Karan, 169
Artaud, Antonin, 194–95
assault, 23, 87, 91, 151. *See also* violence

Babylon Berlin (2017), 157
Bacci, Tamara, 130*fig.*
Bal, Mieke, 19, 55–57
ballet, 38, 41, 186–87
Baranello, Micaela, 41
Bardouil, Claude, 186
baroque, 8, 12, 18–19, 51–53, 55–56. *See also* baroque opera
baroque opera, 12, 18–19, 53–55, 58–59; contemporary, 51–84; voice in, 64. *See also* baroque
Barthes, Roland, 28, 34
Bartoli, Cecilia, 29
Baudelaire, Charles, 24, 99, 121
Bauer, Robin, 147, 217n64

gender *(continued)*
  politics of the opera canon, 8–9; post-
  Enlightenment conception of, 19, 61,
  84–85, 116; roles in the music world, 30,
  118–119, 129, 188–193; scholarship on
  opera and, 8–10, 12, 28–30: of stage
  directors, 7–8, 38. *See also* LGBTQ;
  sexuality
Genette, Gérard, 52, 218n6
Gens, Véronique, 91
Gill, André, 122
Giulio Cesare (Handel), 54
Glyndebourne Festival Opera, 54, 56–58, 61,
  64–65, 73, 78, 80–83
Gobbi, Tito, 148–50
Gordon, Mel, 156, 170; *Voluptuous Panic:
  The Erotic World of Weimar Berlin* of,
  172*fig.*
Gorham, Sammie, xiv, 7, 21, 198–200,
  199*fig.*, 201–2
Grand Macabre, The (Ligeti), 159
Gran Teatre del Liceu (Barcelona), 90–92,
  104–5, 116
Guillaume Tell (Rossini), 38, 41
Guth, Claus: staging of *Don Giovanni*, 19,
  89–90, 105–17, 223n41–42

Haenchen, Hartmut, 128
Hammers, Corie, 216n57
Hampson, Thomas, 140, 142, 143*fig.*, 144,
  145*fig.*
Handel, George Frideric, xv, 12, 18, 53–64,
  218n7. See also *Alcina, Aci, Galatea e
  Polifemo, Giulio Cesare, Rinaldo, Theo-
  dora, Xerxes*
Hannigan, Barbara, 184–93, 190*fig.*,
  229n29; performance of *The Mysteries of
  the Macabre*, 7, 20, 159, 190–93, 198;
  performance of *Lulu*, 20, 159, 168, 173–
  74, 185–87; performance of *Lulu Suite*,
  20, 159, 189, 191–92
Haunstein, Rolf, 178*fig.*
Haus für Mozart (Salzburg), 116
Helgesson, Joa, 21, 200–202, 201*fig.*
Heller, Wendy, 59
Herz, Joachim, 16
Hirschfeld, Magnus, 170
Hisama, Ellie M., 37
Hoeckner, Berthold, 87
Hoffmann, E. T. A., 85
Holland, Ashley, 171*fig.*
Holten, Kasper, 38

homosexuality, 23, 28–29, 157. *See also*
  LGBTQ
Hoomes, John, xiii
Hutcheon, Linda, 30
Hutcheon, Michael, 30
Huysmans, Joris-Karl, 126
hyperbole: baroque, 52–53, 66, 77, 83;
  BDSM as, 18, 35–36; as link between
  opera and BDSM, 18, 38, 45, 195, 202;
  literalization of, 39, 47–48, 77, 83, 87,
  101, 137; opera as, 18, 34–35; hyperbolic gambit, 33, 41–44, 97; in "Batti,
  batti", 89, 97–98, 101, 110–112, 115–
  116, 197; as subversive, 35–36, 215n43

iconography of perversion, 4-6, 18, 21, 26,
  31–34, 118–19; and contemporary opera
  culture, 12, 13, 17, 22, 45; in Hannigan's
  performance of *Mysteries of the Macabre*,
  191; in productions of Berg, 20, 52, 157,
  168, 185; in productions of Handel, 18,
  63, 65, 76, 83; in productions of Mozart,
  85; in productions of Puccini, 120, 135–
  36; in productions of Wagner, 120; in
  relation to opera's past, 6, 51, 56, 58; in
  Weimar Berlin, 156. *See also* perversion
Il segreto di Susanna (Wolf-Ferrari), 20–21,
  198. See also *Susanna's Secret*
infidelity, 109, 198
Institute for Sexual Science (Berlin), 170
International Body Suspension Symposium,
  200
interpretation, 31, 42
Italian opera (English), 23, 57, 62

Jack the Ripper, 155–57, 158*fig.*, 168–70,
  182, 187
James, E. L.: *Fifty Shades of Grey* trilogy of,
  7, 10, 13, 15, 210n45
Jardin des Supplices (Mirbeau), 126
Jung, Carl Gustav, 25

Kaiser, Joachim, 93
Kentridge, William, 170
Kerman, Joseph, 52, 54, 134, 218n3
Kierkegaard, Søren, 23, 85; *Either/Or* of, 23
Klein, J. L.: *Geschichte des Dramas* of, 122
Knapp, John Merrill, 57
Kocherga, Anatoly, 91
Koestenbaum, Wayne, 24, 28–29
Komische Oper, 16, 38–39, 42–43, 49,
  90–91, 196

Society of Janus, 15
Sommer, Dasnyia, 150
Sontag, Susan, 13–14, 155, 191, 214n34
spanking, xiii, 3, 14, 25, 170. *See also* BDSM
Spears, Britney, 13
Spielberg, Steven, 57
Staatsoper Stuttgart, 53, 58, 60–61, 73,
    78–79, 83
staging, 6, 11, 16–18, 47, 66, 79, 80*fig.*, 81,
    91, 110–11, 118, 162, 191; actuality
    effect in, 45–50, 83, 117–18; deviant, 26,
    36, 50; disturbing, 84; radical, 52. *See
    also* opera
Stemme, Nina, 119
Stonewall riots, 14
Straka, Peter, 181*fig.*
Stratas, Teresa, 169
Strauss, Richard, 29
Susanna's Secret (Gorham), xiii, xv, 7, 20,
    198–200, 199*fig.*, 202. See also *Il segreto
    di Susanna*
Sutcliffe, Tom: *Believing in Opera* of, 10–11
Sweet Gwendoline, 14
switching, xiv, 4, 111–112, 192, 199
Switch, Gary, 44

Tarantino, Quentin, 91
Taymor, Julie, 7
Tcherniakov, Dmitri: staging of *Wozzeck*,
    20, 157, 159–66, 161*fig.*, 164*fig.*,
    182
Terfel, Bryn, 136–37, 138*fig.*, 139, 140*fig.*
theater, 34; avant-garde, 46; of cruelty
    (Artaud), 194–195; epic, 46; music, 188;
    naturalistic, 46; postdramatic, 197; space
    of, 146–52. *See also* opera
Theodora (Handel), 54
Tómasson, Tómas, 124, 125*fig.*, 126*fig.*
Torrefranca, Fausto, 134; *Giacomo Puccini e
    l'opera internazionale* of, 134
torture, 23–24, 170; in Bieito's staging of
    Entführung aus dem Serail, 39–42,
    40*fig.*, 48, 102; in Castellucci's staging of
    Parsifal, 126, 150, 152; as public enter-
    tainment, 41, 196; in *Tosca*, 3, 135–36,
    141. *See also* violence
Tosca (Puccini), 20, 119, 134–46, 138*fig.*,
    140*fig.*, 143*fig.*, 145*fig.*, 148–51, 168,
    198
toxicology, 123
tragic opera, 61
Tristan und Isolde (Wagner), 24–25, 121,
    128

Un ballo in maschera (Verdi), 90

Venus in Fur (Polanski, 2013), 25
Verdi, Giuseppe, 25
Verfremdungseffekt (estrangement effect), 46
Vickers, Jon, 148–49, 196
Viebrock, Anna, 79
Vienna, 88, 113
violence, xv–vii, 3–4, 8, 21, 23, 58, 91–105;
    aural, 29, 122; extremes of, 39, 41, 103;
    hyperbole and, 44, 49, 77, 90–105; of
    opera plots, xv, xvii, 8, 51, 187; real vs.
    enacted, 19, 41–2, 82, 89, 148, 164,
    182, 184; repetitive, 19, 103; representa-
    tion of, 8, 36, 41–45, 49, 58, 155, 196;
    Sadean commitment to, 92, 102–105;
    war and, 38, 66; to women, 9, 39, 40*fig.*,
    159. *See also* assault; domestic violence;
    sexual violence; torture
voice, 2, 25–33, 49, 85, 197–98; control, 49,
    65–66, 165, 196, 198; disembodied,
    144–45; eroticism/sensuality of, 28, 43,
    51, 65, 77; as expression of humanity,
    153; as hyperbole, 35; pleasure of, xvi, 2,
    5, 18; power of, 9, 129, 153; female, 9,
    30, 64–65, 129, 140-46, 183–84; as
    object, 20, 28, 131, 142, 144, 146; of the
    castrati, 23, 35, 59, 61–62; scholarship
    on, 27–30; as expression of subjectivity,
    29–30, 153, 186, 188; fetishism, 20,
    32–33, 140-45
Volle, Michael, 170, 171*fig.*
von Otter, Anne Sofie, 119
von Trier, Lars, 25

Wagner, Richard, xv, 12, 16, 19, 119–34; as
    icon of perversion, 24–25; eroticism of
    music of, 24, 121–22, 168; "Über
    Schauspieler und Sänger" of, 132.
    See also *Das Rheingold, Der Ring des
    Nibelungen, Die Walküre, Parsifal,
    Siegfried*
Wagner, Wieland, 16
Wahlfors, Laura, 2,
Walter, Scott, 119
Warlikowski, Krzysztof, 20, 159, 168, 173–
    74, 185–86
Wedekind, Frank, 176, 180, 182, 229n30;
    The Earth Spirit of, 155; *Pandora's Box*
    of, 155, 157
Weimar Republic, 156–57. *See also* Berlin
Weiss, Margot: *Techniques of Pleasure* of,
    147

Founded in 1893,
UNIVERSITY OF CALIFORNIA PRESS
publishes bold, progressive books and journals
on topics in the arts, humanities, social sciences,
and natural sciences—with a focus on social
justice issues—that inspire thought and action
among readers worldwide.

The UC PRESS FOUNDATION
raises funds to uphold the press's vital role
as an independent, nonprofit publisher, and
receives philanthropic support from a wide
range of individuals and institutions—and from
committed readers like you. To learn more, visit
ucpress.edu/supportus.